VAR. I [Dorothy Perkins (rambler) rose]

Allegretto animato (♩ = 108) sempre leggiero

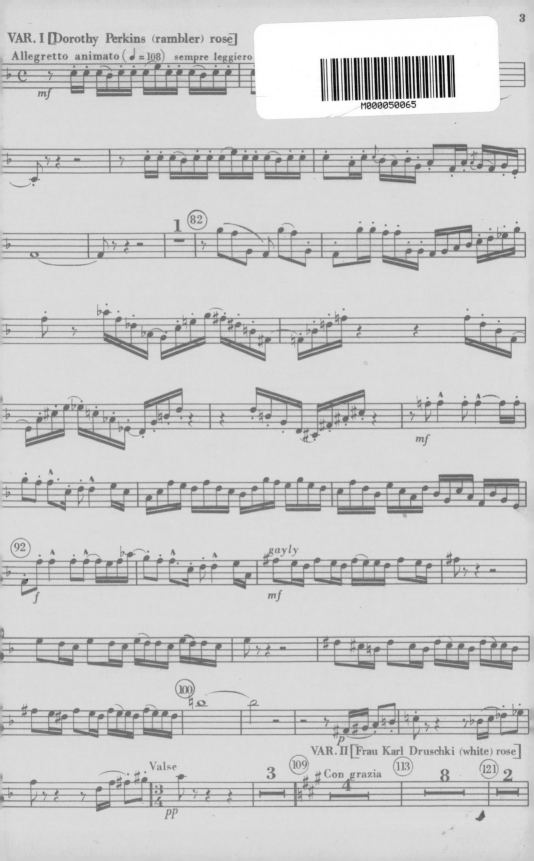

VAR. II [Frau Karl Druschki (white) rose]

Valse   Con grazia

Inside John Haynie's Studio

John James Haynie, 1986

Inside
John Haynie's
Studio

A Master Teacher's Lessons on
Trumpet and Life

Essays by John Haynie

compiled and edited by
Anne Hardin

University of North Texas Press
Denton, Texas

Grateful acknowledgment is made for permission to reprint the following excerpts and use images:

"Basic Respiration for Wind Instrument Playing" by James Lakin
©1969 The Instrumentalist Company. Used by permission.

"Course of Study: North Texas State University" compiled by John J. Haynie and Leonard A. Candelaria
©1983 International Trumpet Guild Journal. Used by permission.

Rose Variations by Robert Russell Bennett
©1955 (Renewed) Chappell & Co.
Reprinted by permission of Alfred Publishing Co., Inc. All Rights Reserved.

Original art for the essay "A Comparison of Cornets and Trumpets and the People Who Play Them: A Two-Part Story" created by Bucky Milam.

Book design by Anne Hardin
Dust jacket design by Joe Parenteau
Frontispiece photograph by Ivan Goodwin

Library of Congress Cataloging-in-Publication Data

Haynie, John J.
  Inside John Haynie's studio : a master teacher's lessons on trumpet and life / essays by John Haynie ; compiled and edited by Anne Hardin.
      p. cm.
  Includes bibliographical references and index.
  ISBN-13: 978-1-57441-226-0 (cloth : alk. paper)
  ISBN-10: 1-57441-226-4 (cloth : alk. paper)
  1. Trumpet--Instruction and study. 2. Haynie, John J. I. Hardin, Anne F. (Anne Farr), 1954- II. Title.
  MT440.H39 2007
  788.9'2193--dc22
                                    2006031719

10 9 8 7 6 5 4 3 2 1

Permissions: University of North Texas Press, P.O. Box 311336, Denton, TX 76203-1336

∞The paper used in this book meets the minimum requirements of the American National Standard for Permanence of Paper for Printed Library Materials, z39.48.1984. Binding materials have been chosen for durability.

For Marilyn—
loving wife, caring mother, accomplished musician, gracious lady—
her presence in my life has made all things possible

and

Anne's parents, F.M. and Evelyn Farr,
whose purchase of that beginner cornet set her on the path in music
that, half-a-lifetime later, crossed mine

CONTENTS

FOREWORD

Much of what I learned about playing the trumpet from John James Haynie shows on a daily basis in my playing and teaching. His attention to detail, to exactness in rhythm, articulation, intonation, and musical style are hallmarks of excellence, and the hundreds of fine players who came through his studio are greater testimony to the brilliance of his teaching abilities than words by me or anyone else could express.

Yet the things I remember most are the lessons I learned from him about how to live one's life. I believe strongly that the great teachers are those who teach by example, by what they *are* even more than by what they might say.

John Haynie exemplifies all the qualities of dedication, integrity, courage, and loyalty that should be the hallmark of anyone who claims to be a teacher of young people. He taught most effectively by example. His devotion to his work, both as player and teacher, is marked by the highest professional and personal standards. He expected no less from his students.

I remember asking once if he thought I would be able to get a job upon graduating. I remember clearly his response. He said, "I can't really tell you for sure. All I know is that the middle is crowded, but there is always room at the top." That sums up his approach to everything he has ever done. Settle for nothing less than the highest standards, and the rest will take care of itself.

This man is the stuff of legend, and the effects of his brilliant career reach far beyond anything he or any of us can imagine. To have the privilege of studying and working with him is to be in the presence of greatness.

Keith Johnson
Regents Professor of Music
University of North Texas

PREFACE

"Come on, come on,
whoever you are.
Come travel with me!"

These are the opening words to *Song of the Open Road*, a delightful piece for chorus, trumpet, and piano written by Norman Dello Joio, one that I performed many times with Frank McKinley's North Texas Choir in the 1950s. As you read this book, you will meet over a hundred of my students who describe the things they learned while "traveling with me."

From the beginning of my teaching career, I have been gratified to receive letters of appreciation for my teaching and interest in their lives from my students, and frequently also from their parents. I promised that one day I would write a book about the things I did that helped them play better, think better, and teach better. Most of all, the book would be about developing confidence in themselves and having compassion for others.

But when I began to write, I found that I needed their help. I wrote many of them and asked three things: What did I teach? What did they learn? What did they remember? The response was tremendous, and I now had the inspiration I needed to get going on my essays. Some were written with tongue-in-cheek, because that is the way I think. Often this casual approach produced a better understanding of the point to be made. All the essays, however, were written as lessons to be learned.

In the spring of 2004 I became acquainted with Anne Hardin, and I sent her some of my rather informal writings, recordings, and other materials. She responded, "John, you have enough material here to write a book like no other." I asked her if she would help put the book together, and she agreed. From the title to the format for student comments called "The Other Side of the Stand," she created this book from my pedagogical and autobiographical essays.

Other friends helped along the way. I wish to thank Dr. James Scott, Dean of the College of Music at the University of North Texas, Dr. Bill Nugent, former Director of the University of Illinois Foundation, and Elida Tamez, Director of Development for the College of Music who encouraged and supported this project from the very beginning. Staying in touch with the "troops" all these years would have been impossible without the help of former student and master communicator, Melvin Gordy. Way to go, Melvin! I offer thanks also to Morris Martin, University of North Texas Music Librarian, and his student assistant, Jonathan Thorn. My thanks go to Bucky Milam, former student and professional artist, for his clever illustration in the essay "A Comparison of Cornets and Trumpets and the People Who Play Them." And last, a special thanks to former University of North Texas President, C. C. "Jitter" Nolen, for suggesting the Press add a special touch—endpapers printed with my signature solo, *Rose Variations*.

Of course, there would be no book without the students' "go for it" attitude expressed in their wonderful letters. From that first class of 1950 to the last class of 1990, I thank them with all my heart.

Now, come on, come on, whoever you are. Come travel with me *Inside John Haynie's Studio* for that first lesson.

John Haynie
Professor Emeritus of Trumpet
University of North Texas

He who has not eaten his bread in tears
does not know the meaning of work.

Giovanni Battista Lamperti

THE OTHER SIDE OF THE STAND

Mr. Haynie's discussion with me about changing my embouchure has been an important guide in my teaching over the past twenty-five years. He told me that he never forced an embouchure change on any student because it was a big step with serious consequences. The student had to make the decision and accept the responsibility and commitment. This bit of wisdom helped me avoid painful situations with students early in my career when I thought I would be able to fix every problem.

Al Moore

Trumpet players were always looking for the ideal mouthpiece, and Mr. Haynie always pointed out that the most important thing to do was to build a good embouchure first.

Mike Olson

I returned to Denton after having been with the Kenton Orchestra for a year. I approached John with a problem I was having—cutting my lip from the strenuous playing on that band. Though I was no longer in school, John nevertheless took time to coach me through the initial stages of making changes in my embouchure and helped me to understand that this was the correct though difficult move to make at this crucial time. This was a most arduous task for me, but John encouraged me while I was going through this terribly frustrating ordeal—probably the most difficult episode of my trumpet life.

Marvin Stamm

John was always patient with our embouchure problems, and he helped us solve them, no matter what they were. I sincerely appreciate his patience, encouragement, and understanding.

Doug Wiehe

THE BIG FOUR: EMBOUCHURE

In the early 1990s, I happened to be in the office of Richard Jones, M.D., and at the registration desk I picked up a little card on which appeared these words: *What the mind conceives and the heart believes, the body achieves.* Dr. Jones was a surgeon, and I was there to make a decision about a procedure I needed but didn't want to have! Just meeting him was an experience all its own. He was an imposing figure, which you would expect of a former linebacker of a major college football team. He was also gentle and kind. Immediately I knew that he was the person I wanted to replace my knees. From the beginning I also knew that "what *his* mind conceived and *his* heart believed, *my* body would achieve."

The same concept has been in my heart all these years because I've watched my students accomplish things they never dreamed possible. Douglas Smith, now a professor of music at the Southern Baptist Theological Seminary, once quoted me as saying, "No matter how well you perform, or how much you know about the trumpet, the best thing you can do for your students is to create an environment where learning is a desirable commodity."

Surely more is written about embouchure than any other technique involved in playing the trumpet, and from the beginning, a student must search for something in which he truly believes. I advise everyone to read everything he can get his hands on to develop an awareness of the many ways that the trumpet is played.

1. Jaw Position

In my method book, *How to Play High Notes, Low Notes and All Those In Between*, I wrote that possibly the most important factor involved in trumpet playing is the preparation of the jaw position to give the mouthpiece a solid foundation. Often the normal overbite allows the lower lip to roll too far under the upper lip. It is important that the lower lip support the mouthpiece in order to give the upper lip freedom to vibrate with a minimum of pressure. The extent to which the jaw is thrust forward can easily be determined by the following simple test: Moisten a finger and hold it near the pursed lips; blow a column of air and locate the air stream with the finger; project the jaw forward and observe that the air stream goes upward; continue to project the jaw until the air stream follows a horizontal line parallel to the floor. This basic position is satisfactory for tones from low F-sharp to approximately second line G. For notes above this tone, the jaw will probably begin to recede ever so slightly. The ultimate range a person achieves can be largely determined by the discretion used in allowing the jaw to recede. A receding jaw causes the air stream to be directed downward, yet it is important to keep some red of the lower lip visible at all times.

2. Wet or Dry

The old argument about playing with the lips wet or dry has no basis, since there is no such thing as playing with the lips dry. The argument should be whether or not to **begin** playing with the lips dry. The instant one starts blowing air into the mouthpiece condensation forms. Then the question becomes how much moisture is too much.

3. Mouthpiece Placement

Eminent authorities have stated that it is not possible to play the trumpet except with the mouthpiece placed one-third on the upper lip and two-thirds on the lower lip. Others argue the exact opposite. It is agreed, however, that the mouthpiece should be as near the center as possible. In my opinion, the young student should be encouraged to place the mouthpiece about half on the upper lip and half on the lower lip. In time the mouthpiece will find its most natural position whether it remains half and half or adjusts itself to one-third upper, two-thirds lower, or the opposite. The reason for centering the mouthpiece is to allow an equal use of the facial and lip muscles both up and down, and side to side.

4. Upper and Lower Lip Vibration

As has been mentioned, the upper lip must vibrate, and it is possible that the lower lip vibrates sympathetically if the jaw-lower lip position is fixed as previously described. A simple test to see which lip vibrates goes like this: Place a 3 x 5 card between the lower lip and mouthpiece and play any sustained note. The tone will continue in all likelihood but will lose its sparkle, and nature will automatically increase the wind pressure or the tone will stop. Now, see if you can play a note when placing the 3 x 5 card between the mouthpiece and upper lip. Anyone who can accomplish this is one of the rare players whose lower lip is the primary vibrator. It is important that the lower lip support the mouthpiece in order to give the upper lip freedom to vibrate.

5. Buzzing the Lips and Mouthpiece

Buzzing the lips and buzzing the mouthpiece help to ensure this vibration of the lips. In addition, buzzing the lips alone is especially helpful for the beginning student and for the advanced student who has some problem of embouchure, a problem that usually results in excessive mouthpiece pressure on the lips. For the trumpeter who has no particular embouchure problem, prolonged lip-buzzing sessions probably serve little purpose, because too much lip buzzing can result in tension that produces a pinched, forced tone. Buzzing the mouthpiece, on the other hand, should be encouraged as a part of the warm-up routine.

6. Changing Notes

It is obvious that not all the notes in the range of the trumpet can be played by merely pushing down three valves. At least three things can be manipulated to interact with the wind and cause the tones to go up or down exclusive of the use of the valves. These three things are: 1) contracting and relaxing the lips, 2) arching and flattening the tongue, and 3) pivoting the instrument and head. The three are not options, but rather desirable traits that must occur simultaneously.

7. Smile or Pucker

For many years authorities have argued whether to use the smile system or the pucker system. They are generally agreed now that it is not a matter of either/or, but a combination of both the smile and the pucker. On the other hand, it could be said that both systems are incorrect and, therefore, we should avoid mentioning either term, smile or pucker. The student could be directed to contract his lips by firming the corners of the mouth as he wishes to play higher tones. Such direction might avoid all confusion of the controversial smile-pucker systems because the student will almost automatically accomplish the desirable feat of pulling the muscles of the corners of the mouth against the muscles of the lips.

8. To "Ah-ee" or not to "Ah-ee"

That is the question. As the lips contract and relax, the tongue arches and flattens, which might be described as contracting and relaxing the tongue. To understand this action of the tongue, the syllables "ah" and "ee" are used. If these syllables are meaningless to the student, tell him to place his fingers on his tongue and say "ah" and "ee." Now he can actually feel the action of the tongue as it raises and lowers itself, the "ah" position for the lowest notes, progressing toward "ee" for the highest notes. It must be mentioned that pronouncing these syllables vocally is at best a rough indication of the action of the tongue. Each note has its own position or elevation of the tongue, and the tongue must be allowed to move in coordination with the contracting and relaxing of the facial muscles.

9. Pivot

An interesting thing happens automatically when the jaw, lips, and tongue function as previously described. These motions encourage what is commonly known as the pivot. Observe that as the pitch ascends, the bell of the trumpet tilts downward and the forehead tips backward very slightly. When this pivot occurs in reverse, too much pressure is applied to the upper lip when ascending; and when descending, the lower lip is restricted. The result is poor tone and attack on low notes. On the other hand, the person who has an abnormal occlusion of the teeth (lower teeth are farther forward than the upper teeth when the jaw is clamped) will be expected to pivot in reverse. This is his natural pivot and should be encouraged.

THE OTHER SIDE OF THE STAND

I expanded John's research with videofluorography for my doctoral work at the University of Oklahoma. My dissertation was "A Videofluorographic Study of the Teeth Aperture, Instrument Pivot, and Tongue Arch, and Their Influence on Trumpet Performance." John's work in this area created a lasting interest in the physiological phenomena of brass performance. His research led to the confirmation of the roles of the tongue arch, instrument pivot, and teeth aperture variance during trumpet performance.

Keith Amstutz

I asked Mr. Haynie how he did lip trills. He said, "I do them with my jaw." That comment opened up a whole new concept of slurring for me, especially in the upper register.

Conrad Bauschka

Using the pivot system was very important to me as a trumpet player. Mr. Haynie always emphasized that the tilt of the bell was a result of the jaw movement, not the hands. The hands were simply the rotating points.

Mike Olson

*During my North Texas sojourn I struggled bravely to cope with what was called a reverse pivot. Before my study with Mr. Haynie I had never heard of the brass player's pivot or Donald Reinhardt's system, but once I understood the problem, I had to decide whether to change it, or to rationalize its existence and make the best of it. I even wrote an article entitled, "The Upstream Embouchure," published in **The Instrumentalist**, complete with parallel pictures of Keith Amstutz and me going from low pitch to high pitch. While teaching with Mr. Haynie, I invested in a camera with extension rings, capable of taking close-up shots of the embouchures of my friends and students. The collection still exists. I use them to this day.*

Douglas Smith

DO THEY PIVOT IN PEORIA?

I was visiting a friend's studio one day and on the wall was an advertisement poster for a new razor, with the caption asking, "Do They Pivot in Peoria?" My answer would be, "If there are brass players and men that shave, then *yes*, they pivot in Peoria." Let me say at the outset that the pivot is not for everyone, especially those with a malocclusion of the teeth. This person will use a reverse pivot, if he or she pivots at all. It must be said over and over that the pivot is a result and not an end in itself. Observation of the pivot is only a clue that a lot of things are working correctly.

The jaw works on a hinge, and I have seen very fine players whose jaws are prone to move more than necessary. Each day as part of the warm-up, sustain a second-line G, drop the jaw and relax the lips, and with ease and smoothness the low C will respond. Observe the pivot. Proceed chromatically down to low F-sharp. Now start on that low F-sharp and slur up to C-sharp, observing the pivot. This is about all a student needs to know or think about. The interconnection of jaw and tongue forms an alliance that will adjust to all intervals.

I let nature teach the student that for the same reason a doctor places a tongue depressor on his patient's tongue and asks him to say "ah." The trumpet player imagines that tongue depressor, drops his jaw, allowing the tongue to flatten. With the "ah" tongue position the doctor can see a more open throat, and the trumpet student will have a more open, relaxed, full tone.

The open throat allows a greater flow of air, a greater volume at a slower velocity. Playing higher, the jaw and tongue go up. This reduces the size of the airway and offers greater resistance to the column of air, which makes the air move faster. The higher you play, the faster the air.

Do not forget the lips. The lips must relax in comradeship with the jaw and tongue to play low notes. The lips contract as the tongue and jaw are elevated. That is not all. When everything is working together as a team, then you are set up for a natural pivot. *Tilting the trumpet up and down with the hands could be hazardous to the overall coordination of the whole mechanism, called embouchure.* In my mind, embouchure equals lips, air, jaw, tongue, and pivot. I have never seen or heard a fine performer who does not coordinate these elements of tone production.

Some excellent teachers talk about the "jaw thrust," which seems to me to be a bit harsh. I suggest pushing the chin forward to even-up the teeth as a starting position for a second-line G. One teacher I know urges his students to have a rock-solid jaw and that it should never move. Absolute non-movement of the jaw places a great burden on the other things that create the flexibility and agility you need to move from low to high notes. This reasoning possibly accounts for the difference in players. There are power players lacking finesse and agility who play with the rock-solid jaw. Then there are the coloratura solo players with great flexibility who allow more and quicker movements of the jaw. There is no right or wrong. It can be a matter of choice, or it can be using best the physical attributes with which you were born.

I have observed with my own eyes many of the finest players in the world who use the pivot, whether they know it or not. Their *not* knowing that they use the pivot is important, since they make all the natural movements that produce the pivot.

Yes, they pivot in Peoria. They also pivot in Ponder and Paradise.

John James Haynie, age six, on his baptism day
First Christian Church, Breckenridge, Texas, 1931

THE OTHER SIDE OF THE STAND

One Monday Mr. Haynie took my horns away from me and wouldn't let me practice for the week—gave me forty dollars and ordered me to go to the Texas Music Educators Association meeting in Dallas and just hang out. Why? Because I had literally practiced my way into total exhaustion of my embouchure! Did it work? Absolutely. On the following Monday when he gave my horns back, I played perhaps the best lesson of my life, and that following weekend gave a near-flawless concerto performance with the University Graduate Chamber Orchestra.

James Linahon

During my junior year of high school I started having serious problems playing the trumpet. I was frustrated. My playing was falling apart, and I didn't have a clue—after all, I was playing in band, orchestra, brass quintet, and stage band, where I was reaching some phenomenal high notes with the assistance of a quite small mouthpiece. Out of desperation I called Mr. Haynie for a "pow-wow" lesson. I hadn't studied with him for over four years by that time. I was very nearly terrified that my playing was dissolving. With endless patience, that keen analytical mind of his, and some direct questioning, it soon became evident that I was not actually practicing—only playing, and overworking, at that. I was under the assumption that I didn't have enough time, and he helped me study my weekly schedule to find a number of places where I could get some good work done. Thanks to that meeting, I redoubled my effort and commitment during the summer before my senior year, a year that saw me once again studying with Mr. Haynie. There is no doubt that his guidance helped me recover my skills and a good portion of my lagging self-confidence, so that I achieved several honors that last year in high school. He instilled in me a level of inspiration that has never left.

Richard Waddell

ENDURANCE

How nice it would be to always have a fresh lip. It can be managed in the practice room, even though few people will rest as much as they practice. We are always very impatient about learning to play. Our schedules are so full that too much has to be learned in such a short time, usually the day of or the night before the lesson. Then there are the organizations that students meet daily, and parts to be learned, and who would pass up a chance to make a few bucks playing a gig? It comes down to this: University students are not in the right environment to practice the way they should and would like to. The setting is all wrong, that is, until they lose their lips. When this happens the student suddenly has plenty of time to practice and to practice correctly, since he or she no longer is welcomed to play in the groups. It is a sad state of affairs when one must lose his chops so he will have time to learn how ***not*** to lose his chops.

I have seen it happen over and over, where musically talented people with a little flaw in their playing just use themselves up, never having the time to do some corrective work. I have thought a lot about creating the perfect environment for really learning to play well. Possibly a first- and second-year student should not be allowed to play in any organization at all, just like the freshmen athletes who are "red-shirted." They practice with the more experienced players, but they forego the game. Too many freshman music majors take all the hits of being on the front line from day one. Instead, I would add the performance-organization credit to the lesson credit and expect a greater effort in learning how to play correctly. It could become a controlled situation in which the student could, at his own pace, make whatever changes are necessary. Practice several short periods, rest and play, rest and play. Each week play a little more, and rest less. Always follow the rule that you should put the horn down at the first sign of fatigue, which can vary from day to day. Over the years I saw many students who were just ordinary players at first. Since they were not in demand, they had the perfect opportunity to work out their problems, practice correctly, and improve. By the time they became upperclassmen, they were on the way to becoming something special. On the other hand, some potential stars used themselves up at school, and when they went out in the big world, they had to start all over, with a job on the line. Fortunately there is a happy ending, because all those I know faced with this situation became serious students whose playing improved as the years passed.

At some point we must consider endurance in our practice periods. Webster defines **endurance** as "the ability to withstand hardship, adversity, or stress." How can one develop endurance if you never endure anything? By learning to practice exactly that. How do you do it? Those students who have everything going well—those without serious problems who really have the prospects of a professional career ahead of them—should consider going to the practice room once a week when free of other playing obligations, and **enduring**. Take your hardest music to the practice room and woodshed those tunes until you can't play any more. A good test will be to see how long you have to rest before your lip comes back. Time it. Good endurance not only means you can play loud and high for an unusual period, but also how quickly you can recover and be able to play the second or third show. When first beginning this experiment, schedule it when you do not have to play the next day because your recovery time might demand a day of rest. When I say "Play until you can't play any more," I mean play until you cannot play reasonably well any more.

I do not mean for you to play until you bleed.

Cisco High School Band, G. C. Collum, director, 1934
John Haynie, age nine, is the little boy in front, on the right

THE OTHER SIDE OF THE STAND

*One day the position of my bell dropped significantly when I tried to go into the lower register (actually, up to that day, it dropped all the time when I attempted the low register). Mr. Haynie quietly put his hand on the back of my head while slightly raising the bell, and the sound got **big**! I burst out laughing because the change was so immediate and for the good.*

Robert Bailey

As a young trumpeter I consistently had problems maintaining a tonal center in the register below the staff. John started me on a series of isometric lip exercises combined with long tones in the extreme low register. You can imagine that this was not glamorous playing, but John was insistent, and I thank him for that every day. John's methodology proved to me that with consistent embouchure "firmness," which was his word, it was like having a steel line attached to every note on the horn. You simply change air speed, tongue position and focus, and muscle tension for the various registers on the instrument. Without this consistent muscle tension you will never know for sure what note will come out when large intervals and drastic dynamic changes are involved.

Did this methodology pay off? You bet it did. I can't tell you how many eight o'clock AM recording sessions or film dates I have been on with overworked chops and a dead-tired physical condition. But fear never entered in because I was used to playing from a different perspective. I have had probably a hundred players ask me, "How do you get your chops to work so early in the morning after last night's gig?" I just smile and tell them I went to North Texas and there was this trumpet teacher I had named John Haynie.

James Linahon

THE LOW-DOWN ON PEDAL TONES

In those formative years as a child, I had private lessons with the city band director, G. C. Collum. My grandmother paid for a few lessons to get me started and to determine if I had a talent to play the cornet. Certainly Mr. Collum never mentioned pedal tones. I do recall that he gave me a lip-building exercise that I have never heard from any other source. He had me open a hymnal, and from the middle of the book, place several pages between my lips. Then I would hold the book with my lips with no use of the teeth clamping against the lips. Is this not a form of isometric contraction?

Pedal tones were never a part of my development, and I learned to play them only after becoming a seasoned player. Did pedal tones help me? I don't know if they did, but I have high regard for the use of pedal tones for my developing students. There is little practical use for the performance of pedal tones in trumpet literature, but I do highly recommend that students spend a lot of time practicing in the lower register, not only for the relaxation of the lips but also for developing a rich open tone quality and dexterity of the more difficult fingering combinations in the lower register.

For those students with endurance problems, pedal tones have proven to be a wonderful aid in relaxing the jaw, tongue, and lips. It makes sense to me that the more relaxed the lower register can be performed, the less strain and effort will be encountered in the upper register.

Since I am not a product of pedal tone development, I only refer to its use in my books without providing exercises. I do, however, wish to point out that others have covered the matter of pedal tones much more effectively than I could. Carlton McBeth, a Louis Maggio student, is probably the best-known advocate of the pedal tone system, and I strongly urge my students to learn all they can from his expertise and experience with this technique.

I first heard of the pedal tone system when I learned how it saved the career of Rafael Mendez. His embouchure was damaged in a freak accident, and I am told he sought help from Louis Maggio. Maggio never published his studies because he handled his students in different ways. The consistent use of pedal tones for all students' problems was the common bond.

There is strong evidence that the utilization of pedal tones can be effective and that overuse can be destructive. A common sense approach is the answer for those who adopt this method of embouchure development.

Since I seldom played pedal tones, most of my students didn't either. I would prescribe them as the need arose. Practicing in the lower register is a different matter. I insisted on it, especially with those who chose to play small mouthpieces just to help with the high notes.

It is too simple to just say, "Work on the low register." Not many realize that low register practice actually builds the high register, or even if they know it, they are not convinced enough to actually spend much time at this necessity of embouchure development. Just being able to play the low notes is not enough. The goal should be to play every note in a chromatic scale from low F-sharp to at least high F or G with exactly the same quality of tone. Often I hear three different tone qualities played by the same person, which is evidence that they try to use three different embouchures. I maintain that there is a different embouchure for every note. Tongue arch, mouthpiece pressure, and the angle of the horn are all different on every note to produce the most even sound. Observe the pro golfer on the putting green. He practices putting to develop a "feel" for how much energy it takes to strike a ball to move it two inches or sixty feet, just like a trumpet player does his chromatic scale.

Except as a compositional technique, pedal tones were not really meant to be performed, and many performers, if not most, alter the embouchure drastically to force the notes to respond. Some can maintain their basic embouchure without "setting in" the lower lip. It is admirable of those who can spend the time it takes to play the pedal notes with a proper embouchure; however, I wish to accomplish my goals going no lower than the F-sharp in search of the perfect embouchure for every note above.

William Latham wrote a piece for me with band accompaniment called *Fantasy for Trumpet and Band*. I premiered it at the University of South Alabama at Mobile. The first four notes were low F-sharps. Each F-sharp was to be as loud as possible and held for four counts, and the composer urged me to play these four notes so loud they bordered on ugliness. After the final F-sharp, he wrote a fast chromatic scale to high D. This was a real test of a full-sounding low register and the ability to make a smooth transition with the same full tone quality to the top.

Where to start and what to practice? Start with easy slurs—second-line G slurring down to C, then F-sharp down to B, etc., then go back up. Next I suggest playing the well-known *Flow Studies* by Vincent Cichowicz. Finally, go to my *High Notes, Low Notes* exercises 5A and B known as Coordination Studies, which use different articulations on each line and in each key.

As you practice these long tones think of the luxury of relaxing in a hot tub when slurring down to those low notes. There is no hurry. Linger on each note. Right now you need to learn to relax all over, except there must be a certain firmness in the lips to maintain a vibration. This is one time you can tell your metronome to stay at home.

THE OTHER SIDE OF THE STAND

I remember a lesson the morning after having performed a long and arduous concert with the One O'Clock Lab Band. Needless to say, my chops felt stiff and uncooperative. I was playing a difficult and awkward lyrical etude by Marcel Bitsch and, as predicted, having more than my share of difficulties. Mr. Haynie had attended the Lab Band concert and commented on how well the band played, and he suggested that I play the etude with the same intensity and passion. His suggestion worked. It was the best I played the etude all week. My chops suddenly felt "just right."

Ray Sasaki

I started lessons with John Haynie as a high school senior after I had hit my upper lip with the claw of a hammer. In my 7:00 AM lessons, we started our long relationship with a complete embouchure change. John's ability to do this was nearly unique in the world at the time. I benefit to this day from that early hour of work, having spent the past forty-one years earning my living playing in symphony orchestras.

Fred Sautter

I had been a member of a small U.S. Army post band during the height of the Vietnam War. One week all four of us trumpet players were out on funeral detail. Because of that, I was chosen to stay on base all the time to do the band work. When I arrived at North Texas my face was just too pooped to pucker anymore. More than anything, I wanted to be a professional trumpeter and the harder I tried, the worse I got. I went to Mr. Haynie to talk things over. He said I should give the trumpet one more year and if things were not better I should look for another career. He made me limit my practice and get my embouchure back in shape. A year later I was playing lead trumpet in the One O'Clock Lab Band.

Richard Steffen

SMASHING THE LIPS

Did that get your attention? Even though this is usually referred to simply as *mouthpiece pressure*, it's true that a trumpet player's lips are constantly being "smashed" between two solid objects—the mouthpiece and the teeth. I would venture to say that every trumpet player, even a beginner having that first concert dress rehearsal, has used too much pressure and suffered with this problem at one time or other. With many, the problem is chronic; every time they blow the horn, they hurt.

Using too much mouthpiece pressure is not unlike hitting your finger with a hammer; when you miss the nail the poor old finger is smashed between two solid objects. When trumpet players use too much pressure, they "smash" their lips, which, at the very least, reduces lip vibration. Sooner or later the vibration will stop entirely, probably sooner! Is there any player out there who has not experienced this pain, embarrassment, and discouragement? Having listened to thousands of solo performances in recitals, jury exams, or lessons, it is very easy to know when too much pressure is being applied to the lips. I hear that telltale sound well before things start coming apart, and sometimes I know the player is in trouble before he does. A less-experienced player might not even recognize the warning and will keep on pressing away, falling deeper and deeper into the mouthpiece, until the sound stops completely. No buzz, no sound, no nothing.

Some years ago I attended a family wedding in Chicago. All the music before, during, and after the wedding was played by a brass quintet. The first few selections were tastefully played and enjoyable to hear, but then I heard that warning sound. Sitting in the same row with me was my son-in-law Dave Zeagler, who was a trumpet player in the One O'Clock Lab Band at North

Texas, who toured with Stan Kenton, and who is currently "on call" in Houston. I looked at Dave and I knew instantly that he knew what I knew. After another selection or so, the whole audience knew. We heard a lot of second trumpet from then on.

The reason so many players have serious problems is because they abuse this very precious thing, the embouchure. They do not recognize the signs of lip fatigue and if they do, they ignore them. Maybe they should be arrested for embouchure abuse!

Apparently, there are those who can play their way through the initial breakdown and catch their "second lip"; when they have the mouthpiece sufficiently screwed into the lips, away they go. I cannot imagine that such an experience is enjoyable. Some players with weak facial muscles will never be free of this pressure and fatigue problem.

Another symptom of excessive pressure is that the mouthpiece moves all over the lips searching for "fresh meat"—off-center, too high, too low, lower lip rolled under too far. Therefore, one must start all over and discover a proper mouthpiece placement. One of the reasons the player is in trouble may be that he or she never had a proper embouchure in the first place.

My preference for mouthpiece placement is about half on the upper lip, half on the bottom lip, and centered from side to side. I know this is contrary to what some eminent pedagogues suggest. The one-third upper and two-third lower group can be very fine performers, but so can the half-and-half guys and gals. My reasoning is that when people are different in so many ways, why should we expect everyone to play with exactly the same mouthpiece placement? Starting at half-and-half, the mouthpiece can adjust itself to the jaw and teeth formation, whatever is most comfortable and gets the best results in sound, range, and endurance.

I just used the word "jaw." ***Don't underestimate the importance of setting the jaw as a part of mouthpiece placement.*** Most people have a normal occlusion of the teeth, which means that the lower teeth go behind the upper teeth when closing the mouth and elevating the chin. If we go with that position and relationship to start with in the middle register, the teeth and jaw have nowhere to go when ascending into the upper register. That is presuming that the teeth come close together in the upper register with the lower lip wanting to ride under the upper lip. There are other embouchure considerations to be discussed, but for now we are just trying to establish a jaw position to receive the weight of the mouthpiece in a position where the lips are most free to vibrate.

If one can buzz the lips without the mouthpiece, it is an excellent idea to do so if done with the jaw position and placement suggested. If you have to roll either the upper or lower lip under the other, it not only is a waste of time but also in conflict with the embouchure and mouthpiece placement we are trying to establish. It is imperative that buzzing the mouthpiece is practiced many times each day in short sessions, using a mirror. Ideally, start by buzzing the lips alone and then place the mouthpiece on the lips and keep that buzz going from lip buzz to mouthpiece buzz.

A reminder: Take full breaths and make the buzz loud and aggressive all the time, disallowing unusual pressure on the lips. Hold the mouthpiece at the end of the stem, and practice using minimum pressure of the mouthpiece and maximum pressure with the air. After about a week of this placement and buzz routine, add the trumpet. Sam Snead once told his golfing students, that when gripping the golf club, to imagine they were holding a little bird in their right hand, being careful not to grip the bird so loosely that it will fly away, nor grip or squeeze the bird so tightly that they will crush it. The point as it relates to the trumpet is to develop just the right amount of firm grip, but not encourage a pressure that would be offensive to the embouchure. How about calling it a relaxed firmness? What we want is a warm, free, and easy sound before going on to the next step.

Just because we will now add the horn does not mean that buzzing is no longer necessary. Are you ready for this? Buzzing is here to stay, forever. Each time you take the horn out of the case, buzzing is necessary to get the blood flowing in the lips to warm up to that foreign object being placed there.

I can imagine the upper lip saying to the lower lip, "Look out, here comes the hammer again. Won't that guy ever learn that we are his bread and butter, and instead of beating us up all the time he should take it easy? Haynie forgot something, because he was in a hurry to get to the golf course. He surely meant to tell everyone that when buzzing with the mouthpiece, they should match pitches with the piano. Better still, they should record long tones with the trumpet, then buzz the mouthpiece along with the tape. Haynie always mentioned some trumpet player who wrote those *Flow Studies*. What's his name? Oh yes, that famous Chicago trumpet player, Vincent Cichowicz."

John James Haynie, age eleven, 1936

THE OTHER SIDE OF THE STAND

Mr. Haynie said that air without embouchure development will not let you play high. You might have a Rolls Royce, but if you have no gas, it won't run. If you own a refinery and no car, that's no good either. You have to have both.

Duncan Brown

I would come into my lessons and squeal a few skinny high notes before playing for Mr. Haynie. He would invariably ask, "Is that the best sound you can make?" Though I was interested in playing high notes any way I could, he was telling me that a beautiful sound guides us to those notes.

Frank Campos

Mr. Haynie once put my music on the floor to demonstrate a different way of looking at things. He said, "See, now there are no high notes or low notes." In another lesson, he measured the distance between two pitches with his thumb and forefinger. "Look, these notes are only this far apart."

Cynthia Thompson Carrell

I was attempting to play one of Michael Gisondi's J. S. Bach transcriptions and was becoming more than a little frustrated with my lack of accuracy, particularly in the upper register. Mr. Haynie noted that my attitude toward the upper register was "coming up short," observing apprehension and fear of missing in my playing. He used a golf analogy to help describe and solve my dilemma. He explained to me that if you miss a putt, miss it long. At least if the ball is on the line, it has a chance to fall in the cup. If it comes up short, it has no chance, however accurate the line. The accuracy in my trumpet playing immediately improved, just by changing my approach from avoiding the miss and "coming up short," to "if you are to miss, miss it long."

Ray Sasaki

HIGH NOTES

At last you can read about the high notes on trumpet. Trumpet players enjoy a certain thrill in playing high notes, especially when the notes respond easily. Even players who struggle with range get pleasure just "eeking" out something above the staff. This feeling is sought by daredevils on snow boards and skis, by race car drivers, high divers, and sky divers. The list goes on. Big Band lead players say there is nothing like the feel of soaring over the band, and orchestral players enjoy high Baroque music and their little horns. There is a market for the high-note players. Those capable relish it, but there is another side of the picture. Fine trumpet performers lacking in embouchure strength live in fear that they will be limited in their choice of music for a degree recital, not making a top chair in band and orchestra, or even qualifying for a chair in a lab band. Worse still is the fear that they can not seriously consider a performance career in any field.

When I was a child I was known as a high-note player, and certainly I did not develop this ability through having lessons. I could squeal around with no idea of what notes I was playing. At age fourteen I played a solo called *Emerald Isle* by Colonel Earl Irons. It has many high C's and ends on a high F. I was quite comfortable playing in this register and I never tried to become the kind of high-note player we know today. No one was writing dissertations at the time of my youth. I would not have known about it anyway since there were no trumpet teachers where I grew up. In fact, after I began teaching at North Texas, I still didn't enjoy playing the higher-pitched trumpets because the literature was quite limited at that time. No one had been to the catacombs to excavate. In recent years, students have written about my high-note playing, and I think what was impressive to them was that I could just pick up my horn without any special warm-up, and demonstrate how to play something. I considered my range to include F and G above the staff. I would play a few double C's occasionally to see if I still could.

Now would be good time to mention that your actual performance range must be exceeded by several notes. Do not expect much of a dependable high C unless you can squeal out a few higher notes. If you want a good solid high F for performance, you'd better work at going a bit higher. It will develop your confidence to have a little reserve.

An analogy might clarify my point. You drive a Volkswagen Beetle, which is an excellent little car and still very popular to own. The car's speedometer says top speed is 60 mph, and on the highway that's how fast people drove them. On the other hand, a Lexus speedometer reads 140 mph as top speed. The point is that a sixty-mile-an-hour trumpet player is maxed out and has nothing in reserve in case he needs to go faster (higher). The Lexus trumpet player at 60 mph is still playing notes in the staff if 140 mph represents a double C.

What we have to work at is developing a reserve, and before we can do that, we must determine what your top range is right now. We must eliminate the fear-factor right now. From the beginning we must think of "notes as notes." It will take some doing, but not as long as you think. It all depends on your attitude. With this new attitude, here's what we will work on:

1. At this stage of confidence-building, the last thing I would have you do is go out and buy a high-note book where everything is above the staff.
2. I talked about relaxation in "The Low-Down on Pedal Tones" essay. Spend a few weeks working on total relaxation. Eliminate the tension from your body.

3. After that few weeks, strive for getting the same relaxation without pedal tones, playing down to no lower than F-sharp below the staff.

4. Our goal is to play third-space C with no more effort than low C. Ultimately the high C will be just another C.

5. You must spend more time buzzing the lips and buzzing the mouthpiece to create vitality in your sound.

6. Coordinating the air with the embouchure is an absolute must. Play those long tones in all registers. In everything you play double, triple, and quadruple your phrases.

7. Most of the playing up to this point is related to isometric contractions, but from this one movement we will use lip slurs. That is movement of the muscles of the face contracting the lips largely with the corners of the mouth

8. Take your Irons book, *27 Groups of Exercises*, and make fast slurs from bottom to top in a glissando manner.

9. Now is the time to use the coordination studies, exercises 5A and 5B found in *High Notes, Low Notes, and All Those In Between*. Mix the slurring and tonguing, changing articulations on every line and in every key.

10. You don't have time for two hours of this routine every day? Make time if you really want to improve your range and endurance.

Other considerations for learning to play comfortably and improving range could be finding a mouthpiece that will fit you and your horn. Even consider a new horn that is popular with high-note players. After you have paid your dues in the practice routine as outlined above, take the next step and use Clarke's *Technical Studies*, playing each exercise up an octave. Take it easy, and do not undo all your progress.

Best wishes. You can do it.

THE OTHER SIDE OF THE STAND

I recall my first lessons with John at a Texas Tech summer band camp in 1946 or 1947. He was holding a trumpet master class in a barn that had sawdust on the floor. Man, was it hot! I can hear him now, "Sit up straight! Support your sound with your diaphragm!" I recall with pride that he complimented my "good sound." Then I became a student at North Texas, and he took me under his wing. Trumpet became secondary to my growth as a composer, but to this day I pucker automatically when I hear good trumpet playing—all because of him.

Larry Austin

On one occasion, Mr. Haynie was listening to me play, telling me to breathe deeper, and he yelled, "Stop!!" Just scared me to death. I said, "What?" He replied," That sounded really good." The shock was worth the compliment.

Robert Bailey

My first lessons, the summer before graduate school, covered the entire course of study in huge chunks—very challenging and exciting. Mr. Haynie had me play a single slur from the Lowell Little book and to explain (and draw) the "perfect slur" between two notes. Then he told me to play the Clarke Technical study number two—five times in one breath. After I played it about three and one-half times (a great victory, I thought), he told me to either run or swim every night, to build up my wind. I did as instructed, and thirty days later there was a significant improvement in my breathing, which was reflected in my playing.

Ross Grant

Mr. Haynie taught me how the breathing apparatus works. This was in the days when there was lots of confusion "out there."

Dave Ritter

THE BIG FOUR: BREATH

Much has been said about the need to practice long tones in order to develop a good tone. Few teachers would disagree; not many, however, follow through by insisting that long tones be practiced regularly. It is assumed that the student will be encouraged to sit or stand with good posture in order for the breathing apparatus to function properly. The idea of "sitting tall" is sometimes helpful in the effort to foster "sit like we stand" posture.

Not only should the student have good posture and practice long tones, but he should also be aware that the volume of tone should be bold and aggressive. Nothing is accomplished practicing long tones with a weak sound. The student should work for a full, rich tone. Then, as he gains more control of the breathing process, he should reduce the dynamic level. Rarely does a young student play a "soft tone"; it is characteristically a "weak tone." Long-tone practice at all dynamic levels should be encouraged as the student progresses.

In working with students on improving breath control, I do not concern myself with how the initial breath is taken. It is far more important to be concerned with those muscles that get rid of the air rather than those that cause the air to be taken in. In telling young students to take a big breath several things can happen that are detrimental to a good tone. The inevitable problems of excessively lifting the shoulders and the subsequent tightening of the throat causing restriction of the tone are the most obvious results of artificial deep breaths. It is far better to use more of the air that is taken in normally than to take in too much air and then hold it back while playing the instrument. As stated before, a person has a much more positive control of the muscles that expel the air than he has of those muscles that cause the air to be taken in. If a student sustains a tone for maximum length, the next breath will be a full breath through necessity, and nature will see to it that it is taken correctly. This process of long-tone practice then is truly a forced expiration followed by an automatic forced inhalation. By going beyond the limits of normal breathing, the lung capacity can be increased and breath control can be improved.

Through this procedure the student can become artistic in his breath control without ever hearing the word "diaphragm." For those who want the whole truth, a study of the breathing process from an anatomical standpoint must be made. When Dr. James Lakin's article "Basic Respiration for Wind Instrument Playing," appeared in the April 1969 issue of *The Instrumentalist*, it was the best explanation I'd seen of the complete process of respiration in laymen's terms. Dr. Lakin allowed me to copy the article to distribute to my teaching assistants that year.

Lakin wrote:

Expiration, the mechanics of releasing the breath, is that part of the respiratory cycle which should be of greatest interest to the teacher and wind instrumentalist. The release of the breath, in conjunction with proper embouchure formation, enables the player to produce a tone on his instrument. The quality of the resulting sound depends, in large part, upon the degree of control which he is able to exert upon the expiratory mechanism. The greater the control of the breath, the greater the control of the tone produced. Thus, to produce a tone which is controlled in every aspect, the performer needs to be able to affect the maximum amount of control over the muscles of expiration.

Notice that no mention has been made concerning the diaphragm. [...] the diaphragm is the chief muscle of inspiration, contracting in a downward direction. Since a muscle may contract in only one direction, let us state once and for all that air cannot be pushed out of the lungs by tightening the diaphragm. On the contrary, the diaphragm must be in a state of relaxation during expiration. When the expiratory muscles contract they serve as a second-hand hammer to push the air out of the lungs. Thus, it may be said that the diaphragm does nothing voluntarily to assist in expiration. It serves only as the middle-man, so to speak, between the abdominal muscles and the lungs.

Often students say, "I can't do that," but the truth is they always have and always will. The breathing process is involuntary and no person can change the action of the muscles that take the air in and those muscles that help to blow air through the instrument. Students can concentrate on getting rid of the air, and then taking air in will be both natural and effective.

THE OTHER SIDE OF THE STAND

During my sophomore and junior years, I developed a tight-chest, throat-pinched quality in my playing. John couldn't find the right buttons to push and consequently became increasingly frustrated. At a pivotal lesson he said, "I am going to tie you up, Wayne, and throw you on the next boxcar out of town." I remember then that it was time I addressed the problem, if only in self-defense! I made myself relax, drop the shoulders, and have zero tension in my body while playing, concentrating only on tone and projection. It worked! I have taught that concept with great success for over forty years.

Wayne Cook

*One of my favorite memories of trumpet lessons with Mr. Haynie is the time he tricked me. I was having some "chop" problems and was losing confidence in my ability to cleanly and accurately hit notes above the staff. So in one of my lessons, Mr. Haynie told me to play a G at the top of the staff and then slur up to a high C. Knowing that I was going to have trouble playing the G in tune and even more trouble slurring up to the high C, I took a **huge** breath and proceeded to play the most beautiful, centered, in-tune G that I have ever played in my life. Immediately Mr. Haynie stopped me, before I slurred up to the high C and asked me what I was thinking about. I said, "The high C, of course." Then, as Aristotle might have done, he asked me what I had just learned. I thought a few seconds and said something about thinking less and just playing the horn. He broke out into the famous "Haynie grin" that he always got when he could tell that the light bulb had come on in one of his student's brains. And here I am, thirty-five years later, still trying to think less and play better, and you know what—when I do that, it still works!*

Bob Nero

OPEN UP—FOR TONE'S SAKE!

This was the title of an article written by James Jorgenson, a trombonist/graduate student who was in his year of residency at North Texas State College in 1951. We had much in common—we were the same age, graduates of Big Ten Universities of Wisconsin and Illinois, avid fishermen from our youth, and most of all, both of us were married to talented and enduring wives, Lorraine and Marilyn.

So what does "Open up—For Tone's Sake" mean? The first thing that comes to my mind to fit the description of beautiful tone is the so-called Chicago Sound, the rich sound of the Chicago Symphony brass section. OK, then what is the Chicago Sound? To my ears I hear a freedom from any nervous tension and great control over the other kinds of tension necessary for the body to perform the myriad tasks in performance. Therefore, the first element of good tone is control of the nervous system. I hear teachers and conductors scream at their pupils, "Relax! Relax!" This results in even more tension and poor tone.

The next requirement for attaining a good sound, the Chicago Sound, or even the Denton Sound, is good physical health and body conditioning. Fine players say that they use every muscle in their bodies in performance. Walking, running, swimming, lifting weights, and diet all play a part in maintaining good muscle tone in brass tone.

Practice is next on my list. Practice what? Start with careful attention to mouthpiece buzzing, always matching pitches with recordings and with the piano. Tuning CDs are available now. It is important to the embouchure and the breath to place each note exactly and to know how it feels. Random noises while buzzing may loosen up the lips but will not teach all parts of the anatomy where each pitch is located.

Practice long tones. Use up the air in what is called a *forced exhalation* and this will cause *forced inhalation*. Blow and keep blowing, and you cannot go wrong.

I cannot separate breath and embouchure in creating a sound; therefore, the embouchure must be conditioned. Vibration and buzzing were the first parts of embouchure development; next is development of strength, endurance, and flexibility. This is accomplished through lip slurs. Not only do the lips contract and relax, the tongue is the partner in making notes ascend and descend. Imagine saying "ah," which would represent the position for the lowest single note, and "ee," which would be the position for the highest. The lips and tongue elevation must find the correct adjustment for every chromatic tone from low F-sharp to as high as you can play. "Practice what?" you ask. Lip slurs.

Open up. This means to avoid elevating the tongue any more than necessary. This can only happen as the lip contraction gets stronger and the air goes faster through the horn.

Songs and melodies must all be played with full tone, as all your practice should be. Do not confuse a soft tone with a weak tone. Practice out of the box. Project the tone. Go out on a country road and play a concert for the cows. See that black cow way over there? Concentrate your mind and project your energy, mind, and sound on that one cow. Do not be surprised if that cow responds with a great big "*Moo*." You know, I think a cow uses the same muscles that we do when she sounds her best "*Moo*." Hear how she crescendos. Did you see that contraction of the abdominals? This all started with lessons from Jim Jorgenson. Now I am taking lessons from cows. You can bet the cows do it right. They have not had lessons on how to breathe.

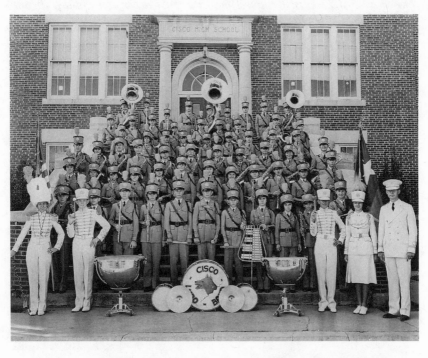

Cisco High School Band, Robert L. Maddox, director, 1938
John Haynie, 4th row, 2nd from right

THE OTHER SIDE OF THE STAND

Mr. Haynie always said, "Sit tall and sit as you stand. Try to stand up from a seated position without moving the feet. If you can do this, your posture will enhance your airway." He was right.

Duncan Brown

I was a horn player in that first class of John's "other" brass students. The most impressive thing about our lessons was the emphasis on tone quality. As we worked on the importance of having a mental image of good tone quality, there was a natural application of this mental image to characteristic tone in all instruments. I know I was a better teacher as I applied the importance of tone quality to my daily teaching.

Ivan Goodwin

When I started at North Texas, I had a small, tight sound. Mr. Haynie encouraged me to keep my head up and use more air. No one had ever made that simple suggestion. My tone then had that nice "round" quality.

Cathy Myer Kliebenstein

JJ taught me to direct my air in my horn playing, and that has helped me become a more confident player. He told me that you can never play too musically, and focusing on the air has made that happen.

Katie Zeagler

THE HEAD POSITION AND THE AIRWAY

A flaw that frequently contributes to a weak or inconsistent tone and air flow is the angle of the head and the subsequent distance of the chin to the chest. Every student should be taught from the beginning that before placing the mouthpiece (and horn) on the lips, the head, chin, and chest position should be normal. There should be no elevating or lowering the chin, just the ordinary day-to-day position that will assure the natural air flow. Projecting the jaw forward to even up the teeth is recommended. If the chin/head position is dropped too much the airway is partially blocked, the tone thins out, and the unstable air can cause poor attacks. It is rarely seen, but if the head is cocked backward to the point of stretching the muscles of the neck, the air flow will be inconsistent at best.

The Cure: Stand up tall and look straight ahead while using a mirror and move your head up and down as you try to determine the most natural and normal position of your head. When you find this most natural position you will discover that the normal functions of the embouchure (including the pivot of the jaw) will be in the most efficient position possible. It is important that one learn to sit using the same precautions.

Beware: I observed one of my finest and most successful students give evidence of cutting off the air supply by lowering and pointing the head and horn downward on the final few notes of the music. It was a means of forcing a decrescendo to a whisper by physically reducing the airway to zero. Not a problem unless one remains in that head/horn position on the next piece.

Simply stated, be sure the airway is open by adjusting the head position for all registers.

THE OTHER SIDE OF THE STAND

One thing that I remember John Haynie taught me was his concept of play-
ing sweet tones and long tones for breath control, volume, and embouchure
development.

Bud Cothern

I remember long-tone clinics where I, as a ten-year-old, would whip many
older students because JJ had taught me the importance of long tones in im-
proving the breathing process. I also remember that he challenged the audi-
ence just to hold its breath while he played a long passage from Goedicke's
Concert Etude *in one breath. They had to breathe before he did.*

Mark Haynie

During one lesson, Mr. Haynie told me something about the first three stud-
*ies of his **Development and Maintenance** book that has been the main*
idea of my teaching and playing. The first study is a long tone—think about
a relaxed breath in and a relaxed breath out. The second study is chromatic,
and he said to play it like a long tone and just "wiggle my fingers." The
third study is a lip slur. Again, he said to keep things simple and to think
about it as a single long tone. I've tried to approach playing in just this way
ever since.

Richard Steffen

Every Saturday morning I would wake up hearing the same trumpet long-
tone warm-ups coming from the living room. After I had married David
*Zeagler and **he** gave trumpet lessons at home on Saturday mornings, I heard*
those same warm-ups and I wondered, "What have I done to myself?"

Melinda Haynie Zeagler

HOW LONG IS A LONG TONE?

How long is a long tone? I would ask people that question and virtually all would say that long tones last for four beats. Some said it was as many as twenty counts, but I never heard the answer I was looking for. I believe that a long tone is held as long as you can sustain a sound *plus four beats when there is no tone coming from the horn*. Holding these long tones will make you aware of muscles you've never become acquainted with, especially when blowing. Taking in the air uses completely different muscles that may or may not function properly unless the previous breath is depleted. The object is to use up the air, forcing the resulting natural full breath. The tone should be full, robust, and aggressive. A skinny, little, whispery tone misses the whole point.

I let the body itself teach a student how to take a big breath. If you use all the air, then the body will replace what you used by necessity. A student must experience being completely out of air before the anatomy takes over and breathes for him. This, then, is truly a natural breath and cannot be done incorrectly.

Throughout my book *How to Play High Notes, Low Notes and All Those In Between*, I require these long tones in almost every study. Of course, long tones are good for purposes other than to improve control of the air. They are a form of isometric contraction, which is a part of embouchure building.

A fine, flexible embouchure that has a lot of vibration is a must for long phrases. Aha! Lip and mouthpiece buzzing to the rescue. Trying to play music with the mouthpiece takes a lot more air than blowing the horn.

Breath capacity can be improved in learning to use the reserve air supply. The use of long tones is possibly the most agreed-upon practice routine to develop that control.

THE OTHER SIDE OF THE STAND

In my lessons, Mr. Haynie wouldn't let me continue a scale if I didn't begin with a good attack. This was also the case with the Arban studies and pieces of music he would have me sight read. I was prompted to concentrate on my attack to have a quality sound. It's true what he also said, that you can apply the rules and fundamentals of playing to everyday life.

Anna Cox

The other point of emphasis was attack. JJ was always interested in how the tone started. His videofluorographic studies revealed much of what we understand today about the attack. He also loved listening to vocalists because of the different ways they could shape the beginning and release of notes. He insisted that every note begin with a good attack. He always found analogies that the student could relate to specifically in this regard. With me, he used golf and fly fishing. He said making a clean, soft entrance on a top-line F was like "hitting a wedge over a bunker to a tight pin," or "softly dropping a dry fly in the quiet water just below a big rock—like a butterfly with sore feet."

Mark Haynie

*I remember a great lesson on the Martini **Toccata** when Mr. Haynie had me change the articulation to bring out the musical line. It made a huge difference in the way I expressed the melody.*

Greg Jones

*When I played out of either the **Development and Maintenance** book or the Bitsch etude book, Mr. Haynie would ask, "What do you do to tongue fast like that?" I grew up on the spicy food of New Mexico, and I always said, "It must be the chili." Since Mr. Haynie was a master of tonguing technique, I took that as quite a compliment.*

Frank "Pancho" Romero

THE BIG FOUR: TONGUE

When I first started to teach in 1950, I was well aware that it was wrong to ever let the tongue come between the teeth and lips in making an attack. Conventional wisdom stipulated that the tongue must be placed just behind the upper teeth where the teeth and gums meet. In fact, my own tonguing did not follow this rule.

It bothered me that I was doing one thing, but trying to teach another. Then in 1952, a fine baritone player, Lida Oliver Beasley, became my student. Her tonguing was sensational. After hearing her play, I asked her if she knew how she did that so well. She blushed and said, "Mr. Haynie, I don't tongue correctly. I tongue between my teeth."

Well, that did it. No longer was I going to teach something I didn't follow myself. Since that time I have taught students to let the tongue go where it wants to go. Let the tongue find where it works best. It will take some experimentation and you will know what works best for you.

The misconception of tongue placement stems from the notion that the tongue is in the identical place for every note regardless of whether the tone is high or low. It is inconceivable that all notes could be tongued from the same position when there are so many other obvious physical changes—that is, the arching and flattening of the tongue, the motion of the jaw, and contracting and relaxing the lips.

Many fine players know that their tongue goes between the teeth and might even touch the lips to attack notes in the lower register. This "touching" position is directly related to the position of the tongue. When the tongue is in a higher "ee" position, the tongue easily touches the palate behind the teeth; when the tongue is in a lower "ah" position, the tongue might touch between the teeth. Playing "ta," "tee," or "tu," changes the arch of the tongue, but does not necessarily indicate the position of the tongue for attack. Vocal syllables help identify a concept of starting the tone. For that reason, any vowels following the letter "t" are satisfactory.

As the student masters a clear, definite "tu" attack, he already has learned two-thirds of triple tonguing and one-half of double tonguing. The remaining one-third or one-half is referred to as the "ku" attack. Actually, the "ku" is produced by building up the air pressure toward the back of the tongue. It's like whispering "ku," not saying "ku." The student should work on the "ku" attack until it sounds as nearly like the "tu" as possible. Then he can mix up the "tu" and "ku" syllables and slowly work on them. The chart in the essay "Triple Tonguing Is as Simple as One, Tu, Three" will be of great help with this.

The two most commonly accepted methods of syllable order in triple tonguing are "tu-tu-ku" and "tu-ku-tu." There is a growing interest in using the double tongued syllables "tu-ku" as the triplet pattern like this: tu-ku-tu, ku-tu-ku. Therefore, the double-tongued triplet should be considered as a third possibility. The preference is an individual matter determined by the nature of the music to be played.

I'll say it one more time. *Let the tongue find where it works best.*

John Haynie's family, 1939

Standing (l to r): grandmother Jessie "Nannie" Benedict, mother Lelia, John, sister Jessie Lee, grandfather John "Papa" Benedict; kneeling (l to r): brother Harvey, father James holding sister Patty, John's squirrel dog Bounce

THE OTHER SIDE OF THE STAND

For those times when I had difficulty finding the first pitch of a piece, Mr. Haynie would say, "You have to 'taste' the note."

Cynthia Thompson Carrell

Mr. Haynie worked to help me use smoother tonguing and use my harder tonguing style for emphasis.

Cathy Myer Kliebenstein

John had an insightful and very skilled awareness of how to improve finger and tongue coordination. He observed that "most players think that a missed note is because of their lips, but I believe that 98% of the time it is because uncoordinated valves and tongue have caused the air stream and lips to misfire." Of course when he said this it was like someone turning on the light in a darkened room at your first boy-girl dance—panic followed by sheepish grins and then the "Oh, I get it" awakening.

James Linahon

I was puzzled by the mechanics of the articulations I heard Clifford Brown do on a recording, so I had Mr. Haynie analyze the recording and he worked it out. I knew he would be able to tell me what I was hearing, based on all his years of teaching so many players.

David Miller

BREATH ATTACKS

Breath attacks are very beneficial in helping students realize that air is the catalyst for producing a tone. So much emphasis has been placed on the importance of the embouchure and tongue in playing an attack that the air is sometimes too little, sometimes too much. The embouchure has a different amount of tension for every note and might be in exactly the right position for an attack on a given note, but if the air does not drive its way through the lips, the result will be a bad attack. In my opinion, the worst sounding attack is the "fu-fu" sound when the tongue action, embouchure, and breath are not coordinated in a positive way. Chances are the air is inadequate to balance the other components of attack.

There is a practical application in performing music where the attack should not be heard. The listener should hear no percussiveness in a normal attack. The *tone* simply appears from nowhere. Many times I have used the silent attack in the performance of vocal repertoire. The human voice is capable of so many variations of beginning a tone that we should listen very carefully and emulate those sounds. The *words* dictate the attack of the vocalist and a vocalist would be horrified at my using the word attack. Nevertheless, I use the word which simply describes a beginning of the tone for an instrumentalist. As an experiment, read the last sentence *out loud*. Read it again and notice the tongue action in speaking. Now, place the trumpet mouthpiece on your lips and again say the words without blowing the horn. Next, on a second-line G play the rhythm of the sentence in a detached, normal everyday trumpet attack. Say the words again. Now the test! With the horn, play the sentence trying to make the same nuances of attack just like a singer sings.

Notice that some attacks may not use the tongue at all, and that is why a trumpeter must learn to make breath attacks.

I use the breath attacks for other reasons. Both double and triple tonguing require making an attack with the infamous "ku" attack. Here the goal is to make the "ku" sound just like the crisp and detached "tu" attack. When I played in band and orchestras I would use the "ku" attack to keep that syllable focused.

Another device I used especially often with my students was this. Many of my younger students rode their bicycles to lessons and parked them in plain view as we had their lesson in my living room. Now, imagine a wimpy sound, no brilliance, no aggressiveness, no energy being used at all. To make a point, I would ask the student to imagine the following:

Someone walks up and gets on your bicycle and starts to ride off. What would you do since you obviously can't catch him? Almost always my student would bristle and tell me that they would at least yell at the thief. I asked him to show me how, and the student would yell, *"Hey!"* with vigor. Then I would tell the student to put that same energy into blowing the horn. **Without using the tongue, blow air through the horn using the "Hey!" attack.**

In the effort to make the breath attacks as described there is a danger of getting lazy with the fingers, and the result will be a delayed "fu-fu" attack. This happens when the valves are not all the way down or up before the air is sent to make the attack.

A common belief is that the air and fingers arrive at the same time for a perfect attack. I say the fingers must get there first. To assure that the fingers *do* get there first, practice scales using a metronome. Depress the valve or valves exactly on the beat and make the attack on the upbeat. This little exercise will guarantee that the fingers are in place waiting for a good attack to happen.

John James Haynie, age 16

*This photo appeared on the cover of the Texas Music Educator conven-
tion issue, February 1941. The note inside the cover read, "John James
Haynie is only a junior in the Mexia High School Band, directed by
Robert L. Maddox, but he has a clinic and contest record that would do
honor to a post-post-graduate."*

THE OTHER SIDE OF THE STAND

When the North Texas boys would play at the Baptist Church, they'd warm up with their scales, and some sure played faster than others. I always told them that John said to warm up with low tones and sweet sounds. Then they could triple tongue to show off!

Bud Cothern

*The most important technical assistance Mr. Haynie gave me was getting my triple-tonguing going. I thought it to be physiologically impossible for me since I had tried unsuccessfully to master it for eight years already. The effective procedure he gave me was simply assigning me Guy Ropartz's **Andante and Allegro**, which required triple tonguing in brief bursts that I could do after much hard work. I had worked before but always "hit the wall." With his instruction and encouragement I broke through that wall.*

Ruth Jane Holmes

I was the "on scholarship" boy from Nocona, Texas, ready to set the world on fire with my fabulous trumpet playing. I walked into my first lesson, decked out in blue jeans and cowboy boots, and Mr. Haynie told me to have a seat. His first question was, "Can you double tongue?" "Yessir." He had me do some. Then he said, "Can you triple tongue?" "Yessir." I did some of that. He reached for his cornet and said, "Shoot, I can single tongue faster than that." My first thought was, "Nobody can do that." Then he did! I thought to myself, "John boy, you got lots of practicing to do!"

John Parnell

I was an oboist, and John and I frequently fished Garner's Lake together. Sometimes I would "sneak in" a brass question. I still remember one question and answer: "When do you teach double tonguing?" "Before they realize it's hard." I've used that same philosophy in teaching almost everything!

Lowry Riggins

Triple Tonguing Is as Simple as One, Tu, Three

Count them. There are two "tu" syllables and one "ku" syllable when you triple tongue, and it is a "must do" to spend a lot of time practicing single tonguing. The faster you can single tongue, the faster you can triple tongue.

I have started absolute beginners on triple tonguing, teaching them to play the "ku" attack just as clean and neat as the "tu" attack. I wish I had learned it this way. I was told to *say* "tu-tu-ku" over and over. I rode my bicycle from the elementary school to the high school for band rehearsals, and I would say "tu-tu-ku" all the way there and back. Following the ride, I would take my horn out and continue to say "tu-tu-ku" into the horn, and I still could not make it sound right. Then quite by accident I just blew the horn without saying anything, made the same tongue action, and lo and behold, I could triple tongue! After this, it was a simple matter to double tongue. All I had to do was leave out one of the "tu's."

When I began teaching at North Texas in 1950, many of my students had never had a private lesson and had tried to triple or double tongue without the good fortune I experienced. The problem with most was that they could not triple tongue any faster than they could single tongue. My remedy for this problem was this: I would have the student pick any note—second-line G is good enough—and then play only one triplet at a time as a pickup to a downbeat. Like this: tu-tu-ku **Tu**. Do it again, again, and again. Now, play two triplets as pickups to the downbeat.

Smoothness and speed will be determined by getting the "ku" attack to sound just as good as the "tu." I would have them mix up the order and number of T's and K's, like this eye-chart of triple tonguing:

☞ T-K-T T-K-T

☞ T-K-K T-K-K

☞ K-K-T K-K-T

☞ K-T-K K-T-K

☞ T-K-T K-T-K

☞ T-T-K T-T-K

   .As soon as the K attack is made with confidence, students should immediately change notes to learn to coordinate the tongue and fingers. Do not allow yourself to develop fast tonguing on the same pitch without learning to coordinate the **Big Four** on moving notes. What is this? ***Embouchure, Breath, Tongue, and Fingers.***

John James Haynie, age seventeen
Mexia High School senior picture, 1942

THE OTHER SIDE OF THE STAND

The cine- and videofluorographic research John initiated and completed during my years at North Texas, which was the basis for my doctoral dissertation in the early 1970s, is still one of the most important pedagogical tools in brass instruction. His work in this area created a lasting interest in the physiological phenomena of brass performance. His research led to the confirmation of the roles of the tongue arch, instrument pivot, and teeth aperture variance during trumpet performance.

Keith Amstutz

I often reflect on the videofluorographic studies that were recorded during my days at North Texas. The discovery of my extremely high palate and subsequent tongue arch was both a puzzle and a curiosity. The conventional wisdom at the time was that I shouldn't have been able to play the trumpet at all! The fact that I played at such a high level was quite the discussion of study for those involved with the project.

Larry Hodgin

During the mid-to-late 1960s, the Haynie studio was characterized by research, through X-ray technology, on the function of the body during trumpet performance. Seventy-three trumpeters (and a few clarinetists) were photographed internally during that time, and the sessions were most enlightening. In fact, when Maurice André came to the campus for a recital some time later, even he was X-rayed—for a price (!)—and his accompanist was hired to translate for him—for a price(!)—so Monsieur André would know when to inhale, to slur, to double tongue, etc. I never got to see those films, but by some accounts his innards did not look significantly different from ours!

Douglas Smith

VIDEOFLUOROGRAPHIC RESEARCH WITH DR. ALEXANDER M. FINLAY

I sometimes just sit and wonder how many golf courses we played together, how many different streams we fly fished, how many tamales and tacos we consumed together, how many trips our families shared, how many times we hunted together, and so on. Ours was a first-class friendship. I could go on and on about Alex Finlay, but I want to tell you about the most important thing we ever did together.

We were out fishing one day and out of the blue, I said to him, "Let me explain to you how the breathing process works." "*What?*" asked Alex, surprised at the break in his day-dreaming. I told him not to interrupt my explanation, as if he were a trumpet student hearing it for the first time.

I then elaborated about the diaphragm being a muscle used for inhalation, which I had learned recently. Fishing was forgotten, and Alex said, "Well, John, let's go to my office and take some X-ray pictures of you playing your trumpet."

Through the use of X-ray film, we verified what was already known about the breathing process. It was a simple thing to film the diaphragm and to see that its function had to do with inhalation, not exhalation, which could be studied in various anatomy books. This session led to telling Alex of my concern about what goes on inside the oral cavity. My really big question, and the one that had puzzled me for years was this: *Did the tongue arch during trumpet playing?*

Some days afterward, Alex called to invite my teaching assistants and me to go to Baylor Hospital and use their recently acquired fluoroscope with an 8mm camera attached. At that time there was no provision for sound. Doug Smith, Keith Johnson, James Smith, and I went to Dallas on a Sunday morning to experiment with the new equipment. That afternoon, Alex took us all to see the Dallas Cowboys play Cleveland. Such was his love of sports and his generous nature.

Not long after this, Dr. Finlay obtained the same equipment for his Denton X-ray lab, and this set the stage for a more thorough study of the oral cavity. With the appropriate approval and a modest faculty grant, the Haynie-Finlay research was about to happen.

Some seventy university students and at least ten additional professional musicians participated in two different formats. My observations were published in a sixteen-page booklet using Doug Smith's title—*A Videofluorographic Presentation of the Physiological Phenomena Influencing Trumpet Performance*. Those observations were as follows:

- Jaw Position: It is desirable to project the jaw to the extent necessary to equalize the teeth.

- Teeth and jaw aperture: The great majority will show that to accommodate the low notes the teeth are opened.

- Tongue arch: All our subjects [whose videotapes were shown during the lecture] show a definite arching of the tongue.

- Pivot: All our subjects [whose videotapes were shown] show some use of the pivot.

- Mouthpiece pressure: Mouthpiece pressure increases in upper register performance and with increased dynamics.

- Position of tongue for attack: The amount of aperture of the teeth and jaw will determine the position for the attack.

- Position of the tongue for double and triple tonguing: The position of the teeth, jaw, and tongue for saying the syllable is different from the position used when actually playing.

The tongue arch as described by Colonel Earl Irons in his book, *27 Groups of Exercises*, was the most revealing in that several subjects claimed they did not arch their tongue, but kept it flat in the bottom of their mouth. They were wrong. The position of the tongue at the beginning of an attack was another belief that was blown out of the water and proved they really did not know how the tongue was functioning. They were guessing.

THE OTHER SIDE OF THE STAND

Scale exams!!! I was so exhilarated when I was one of those fortunate few to play the scale exam over all major/minor/Matteson forms perfectly! I worked diligently for that accomplishment, but I thank Mr. Haynie for the challenge. My students are given scale and technique exams every semester.

Marilynn Mocek Gibson

I remember well what Mr. Haynie said about the scale exam, "Scratch, hesitation, bobble, or chip—the scale is wrong." It has served me well.

John Harbaugh

I have thought about this virtually every time I have had to work in a professional situation. As a studio session player in LA, I have often ended up with the "heat," also known as the "hard part" when there are lots of notes requiring skilled technique. I attribute my ability to handle these challenges to John's sage observations and meticulous approach. His multiple-tongue exercises, awkward finger/tongue routines, and repetitive insistence, while frustrating, did produce the results that one needs to become an artist. His published trumpet books are a gold mine of these exercises.

James Linahon

THE BIG FOUR: FINGERS

The use of the fingers completes the quartet of physical functions involved in playing the trumpet. Embouchure, breath, tongue, and fingers must come together as a team in such perfect coordination that we could say the four entities actually become the instrument. When you purchase a piano, you have a musical instrument. Touch a key and a musical sound is there ready to be refined by touch and sensitivity of a performer. Anyone can play that same piano with the same basic sound. On the other hand, when a person purchases a trumpet all he gets is an open-ended piece of tubing coiled here and straight there, a mouthpiece, and a bottle of valve oil. For music to come from this coil of brass tubing, the trumpet player must develop the *Big Four* before the pretty horn can make a musical sound. In no way am I making light of the effort that must be made to become an accomplished pianist. Different instruments require different physical actions.

The point must be made that training the embouchure, breath, and tongue cannot be totally separated. Finger training is another matter. Not only are the fingers associated with the other three, they are connected the same way to the brain. Embouchure, breath and tongue are so connected and dependent upon each other that a trained trumpet player rarely even thinks about that part of the team. Not often do the embouchure, breath, and tongue cause you to misplay some notes. As stated previously, the fingers are connected to the brain in such a way as to react to what the eyes see in order to read music. When the fingers misfire, the result is mistakes. This misfiring can be the problem of eyesight and focus, a matter of intelligence, or the careless nature of the player. When it is obvious that "woodshedding" is necessary, the first step is to slow down the tempo.

Now why is that? It is the only way the eyes can focus on one note at a time and remain focused until the correct fingering can be applied. This, in turn, will trigger the embouchure to find each note, with the proper amount of breath, and with some kind of articulation. As these steps are improved, the tempo can be gradually increased to the proper tempo of the music.

In order to achieve the greatest control of fingering and to develop the maximum speed, let us first consider hand positions. The trumpet should be held firmly with the left hand, leaving the right hand free to manipulate the valves. This implies that the little finger of the right hand be free of the finger-ring and allowed to move as the other fingers move. Furthermore, the right hand thumb must not be bent in a cramped position, but should be placed between the first and second valves, under the leadpipe, and allowed to bend slightly as required to arch the three fingers. The three fingers should be placed lightly on the valves just back of the fingertips. Caution should be observed in not pulling the valves down, not playing with the fingers straight and stiff, not allowing a double-jointed action of the first joint of the fingers, and not playing with the very tip of the fingers.

What to practice is an important factor in the development of finger execution. Scales are basic and every effort should be made to get the student to enjoy scale practice. With young students, scales can be taught with subtlety and persistence; scales are seldom taught, however, at this level, as evidenced by the few college students who can effectively play all major and minor scales. At a young age, they were never convinced that mastery of scales ensures accurate and disciplined fingers as well as improving sight reading ability. Here's a story about cornet virtuoso Leonard B. Smith and one of his approaches to fingering.

Many years ago Frank Elsass invited me to sit with him at a cornet/trumpet clinic being delivered by Leonard B. Smith. I was in a state of euphoria. After a quarter century, I had now reached a pinnacle of my career when Leonard Smith introduced his beloved friend, Frank Elsass, and me to the audience. Both Mr. Smith and Mr. Elsass were soloists with the Goldman Band.

Much of the clinic was familiar to me at that time since I had followed in their footsteps. A couple of points, however, are still clear in my mind about that clinic. I recall that Mr. Smith removed the valves from his cornet, took the felt pads out, then put the valves back in the horn. He told us that he had his students do this to make a point of depressing the valves with vigor and lifting the fingers quickly without riding the valves up. "Bang the valves down" were the words he used. Even in slow and melodic playing, the movement of the fingers must be as positive as when playing fast and loud. He asked the audience to listen to the clatter of the valves without the felt pads, clackity-clack. In listening to his students he would then determine for sure if the valves were going all the way down and coming all the way back up. Point made.

After this incident Mr. Elsass leaned over and said to me something like this, "There he goes again with one of his teaching examples." Over the years, I had the pleasure of working with many of the students of Frank Elsass. From them, I learned that his style of teaching was characterized by demonstrating his remarkable playing for his students to observe and hear the proper techniques of trumpet performance.

Another lesson learned by the new kid on the block was that here were two giants who had great careers, each allowing his own personality to come forth in the products of his pedagogical procedures. Me? I decided to emulate some of both.

THE OTHER SIDE OF THE STAND

In one of my last lessons with Mr. Haynie, he mentioned my faulty hand position, a topic he had mentioned more than a couple of times in our work that year. He told me that soon I would be sitting in my own studio, with the snow quietly falling outside, and with nothing more important to do than practice. "That will be the best time to address the problem, not in the middle of all this hectic playing activity." I can't tell you how many times I have been sitting in my studio (with the snow falling!) and the trumpet in my hands, when my mind turns to his words. It was a masterful bit of programming: he was setting me up to remember the lesson at the appropriate time.

Frank Campos

I was sixty-five years old when I went to John Haynie for help on the trumpet. He made sure I didn't play holding the trumpet down, but straight in front of me, keeping my fingertips on top of the valves.

Bud Cothern

John would play along with me, giving me the perfect characterization of tone, nuance, and colorful melodic phrases. He would also demonstrate the styles that should come from the written page. Many times he would say, "Pop those fingers, pop those valves, pop those notes out. Don't have lazy fingers."

Joe Harness

THE ARCH OF THE FINGERS

A lot has been said about the "arch of the tongue," but what about the "arch of the fingers?" I see trumpeters with all kinds of detrimental hand and finger positions because not much space in books or in lesson time is devoted to this. We have a lot to learn from artists who play piano and other instruments.

The quickest way for me to bring to mind the proper curvature or arch of the fingers would be for me to toss you a tennis ball. Simply hold that tennis ball in your right hand, grasp it firmly and rotate the wrist to observe both right and left sides. To strengthen your right hand squeeze your hand, relax it, squeeze it, relax it, over and over. For those whose fingers are double-jointed, this ball squeezing routine is a must. First the fingers bend backward and then they go down, resulting in a delay. If the attack is made with the first motion, which happens before the valve actually goes down, a coordination problem arises, often called "sloppy fingering."

When holding the tennis ball you will notice the natural position of the fingers on the valves. The arch will assure the correct position disallowing the straight fingers as used by many. Instead of using the end of the fingers, these players depress the valves very close to the knuckles. Obviously the finger tips are not used at all.

It is possible that for one reason or another some students strike the valve caps with their finger nails, which should be avoided. Either the arch is too straight and down or the finger nails are too long.

A lot of talk about nothing? Maybe. Think about it.

THE OTHER SIDE OF THE STAND

I remember having a make-up lesson in Mr. Haynie's living room during the winter holidays—there was a fire going in the fireplace. We were playing duets, and both were playing well. When we finished, he said, "Isn't it fun to play the trumpet?" He always made it fun.

Bob Blanton

I'll never forget a rehearsal with my accompanist, when Mr. Haynie instructed me to go to the other side of his filing cabinets and begin the solo just by breathing—no eye contact! His point? It doesn't take much activity or motion to begin together. Just breathe naturally in rhythm, and the pianist will commence perfectly with you. It worked!

Marilynn Mocek Gibson

*At North Texas, I quickly learned that my talent was pretty ordinary. In one lesson, when I was preparing for a recital, Mr. Haynie said words to the effect, "You are playing this technically perfect, but you need to play **musically**." His statement really stuck with me as I was re-evaluating my future. I loved the trumpet, but I realized I needed to look elsewhere for my profession. After graduation, I became a Navy pilot, served in Vietnam, and became a commercial pilot. During these thirty-six years, I spent thirty-five of them playing my trumpet in military and local bands. I loved every minute of it. Thank you, Mr. Haynie, for all you did for me.*

Karl Lassey

After each dress rehearsal for my doctoral recitals, Mr. Haynie would make a few general observations about tuning or pacing for endurance and then finish by saying, "Well, Al, you have already passed this recital, because I'm happy with it, and I'm the one you have to satisfy. Now, just go out and enjoy the performance tomorrow."

Al Moore

ON STAGE—THE REASON FOR BEING

There are many reasons for learning to play a trumpet; however, the most important one should be the preparation to play for others. Like it or not you will play for others and, from the beginning, you should be aware that someone is listening to every note you play. That one person you are playing for is yourself, the most critical of all listeners. If you cannot please yourself, then why should anyone else want to hear you?

When you walk out on the stage to play you are bringing along more than your accompanist, trumpet, music, mutes, and a glass of water. The other baggage you are bringing out of the wings is your reputation as a person, as a musician, and as a technician of the instrument. It is good to play for your friends, and the cultivation of their friendship should be a lifetime goal. True friends will want you to play well. That is why they came, to cheer you on. When Maurice André walked onto the stage in the old Main Auditorium at North Texas in 1970, he received an immediate standing ovation. It was spontaneous, as everyone stood as one, not one here and there. It was electric. How we all would like to carry that "baggage" on stage! Monsieur André told me afterward that it was one of his finest recitals. Was there a connection?

The number one cause of nervousness, stage fright, and fear is lack of preparation. Sometimes the music is too difficult or not suited for your style. Certainly we should always be reaching upward, but the reaching upward should be done in the practice room. Good judgment (or lack of it) in selecting repertoire very well may determine the success of your performance. You should be working on a wide range of solo repertoire, including the major works like the Haydn *Concerto*, the great romantic Russian works such as Arutunian's *Concerto for Trumpet*, the French

Morceau de Concours pieces, the cornet virtuoso solos by Clarke, the contemporary and experimental works of our American composers; and by all means, include transcriptions of vocal literature for which you can do the editing.

From this vast amount of music, pick those pieces for the recital stage that are kind to you. Unfortunately, too many advanced degree students have not settled on their degree recital pieces as late as two months before their recital. No wonder they are nervous on the stage with the usual results. It is interesting that no one ever thinks enough of his playing on a degree recital to use that recording as an audition for a teaching position. Yet, the student would be devastated if the faculty failed him on the recital.

Other considerations include the physical preparation for the recital, the mechanics, and the details. For instance, never clean the horn inside and out just the day before the recital. Keep it clean and well-conditioned all the time. A word of caution about your apparel—wear dark clothing in case the excess oil drips on your pants or dress; men, check your zipper one more time before walking out on the stage.

Before the recital and prior to the audience coming into the hall, go on stage and tune your horn thoroughly. Tune and mark your slide in two places: where you are on those first notes, and where you will be as the temperature rises inside the horn. Tuning is a matter of tuning every note of every piece. Call it ***tune as you play***. Often, too much time is taken tuning for the audience and not for yourself. In this situation you very well might be showing the audience how "out of tune" you are. When you enter the stage, followed by your accompanist, give him or her time to sit down and have both eyes on you for an immediate start following the ovation you hope to receive. By all means, acknowledge the warm reception and then begin. Do not empty the water key on stage before you play a note. Avoid all such types of nervous behavior. Example: I attended a concert by Doc Severinsen, and in a two-hour concert he never let the audience see him empty his horn or tune. I held my field glasses on him the entire time. What is recommended before going on the stage and also after you get there, is to take deep breaths, exhausting the air and then refilling. This also can be a fetish, and you should not make a show of it.

At last we have you on stage after a lifetime of preparation. You should have the feeling of supreme confidence saying to yourself that you are as prepared as possible. You know you can play every note. You can play it from memory you know it so well. It is also the time to give thanks to God or the superior being you worship who will play the horn with you. You will not be alone if you have prepared yourself totally. It all comes together right now. Enjoy it.

Our soloist is now on stage and ready to play the performance of his life. In fact he must consider that every time he goes on the stage it will be his finest performance. For a note-by-note, phrase-by-phrase report, let us hear from the principal parts of the anatomy that have been trained for this performance.

Brain: OK, guys, listen up. Do you read me?
Embouchure, Lungs, Tongue, and Fingers: Loud and clear.
Brain: Up here in the control tower I can see clearly that our soloist is on the stage and ready to play. We will let him keep thinking that he is the player. He just doesn't get it. We are the player. He is the instrument.
Lungs: Right now I am taking his first breath.
Embouchure: Lips are set.
Tongue: I am in position to release the air for his first attack.

Fingers: If he misses this note it will not be my fault. The note is third-space C, so I can sit this one out. Hang on to that C, and I will dazzle you with my speed. Embouchure and lungs, here we go.

Embouchure: How did you like that lip trill I just laid on you?

Lungs: I did my part and supplied enough air to have trilled much longer.

And so it goes. The point of this dialogue is to emphasize that the proper preparation will allow you to stay relaxed and confident that your body will do everything you have trained it to do.

Now let's turn our attention to other matters related to a solo performance. Without good posture, the soloist will be taking a chance that the connection of air with embouchure, tongue and fingers will be lost. Stand tall, solidly on both feet with one or the other foot slightly ahead of the other. Keep in mind that you must use this same good posture when sitting in ensembles. At a TMEA convention I observed a very good lesson taught by the All-State orchestra guest clinician. Before playing a note, he gave a command to stand up. As you can imagine, bows, mouthpieces, music were dropped, stands knocked over. Then he asked the orchestra to play a tuning note while standing, and while playing he would direct the musicians to sit and stand until each player learned to keep his feet under his torso. By the end of the three-day event the entire orchestra could either sit or stand with perfect ease. The sound was excellent. The orchestra simply learned to sit and stand in the same manner.

The trumpet is like a rifle. The sound goes in the direction that the horn is pointed; therefore, you should practice in the hall where you expect to perform. Each hall will have a place to point the bell that best amplifies or accepts the timbre of the trumpet. Experimentation is necessary. Eye contact with your pianist is not completely necessary. It is more important that he or she can hear you take the breath for initial attacks. It has been demonstrated over and over that the soloist may be in the next room and still a fine accompanist will be right on the button. Certainly the horn should be nearly parallel to the floor. To avoid directing the sound to the floor, into the music stand, or into any other player's back, get the horn up. Do so by getting the shoulders back and chin up, which allows the throat to be relaxed, permitting a more open tone and greater projection.

Have you ever noticed that trumpet soloists frequently do not listen to their pianist in those interludes where the pianist becomes the soloist? It is a courtesy to the pianist to listen and concentrate on the music being played. It is impolite to wiggle the fingers, blow air through the horn, or make any distractions that would take attention from the pianist.

Intermissions are generally much too long. If a degree recital is so tiring that you must have excessively long intermissions, then there is a good chance you do not have the strength necessary to be in a performance program. Even if the audience does not leave the recital at the long intermission, they might as well since people lose interest in the recital with such a long gap in continuity. Ten to fifteen minutes is long enough.

Post-concert tips: Move briskly on and off the stage, expect at least one curtain call. Return to center stage with your accompanist. If you have an encore piece, play it now. If you have reason to speak to the audience this would be a good time to do so. By all means practice taking bows in front of a mirror. Get your pianist to help by instructing you on the art of bowing. They are schooled in these matters since childhood.

Recital follow-up: Review your music and listen to a recording of the recital. What went wrong? Where? Keep working on this music as it now is a part of your repertoire. Keep the list growing until you have at least a hundred solos ready to play. Did you memorize your music for the last recital? If not before the recital, do it now. You can polish this music even if you never play the music from memory. The act of memorization requires more detail in the study of the music and will elevate the performance level at least fifty percent.

Trumpet players are usually described as being aggressive, self-centered, arrogant, obnoxious, and I suppose some of it is true. These impressions are no doubt a reflection of being self-confident or an attempt by some to appear self-confident. By nature, many trumpeters are just not of an outgoing persona, and my suggestion to them is to work at it. Practice putting on an aggressive attitude even in the practice room. A soloist is an actor or actress just as much as a musician, and through sight and sound there is a story to be told. If you see yourself as a drab person, it will be reflected in your performance. So when the horn comes out of the case think of it as a transformation. Who knows? Maybe that transformation becomes permanent through the joy of sharing your music with others. Remember, the stage is our reason for being trumpet players.

John Haynie
University of Illinois, 1948

THE OTHER SIDE OF THE STAND

There are many approaches to memorization, visualization being just one of them. As a starting point, Mr. Haynie suggested that I visualize my mother's face. As I write this remembrance, I'm making it a point to visualize Mr. Haynie and everyone else I knew then. It sure brings back memories of good times.

Michael Craddock

I remember Mr. Haynie talking about being completely prepared for a recital or concert. He said his rule was that he would never play anything in public that he hadn't memorized six months prior. I always use that line with my students who think that two run-throughs are preparation enough.

Larry Engstrom

The psychology of trumpet playing was very important to Mr. Haynie. When working with us on memorization, he told us to picture ourselves in the most beautiful place in the world and to perform with that concept. I have used this technique in my performing and teaching.

Mike Olson

I was in the 7th grade, and Mr. Haynie helped me learn a Class III solo for the local UIL competition— "Rule Britannia" from Bernard Fitzgerald's **English Suite***. He knew how to challenge me by leading me to this competition, which required solos to be memorized and performed with a piano accompanist. Achieving a First Division on my first effort made me feel very good about what I was learning.*

Richard Waddell

WHO SAYS PLAYING FROM MEMORY IS IMPORTANT?

I do, and for a number of reasons. The most obvious reason is that with the goal of playing from memory, one has to practice the music far more and that, in itself, guarantees a better performance. Appearing before an audience unencumbered looks more professional and prepared. Any public speaker, minister, or politician is more believable when he speaks directly to the audience, congregation, or constituency. As a soloist in my early years, I always felt I could play from the heart and to the hearts of the audience if there was nothing between them and me. Even if you use the music for the sake of safety, do not let this block out the audience. The great Russian trumpet virtuoso, Timofei Dokschitzer, once performed at North Texas. Who in the audience could ever forget how he strode onto the stage with purpose and took his place in front of the orchestra? No music. He played everything from memory.

We all have our excuses for not taking the time to memorize the music. My excuse was that I had rather be learning new music all the time rather than have a repertoire of a half dozen pieces really prepared and from memory.

Teaching "how I memorize" is somewhat startling to the students when I tell them that I know what each page looks like. Their response is, "Oh, you have a photographic memory. I can't do that." Yes, it is a form of photographic memory, but everyone has that ability, and I am usually successful in building upon it. To assure a student that he does have a photographic memory I give a little test. I have the student close his eyes, and I ask him to visualize various things. "Can you see your mother? Your father? Your car? Your trumpet? The music building?" On and on it goes. "Visualize your solo for jury, the cover page, and describe what you see. What is the composer's name? How many pages are there? Where are the page numbers? Who is the publisher? What is the first note? What is the first note on the third page?" By using this approach in practice, a student will eventually have the music before him at all times because it is pictured there and not just learned by ear.

The ears and perceptions of the music should certainly be a part of memory, but it is not complete in itself. Pianists and vocalists generally memorize everything. We wind instrument players, however, have done a pretty good job of convincing the world that it is not necessary for us. The difference in playing a wind instrument carries over into memory. A singer is born with his instrument; a pianist performs on one with all the notes ready to play. A trumpet player must become the instrument, with the trumpet serving as the amplifier. It all comes down to how much a person really wants to play well. Memory work will raise the bar.

Texas Tech Summer Band Clinic, 1948

*The boy in the middle of the front row is Robert L. Maddox, Jr.,
son of John Haynie's band director, Robert L. Maddox, Sr.*

THE OTHER SIDE OF THE STAND

JJ always told me, "Find the story, and you will play it better every time."
Jordan Haynie

I learned more musicianship from John Haynie, both in accompanying him and in private French horn lessons than I did from anyone else in my music education.

Gene Iles Jacob

I first encountered John Haynie in 1950, his first year at North Texas. He was my judge at the UIL solo contest in Odessa, Texas. I was a sixteen-year-old junior from Andrews High School, and I played Del Staiger's's **Carnival of Venice**, *one of Mr. Haynie's signature solos at that time. After my performance, he critiqued my playing in a firm manner and demonstrated the proper rendition of various areas. I was most impressed with his ability to explain and perform so expertly. The theme following the opening cadenza, as you know, is very melodic, and not knowing any better, I played it very straight and exactly as written. John showed me how to give some expression to the tune—a little rubato here and a little sostenuto there, and "make it sing." He said, "Don't play notes, play* **music!**" *I believe that brief lesson, which made me determined to go to North Texas for college, made me a better and more expressive musician for the rest of my life.*

Rex Perrin

I recall so many lessons with John Haynie, especially those during which he would help me prepare for recital performances. He knew how to get me excited about the story in the music, the surprise, and the passion.

Galindo Rodriguez

I COULD HEAR EVERY WORD YOU PLAYED

After I retired from active teaching in 1985, I started practicing more and played at our church a lot. From childhood I played in churches and much of my lyrical playing of songs was a reflection of my exposure to vocal music and hymns. In my early years of teaching I was probably more imaginative, and with retirement and more time to practice, I became really interested in this approach to melodic playing.

It's true that you have to be careful when you try this. There is a bit of a chance when experimenting with attacks. It is much safer to use one style. Some notes are weak, some delayed, some anticipated, some too bombastic and often crack, some sharp, some flat. Nevertheless, I am convinced that my playing and anyone else's could be enhanced with a deliberate effort to do more than play the notes, no matter how well.

I have never liked to use specific syllables that required the tongue to be in a specific position for the note or style. I would use vocal copies of words, and I would let my tongue do whatever it wanted to do in emulating the attacks used in saying the words. I would read and say the words and tell my tongue to make those vowel or consonant sounds.

Here's how I could tell when I'd done that just right, and it was always this kind of comment that meant the most when I played. I'd be packing up my horns after a church service, and I would spot a little old lady making her way up the aisle against the current of people going the other way, and she'd just beam and say, "I could hear every word you played." Sometimes as a child I would be told by a tough old rancher, "Sonny, you sure do make that horn talk."

I tried to use the same technique when I played non-vocal music. On song-style pieces, like *Mont St. Michel*, or any andante second movement, I tried to determine the mood of the music and use my attacks accordingly. Sometimes I would make up words, and I could make many versions of the same notes. Shaping the tones like a potter shapes a vase was my intent. Or, like an artist paints a picture—instead of using paint and brush, I used my embouchure, tongue, and breath.

The goal is to find ways to make the music more expressive. There is an obligation to the composer in playing the music as he intended it to be played, but be imaginative, live dangerously, take a chance, and give it your all. I tried to impart that in my recording of *Black Is the Color of My True Love's Hair*. What if the title had been *Black Is the Color of My True Love's **Heart?*** What a difference ***that*** would make in how I would play it.

John and Marilyn Haynie, August 1951

*The photograph session was part of the
Broadmoor Hotel's "Honeymoon Special"*

THE OTHER SIDE OF THE STAND

Mr. Haynie was the one who told me about the "logic" of the accelerando and ritardando. He said even the untrained listener can hear that music that is speeding up or slowing down has a natural rhythmic sequence to it that is recognized as right and musical. He said an accelerando can be likened to the way a golf ball bounces or a train starts (and the opposite for ritardando). I have used this image countless times with students and it always works.

Frank Campos

There were a couple of times, when I had all the dynamics and phrasing just right, that Mr. Haynie told me I had played incredibly well, and he made a big deal of it. He saved his best praise for those special occasions. It reaffirmed to me what it was like to be "in the zone," so I would know what it felt like when I went there again.

Cathy Myer Kliebenstein

John's exercises of "hairpin-like" crescendo-decrescendo dynamics enabled me to succeed in my first job, because learning to relax into loud passages is necessary in orchestral playing.

Fred Sautter

*When learning to play **Bugler's Holiday** and you think you are playing with enough dynamic contrasts, try playing them double what's written just to hear JJ say, "Getting better, but do it with more dynamics."*

Cole Zeagler

CRESCENDO AND ACCELERANDO

Without it even being indicated on a sheet of music, it is assumed that a crescendo will be played any time the musical line ascends. Let us visualize a piece of music that has a measure of sixteenth notes ending on a high C. Underneath these sixteenth notes is a crescendo climaxing on the high C. There is a tendency to crescendo too much too soon; thus the high C becomes the weakest note rather than the strongest. I suggest to my students that they rewrite the crescendo by delaying its beginning until the third beat of the measure, assuring that the high C will have better air and will soar.

Everyone knows that accelerando means to go faster gradually and evenly; seldom is it played gradually or evenly. To experience a perfect accelerando, a person must have a golf ball. Find a smooth concrete surface, extend the arm straight out, and drop the golf ball from your hand. You will observe a perfect accelerando conducted by the law of nature. The first bounce will be the highest, and as the ball progressively bounces to a lower elevation, the speed of the ball will appear to be faster.

If circumstances permit, take your horn and play an attack each time the ball bounces. Possibly it will be the first time you have ever played a perfect accelerando. When performing, remember and visualize the bouncing golf ball.

THE OTHER SIDE OF THE STAND

It's been a number of years since I studied with Mr. Haynie, but when I developed soreness in my embouchure that would get worse with the high, long, and loud playing I sometimes have to do, he was the first person I turned to for advice. He had immediate suggestions that helped me with this.

Miles Johnson

John taught me that the greatest challenge to "crossover" playing is maintaining a flexible embouchure and minimizing damage to the lips when playing extremely loud and in the high register. He gave me several lip-buzzing exercises for both warm-ups and warm-downs, making sure that I looked at my embouchure as "a set of muscles that cannot be abused or you will lose control, focus, and ability." He talked at length about the critical facet of maintaining corner strength in the embouchure. "The corners are the key to the dime-sized place in the center of your lips where steel meets flesh. The corners are like the foundations of a bridge—strong corners will minimize abuse in your aperture." John helped me develop a daily routine, stating, "Keep focused on maintaining flexibility, and your ability to play softly. These are your yardsticks for a healthy embouchure. If you start having problems with these two facets of your playing, refocus your warm-ups and warm-downs, and spend more time playing simple music delicately. Rest between pieces. Rest as much as you play."

James Linahon

Playing an even crescendo and an even decrescendo was accomplished by using the Conn intensity meter that measured volume. The machine had a tower of many different colored lights that illuminated from the bottom up as the player did a crescendo and the top down as a decrescendo was done. A perfect crescendo made the lights come on in order. This was a terrific visual aid.

Mike Olson

How Loud Is Loud?

Unless you can answer that question where musical dynamics are concerned, you'll miss the answer to question number two, which is "How soft is soft?" Certainly, loud and soft are relative to each other. Each conductor has his or her own concept of loud and soft dynamics, and the ensemble must adapt to the conductor's standard. Therefore, each instrumental student must be flexible and work at both ends of the spectrum of volume to develop the control needed for these extremes.

At one time in my career, I purchased a volume indicator. It consisted of a stack of different colored cubes that would light up to measure different levels of volume. My students loved it and hated it, but it was a marvelous visual aid.

No matter how close your *fortissimo* is to your *pianissimo*, you must leave room in-between for *piano*, *mezzo piano*, *mezzo forte*, and *forte*. Young students rarely have the control to play loud or soft enough to make much difference in the subtleties of dynamic range. In fact, most young bands have only one volume. It might be too loud, maybe even too soft, but most often it sits comfortably in the middle—the Goldilocks effect. These organizations just plod along, rarely being bad, but never being outstanding. Neither the players nor their audience will ever leave a performance having experienced the thrill that great dynamics can provide.

Practicing long tones and scales will make volume control possible. Players must give special attention to practicing while standing and sitting for maintaining good breathing habits.

· Put the word "imagination" in place of your middle name as a reminder to mix up the dynamics in every conceivable way, to stay flexible, and to overcome the temptation to just "get the notes out." Sage advice from Goldie Imagination Locks.

THE OTHER SIDE OF THE STAND

Mr. Haynie's advice was for me to listen closely to the vibrato of my wife Cindy as she played the flute, and then copy her speed and style.

Duncan Brown

For the first few months of my lessons with John, I was always extremely nervous. My primary reason for this apprehension was my too-wide vibrato that he would not tolerate. I knew I had to fix this problem with my playing, but I had a hard time doing it. At the end of my lessons, John would be completely exasperated, having a guarded patience concerning his desire for me to play with a better vibrato. He would say, "Your vibrato is so wide and uncontrolled that someone could walk through it. Get in that practice room and straighten that thing out!" My vibrato did get progressively better as time passed and Mr. Haynie said, "Well, evidently the practice room did a good job for you."

Joe Harness

Mr. Haynie advocated that I use hand vibrato because it was easier for me to control. He also said it would give the audience a nice "visual." That's just like him to think of both the performer and the audience.

Mike Olson

John's vibrato was the first I heard; when I went to Europe and heard trumpet vibrato there, it was like his, like a string's vibrato.

Fred Sautter

VIBRATO

Vibrato is a requirement for great trumpet players and is a vital part in becoming a musical, stylistic performer. Some of us started right out using vibrato without being aware of it or knowing how we produced this delightful technique. Just because one has a natural vibrato does not mean that it is good or appropriately used.

Webster defines *vibrato* as "a slightly tremulous effect imparted to vocal or instrumental tone for added warmth and expressiveness by slight and rapid variations in pitch." This waiver in the tone can be created in several ways:

Hand/arm vibrato is executed by rocking the hand to and fro, allowing the mouthpiece to gently pulse against the embouchure. At one time this was the most common type of trumpet vibrato.

Lip/jaw vibrato is currently popular and requires the jaw to be the catalyst like saying "yah, yah, yah," not too unlike a chewing motion. This vibrato is a deviation in both pitch and wind intensity. I recommend that the student work on both kinds of vibrato right from the beginning, giving each equal practice time. One or the other will emerge as sounding the best and more natural to perform. My rationale is that if you can do something more than one way, then you have a choice of which type is best for you.

Wind intensity vibrato does not require a waiver in pitch since the air will be released in spurts like saying "ha, ha, ha." Most woodwind players use this type.

Head vibrato is rocking the head up and down, like nodding "yes, yes, yes." I made only one exception in allowing a student to use this vibrato. The obvious rocking of the head makes it difficult to read the music.

Nanny goat vibrato—let's call this one the way we hear it. This vibrato involves maintaining a steady stream of air and making a quick goat-like sound: "he, he, he, he." This throaty vibrato is always too fast and uncontrolled, and I discourage its use.

Vibrato is very personal and is an outgrowth of one's basic musicality. I often suggested that my students emulate vocalists, since the words determine different nuance, speed, and amplitude of the vibrato. In the jazz field, delayed vibratos have long been the norm. In fact, jazz soloists have such individualized vibratos they can often be recognized by vibrato alone.

A beautiful effect is possible by starting softly without vibrato and gently adding the pulsation. A world-class performer giving a master class urged my student not to just sustain the tones but to do something with them. My student used the soft, straight tone and then added vibrato as he got louder, which pleased the clinician. Composers seldom indicate anything about the use of vibrato except when ***not*** to use it.

For vocalists, I believe that the speed of the vibrato depends upon the voice classification. The speed of vibrato for the high voice of a coloratura soprano is far faster than a bass vocalist. I observed that virtually every musical performer, whether a vocalist or wind instrumentalist, uses a faster vibrato as he ascends into the upper register.

I urge my students to listen to all sorts of music and to produce a sound that will be established in their heads. They will play to that sound and will include the use of vibrato. For advanced students this was probably already established and I seldom tried to change them.

If the only vibrato training a student will receive occurs in instrumental classes, it is very important for the teacher to be in complete control of the student's use of vibrato. The musical taste of the teacher will determine not only the type of vibrato to be used but also the other aspects of vibrato. Using the metronome would assure uniformity in group performance.

For many of us, the development of vibrato was an accident. It just happened one day. At some point this natural vibrato must come under close observation to be assured that it enhances the quality of tone and is appropriate for the music being played.

Regardless of the type of vibrato you use, a fundamental concern is making sure that the pitch is centered and in tune. To my knowledge there are few, if any, definitive research projects that prove that one method of producing the vibrato is superior to the others. It is simply a matter of which sounds the best not only to your ears but also to the ears of your teacher. I once heard John Holt, professor of trumpet at North Texas, say to his students, "You must learn to listen and hear with *my* ears."

Well said, John.

THE OTHER SIDE OF THE STAND

I have been teaching almost twenty-five years now, and my family is most important in my life. I watched Mr. Haynie balance his work with his family and his hobbies. This has helped me in raising my own two children. I want them to have a love for music, but I know they need other interests to fulfill their lives.

Marsha Millender Adams

I began corresponding with John after a mutual friend sent me CDs of his recordings from the late 1950s. As a "thank you," I sent John the CD my middle school band had made during its recent spring concert. When he wrote back, he said, "Your band, in my opinion, passed my evaluation with flying colors. Very simply I listen for the THREE C's of musical performance. As I write this, I wonder how I have the nerve to do more than to tell you that you are a fine band director, teacher, and administrator. Oh, by the way. How did you become the editor of the ITG Journal? In 1978 you had just finished your MM in trumpet." My answer to **that** *question led to our work on this book. From such small beginnings . . .*

Anne Hardin

JJ taught me to exaggerate dynamics until they seemed too much. "If you think it's too much, it's just barely enough," he always said. And he was right.

Jordan Haynie

During one of my lessons, Mr. Haynie said music should have continuity, contrast, and climax—the three C's. He said my routine should have them, my recitals should have them, and my life should have them. This is a part of balance!

Richard Steffen

THE THREE C'S—
CONTINUITY, CONTRAST, CLIMAX

The word "musicianship" is used to describe a personal reaction to an experience of hearing music played or sung. Comments like "He plays with such feeling," "She has such great style," and "I could just hear the words when he played the song" are wonderful testaments to a meaningful performance. This could be equally true: "Even though he cracked a lot of notes, the overall performance was so musical." What is the formula to develop musicianship?

Mark Hindsley was the Director of Bands at the University of Illinois and, by virtue of the fact that his wonderful daughter accepted my proposal for marriage in 1950, my father-in-law as well. He taught a course of band administration that covered many aspects of band performance. During one lecture, he talked about preparing a halftime performance for a football game and said, "Every performance must abide by the rule of the three C's." He went on to describe what these three C's represented in the thought process: continuity, contrast, and climax.

I have never prepared a band for a halftime show, but I have incorporated the three C's into the preparation of just about everything I played. More importantly, I often used the three C's as a checklist in performances of my students.

Continuity is simply playing the correct notes and time, i.e., being able to play the music fluently. Developing an ability physically and mentally to play the trumpet is a never-ending responsibility and requires constant effort to develop and maintain technique. Embouchure, breath, tongue, and fingers are the elements from which continuity is made possible.

Contrast requires great imagination on the part of the player. Rarely does a composer write in all the nuances and dynamics he hopes will be played by the performer and expected by the listener. Some exaggeration must occur to transfer these dynamics and tempos to the audience. The *fortes* should be louder and the *pianos* should be softer. The *allegros* should be brisker and the *adagios* should be stretched. A great conductor once said, "When you think you have gone too far, it will be almost enough." As a basic rule, make a crescendo when the melodic line ascends. As the line descends, get softer. For special times, do the opposite. Do not become too predictable. Keep the listener a little off-balance and wondering what is yet to come. The listener will pay more attention.

Climax is unique in that there should be a little climax here and a little there while preparing for the big one at the end. What if the music goes against the norm? How clever one would be to start right out with a strong climactic tone, then fading the ending. Of course, the music dictates the dynamics. Sometimes composers sprinkle in dynamic markings that have little relation to the notes they write. The musician in you will make the adjustments.

Some people will say that style and musicianship cannot be taught. It is true that some players instinctively do all the right things to make their playing enjoyable without instruction. I say that even these gifted players will benefit from additional help if some of their natural playing is contrary to what a particular piece of music needs and demands.

John and Marilyn, 1958

This photo appeared inside the Golden Crest record jacket

THE OTHER SIDE OF THE STAND

One of the most important and lasting things that Mr. Haynie always stressed was making music. Etudes were not only for technical development, but also for developing musicianship. I learned so much about phrasing, style, and intonation from the material we worked on. Mr. Haynie taught me how to listen by insisting on good intonation. So many private teachers don't talk much with the students about pitch tendencies and intonation. They teach you how to play, but not how to fit in with the ensemble.

Bob Blanton

When I attended North Texas, I had never seen an electronic tuning device. In the Air Force band, we tuned on the pitch of the first chair clarinet player. John had a StroboConn™. He spent a lot of time with the chromatic charts to establish the problem pitches and how to correct them. I used that technique wherever I taught.

Charles Millender

Mr. Haynie taught me the way intonation works on the trumpet and how to relate it to the other brass instruments. This has been a great help in many ways over the years.

Dave Ritter

John got me to play in tune, as he put it, "like a great string player," simply by calling my attention to it. His teaching methods were non-threatening. When other teachers were issuing deadlines, John was simply patient. He understood that each person grew in his own way and time. As for me, spring came and the grass grew by itself!

Thomas Wirtel

TUNE AS YOU PLAY

The Tune As You Play mechanism was invented by Mark Hindsley at the University of Illinois. It was a trigger device attached to the tuning slide rather than the first valve slide. A double action spring on each side of a fulcrum allowed the player to move the tuning slide either way to raise or lower the pitch of any note. Mr. Hindsley and an engineer designed and installed the mechanisms on the university-owned set of Bach cornets and trumpets in 1951 or thereabout. He had no commercial interest in the mechanism, but he applied for and got a patent for the device. In 1951 or 1952, he showed me the Bach instruments that were equipped with the TAYP trigger, and I was fascinated with how easy it was to tune any note either up or down. Actually, it was easier to tune notes up rather than down, at least on the trumpet, since you had to squeeze with the left thumb to go up and pull back to lower the pitch. I was just getting started using Reynolds instruments, and the company agreed to equip my horns with the device, provided I could borrow a cornet and trumpet from the University of Illinois Bands so the designers could copy and improve upon the Hindsley model. This was all done rather quickly, and I had to learn how to use this trigger device. I spent a lot of time with a StroboConn™ and it was remarkable how easy it was to tune those bad notes that heretofore just had to be lipped.

The major use I had for the TAYP device was when I played solos with piano or with a group. As soloist with band or orchestra it worked just fine, but not in a section when I was the only one with the mechanism. Often I would use it to play out of tune on purpose in order to give my ears a break. One time I was performing with a cornet trio playing second part. I was the only one in the trio equipped with the tuning device. (The Reynolds cornets defy nature by not being flat on the fifth harmonic. Instead they are quite sharp on the 6th and 8th harmonics.) There were a lot of high C's to play in that trio, so to accommodate the group tuning I would use my TAYP tuner to play the upper G's even sharper to make the trio sound in tune. It didn't make any difference that we were out of tune with the band. We were the guest artists, so how could we be wrong? Besides, we played so loud and were so dominant (and I must say the trio was marvelous) that no one cared if we were sharp. I wasn't sure how to take this, but someone once said, "It's better to be sharp than out of tune."

I liked the Reynolds trumpet in particular. It had neither the sparkle of the Benge nor the more solid sound of the Bach, but it was just right for me. The valves were spectacular, and the sound was very even over the entire range. Unfortunately Heinrich Roth sold the company and the Reynolds Company just disappeared. I had no contact person and decided that I must change horns, since I felt I should play a horn that was readily available. During the ten years I played Reynolds horns, the Hindsley **T**une **A**s **Y**ou **P**lay invention was called the "Haynie Gadget." Nearly all my students purchased both cornets and trumpets with the tuning device, and our sectional tuning was outstanding. For a short period I played a Conn cornet, which was also equipped with the **T**une **A**s **Y**ou **P**lay gadget.

When I switched to the Benge trumpet and cornet, Donald Benge effectively copied the Reynolds version of the TAYP. By the time I switched to Bach I never again played the gadget horns. I was convinced that it was a dead issue so I rejoined the "lippers." TAYP had a chance to succeed, but at the time I did not have enough of a reputation to attract much attention to the device.

A person without an ear for tuning would be an intonation threat when moving the tuning slide the wrong way much of the time. That same person might be a good piano player, but certainly not a string instrument or trombone player for exactly the same reason.

If I could, I would start beginners on the TAYP gadget. Why allow them to play the fifth harmonic flat when they don't have to? I would also extend their third slides to accommodate the out-of-tune low D and C-sharp, though I'd create some flat ones at the same time. Then I would have them use the tuning slide trigger to tune the new flat ones upward. Remember, I mentioned it is easier to tune up than down. I've heard timpani players say the same thing. This suggested method is theory only. I decided it is not worth the effort and impossible to defend, especially if a person does not like the Reynolds or Benge anyway. Most of my students who played Reynolds while at North Texas who went on to play professionally could not use the Reynolds. The other players probably said, "Who wants to play with that guy? He can play his horn in tune."

The **T**une **A**s **Y**ou **P**lay attachment was a grand and hopeful experience, but I would not go out on a limb like that if I had to do it over again. Yeah, I probably would because I would use it for my solo playing with piano.

THE OTHER SIDE OF THE STAND

I was playing a scale study in C major one day and not bothering to use my slides to compensate for "bad" tuning. Mr. Haynie stopped me, and told me to use my slides. I replied, "Mr. Haynie, I figure nobody can hear it at this speed." He said, "I can hear it!"

Robert Bailey

I was already at North Texas when Mr. Haynie was hired, and with him, a new era began with diagnostic and technical methods as integral parts of the private lessons. There was a very detailed study with each student on the intonation tendencies of each pitch on the trumpet. Then we were expected to make the adjustments by moving our first or third-valve slides, alternate fingering, direction of air stream, and mouthpiece placement to play each pitch in solo music or band music to match the ever-present, always accurate, "third being" in our lessons—the StroboConn™. Some of us were fitted for custom-made mouthpieces, which I considered very special. So, with my Hruby mouthpiece on my new Reynolds cornet, and my personal chart of intonation tendencies, I would never play out of tune again.

Judie Barker Goodwin

Intonation was greatly emphasized in Mr. Haynie's lessons. All the trumpet players were given a chart that listed the complete chromatic scale. We were to check each note on our instrument with a StroboConn™ and write down the deviance of each note and the solution to play it in tune. I have used this method for thirty-nine years in teaching bands.

Mike Olson

GET THOSE THIRD SLIDES OUT

Can you imagine a trumpet without any means to extend the first and third slide to accommodate the sharp notes? The band instrument manufacturers knew there was a problem when the 1-2, 1-3 and 1-2-3 valve combinations were played. Most would make the individual slides too long, which would improve and reduce the sharpness on these finger combinations.

It wasn't until I was a student at the University of Illinois that I discovered how their solution simply created another problem. My cornet was out of tune! How could this be? It had been tuned at the factory and it was gold-plated, with a sterling silver hand-engraved bell, and it cost a lot of money! Nevertheless, I was called in to see Mark Hindsley, Director of Bands, after a rehearsal one day. The band was playing a thinly-scored transcription by A. A. Harding, which used one cornet with mostly woodwinds. I had to play a sustained second-space A-flat, and Mr. Hindsley said the pitch was flat. He wanted to check out my horn with a new device called a StroboConn™. Sure enough, there it was. The flashing red light was spinning when it should have stopped. Checking other notes we discovered that my low D and C-sharp were not sharp and were actually pretty well in-tune. I couldn't lip the A-flat up enough to match the strobe—to say nothing of the clarinets! The solution was to have an instrument repairman cut off about one inch of the third slide, and then hand-make a first-slide trigger. This very well might have been the first trigger put on a King cornet. It was a fascinating experience to now have a horn that was better in tune, and this event was the catalyst for a lifetime of working at ways to improve intonation.

When I first began teaching, most cornets and trumpets were not equipped with rings or other such devices to move slides for pitch adjustment. As the manufacturers added these to their horns, my students had to learn how to move their slides to compensate for sharp notes. Let me tell you about one of my experiments at getting students to use the third slide extension on low D and C-sharp.

I purchased a bunch of springs that fit neatly on the threaded bar that retains the third slide. This spring extended the third slide to the point that low D and C-sharp were well in-tune. In other words, the extended third slide improved 1-3 and 1-2-3 combinations, so the slide stayed out all the time with the spring. It had to be pulled in and held in, however, on 2-3 combinations. Of course, that spring was stiff enough to create some physical discomfort, so we took the springs off the third slides when the students were made aware that the third slide needs to be out more than it needs to be in.

*The North Texas concert band cornet/trumpet section
with their Reynolds instruments, 1958*

*(l to r): Sherwood Dudley, Randol Webb, Bob Pickering, Bob Foutz,
John Haynie, John Parnell, Marvin Stamm, Mike Fassino, Nancy
Meyers Childress, Pat Deemer Kimbell, Nona Beth Barker*

The Other Side of the Stand

*Sometimes we'd be notified that a bomb threat had been called in. (Thank goodness they were always false.) On one such occasion, Mike Funderburk and I were practicing when a policeman came to tell us we had to leave the building. Mike said, "Let's go see what Mr. Haynie says when they tell him!" We grabbed our stuff and followed the policeman downstairs to the studio. When the officer explained the situation, Mr. Haynie said, "But every time I take my horn out of the case there's the threat of a bomb!" I don't know about **that**, but we got a kick out of it and it showed us that a good sense of humor always comes in handy.*

Michael Craddock

I own a 1959 Reynolds Contempora cornet that originally belonged to Mr. Haynie. My uncle, trombonist Joe Nicholson, was doing masters degree work at North Texas at the time and knew that Mr. Haynie was selling his cornet. A deal was quickly made. It was the most beautiful cornet I had ever seen, and I have never seen another one like it. It has a copper-colored bell with the Reynolds silver ring and has "Contempora" scripted the length of the bell. The rest of the horn is mixed silver and brass. It has real pearl valve caps, a third-valve slide trigger, and an unusual thumb trigger that is attached to the tuning slide, which is in the back rather than on the side. It has a beautiful mellow tone quality—almost like a flugelhorn—in the middle and lower registers. The cornet did indeed go to someone who really wanted to play it. I played this cornet through high school and college. I was the first female trumpet major to graduate at Evangel University (1966–70) in Springfield, Missouri. I played my junior recital on it. I think the knowledge of owning an excellent instrument gave me more confidence—there were few female trumpet majors or graduates in those days. I've kept the cornet all these years through graduate degrees and a teaching career. Only two people have owned this cornet—John Haynie and I.

Joy Maynard

HAYNIE'S HORNS

I had three King cornets as a boy. I got the first one when I was about ten years old. It was plain vanilla rough-finish silver-plate that cost about $100.00. The photo of me in my band uniform wearing the cocky cap was that one. My second King was a much better horn, and it had a sterling silver bell. I'm holding this horn in the photo that featured me on the cover of the *Texas Music Educator* in February 1941. Shortly after this, I got the third one with a gold-plated, hand-engraved bell. It's no wonder that people thought I was "just a cornet player." Truth was, the cornet was all I played, until about 1951, when Colonel Earl Irons set up a deal with Heinrich Roth and the Reynolds Company to provide me with a matching cornet and trumpet. I liked the Reynolds horns, and the trumpet was a real treat. Suddenly, all the trumpet music I'd ever wanted to play was there for the picking—trumpet picking, that is. I played on the Reynolds horns until about 1962, years after Mr. Roth sold the company.

I continued to play my Reynolds trumpet; later, however, I switched to the Conn cornet. Don Hatch was the Conn representative, and he had approached me about playing the new Conn Constellation cornet. He agreed to fit it with the **T**une **A**s **Y**ou **P**lay gadget. I liked the horn even though it was heavy and lacked the flexibility of the Reynolds.

I became interested in Benge trumpets when two graduate students came in with that brand in 1965. John Eckert played a Benge 3X and Ralph Montgomery played a gold-plated Benge 5X. They were both Eastman graduates, excellent players, and I liked Ralph's sound on the 5X. I had Don Benge send me several 5X's, still in raw brass, to try out before buying one.

I switched to the Benge trumpet and cornet, and Don copied the Reynolds version of the TAYP gadget. During this period of my life I seldom played in public, but I used the Benge 5X trumpet and cornet in all the playing I did in my studio.

During the 1970s, through my students and others, I discovered the "Chicago Sound." This was the rich sound of the Chicago Symphony brass section. I liked it. It was the sound I always hoped I fostered. To my ear, the sound had great control and was free from tension. They played Bach. Even though I still think the player is more important to the sound than the horn or mouthpiece, I went with the flow and started to play Bach. A former trombone student of mine, Phil Elliott, was a Selmer/Bach representative, and he supplied me with a number of their horns. From that time on I played and recommended Bach.

I deliberately did not allow myself to be indebted to any company because I believe in freedom of choice, and the possibility always existed that I might want to change without obligation to anyone. I had an excellent relationship with many trumpet manufacturers. I had numerous horns on hand in my studio at any one time, and they were available to me and my students. The students could try out these horns with no strings attached.

After retirement from active teaching in 1985 and going into a five-year modified service program, I could practice and play to my heart's content. My most memorable performance during this time was when I appeared as guest soloist with the North Texas Wind Ensemble at the 1986 Music Educators Association convention. I played the *Carnival of Venice* on the cornet I had played in high school. I had fun, and the cornet had fun.

John Haynie, 1960

THE OTHER SIDE OF THE STAND

I still remember my first order of business when I got to North Texas was to go into the practice building and listen to students practicing trumpet, and to see how many sounded better than I did! Most of my student colleagues were "star" trumpeters from their undergraduate schools. They came to North Texas and immediately heard better players than themselves. Within a matter of weeks, many of them began changing mouthpieces, horns, and undergoing embouchure changes in order to achieve a higher level of playing.

Ross Grant

I was having difficulty getting the high notes, and I was very frustrated during my lessons. At one point, John said, "Stop! Here, I'm gonna give you this mouthpiece. (He retrieved it from his desk drawer.) It is a comfortable mouthpiece. Let's see what you can do with it. It's a Bach 10½CW New York die." John's mouthpiece allowed me to soar. I used that mouthpiece throughout my entire teaching career. What a gift!

Joe Harness

*One day I asked Mr. Haynie about "no-pressure" mouthpieces. He took out his special mouthpiece—the one with the rim cut in saw-toothed-like fashion so you had about eight sharp brass points on your lips. Any pressure, and it's all over. He then showed me how unnecessary pressure was by playing **Willow Echoes** with this mouthpiece, complete with the triplet slurs glissandoing up to high A. He ended with a high F. Unbelievable!*

Craig Konicek

John's studio had drawers and drawers of different trumpet mouthpieces made by all the famous mouthpiece makers. Above this mass of mouthpieces was a sign that read, "When you find the one that does everything, it's a gift from me to you."

Ron Modell

MOUTHPIECES—
THE HOLY GRAIL OF TRUMPETERS

Finding the perfect mouthpiece has been almost as elusive for trumpeters as finding the Holy Grail has been for those of the Christian faith. The most important thing I can say about mouthpieces is that you better have one because that sharp rim of the leadpipe will cut your lips! All kidding aside, it is true that I have practiced, on occasion, without a mouthpiece for the purpose of eliminating the use of pressure. Further, this can only be accomplished by using a very small aperture of the lips, which in turn requires considerable focus of the air. I would not recommend this experimentation to others, but it was interesting to try and was just another example of how far I would go to find a way to help my students.

I began playing at age six, and sometime before I was ten, my grandmother bought me my own King cornet. I played the mouthpiece that came with the horn. It was an M5, whatever that means. I played on that mouthpiece through public schools, college, the army, back to college, and was still playing it when I started teaching at North Texas in 1950. Somewhere along the way I decided I ought to know something about mouthpieces since students were always concerned about what they should use. Most of my students played Bach mouthpieces—wonder how many of them were still playing what came with the horn?—so I thought it was a good place to start. I got the Bach mouthpiece catalogue and made an arrangement with the local Bach representative to have several of the popular model numbers to try out.

I discovered that the Bach mouthpiece most like my King M5 was the Bach 7B. So, I played the 7B for awhile. Then Alois Hruby of the Cleveland Orchestra sent me one of his designs that was also much like the 7B Bach and the King M5, and I played on it for awhile. Still experimenting, I discovered I could play a richer, fuller sound on the Bach 7. From the first time I played the Bach 7, it was the sound I wanted on the Reynolds trumpet and cornet. I stuck with that mouthpiece for many years. In fact, I recorded the Golden Crest Recital album on the Bach 7 cornet and Bach 7 trumpet mouthpieces. I became more informed about mouthpiece makers and mouthpiece characteristics, and since I was now fifty pounds heavier than I was when I first played the Bach 7 diameter, it was time to move on to something wider! After purchasing every Bach mouthpiece in their catalogue for the trumpet department, I finally switched to the Bach 1½B that I played for the rest of my career, probably close to twenty-five years.

Mouthpiece selection is a very personal thing. It must match up to what the trumpet design needs and at the same time fit the player and his expectations. It must be comfortable on the lips, and it should enhance a good tone. Numbers do not mean a whole lot to me because fine players will make the horn sound the same regardless of what they might play. The right mouthpiece will make this easier. Less-gifted players do need to consider which mouthpiece they play because they need all the help they can get.

To keep things simple for most players. I suggest trying the popular Bach sizes—numbers from 1C, 1½B, 1½C, 3C, 5B, 5C, 7, 7B, to 7C. Most players know this, but for those who don't, keep in mind that the numbers 1 through 7 indicate the diameter of the mouthpiece, with 1 being the widest diameter and 7 being the narrowest. The numbers go all the way to 20, but I do not recommend anything more narrow than 7 (which is considered Medium) for standard playing. A smaller diameter is certainly a consideration for smaller F, G, and piccolo trumpets. I used a Bach 20C when I played the *Brandenburg Concerto* in 1950.

The letters indicate the depth of the cup. Size A= very deep; B=deep; C=medium; D=shallow; E=very shallow. Remember that the diameter determines how it feels on the lips and the depth determines the quality of tone.

Some players might need a more comfortable inner rim. Schilke and Yamaha make identical mouthpieces, but the numbering system is exactly the opposite from Bach. A glance at the ads in any International Trumpet Guild *Journal* will reveal that mouthpiece makers probably outnumber trumpet makers these days. Some brands have been around for years; others are quite new, and it would be interesting to compare them to the ones I know best. David Monette even incorporates the mouthpiece into the design of the leadpipe of his high-end horns.

Everyone should experiment with mouthpieces even if they are perfectly satisfied with what they have. You will not know if you have the right mouthpiece until you have played and rejected a variety of mouthpieces. Who knows? There just might be one out there that you cannot reject. Go ahead and buy it. Nothing is forever. You will change again some day.

THE OTHER SIDE OF THE STAND

John once said, "Being a trumpet player is like being a plumber. You must have a full bag of tools to get the job done. If you show up at my house to fix the faucet and don't have a basin wrench, it is impossible to perform your duties. With trumpet, all the tools such as flexibility, range, double tonguing must be in that tool kit ready to go. And you don't need a basin wrench to clean out your horn."

Gary Barrow

One day when I was an undergraduate student, some of us were talking about how moving the braces around on your horn could really help the freeness and the intonation. I was working at that time in the horn rental and repair office. Some friends of mine were taking instrument repair, so we decided to take my horn (a New York Bach), and remove some of the braces and see what changes we could make. You never know if you can find the right thing. We might have been able to find the secret formula for double high C's! Well, that week I went to my lesson with Mr. Haynie and showed him what I had done. He looked at the horn and asked, "Now what does that do for you?" I told him I thought the intonation was a little better and that it seemed a little freer to blow. Mr. Haynie replied, "Well, when I get so good that I can tell the difference, maybe I'll have it done to my horn." That afternoon I went and had all the braces put back where they belonged. Mr. Haynie's words were so true. If I'd only spent that time practicing!

Craig Konicek

THE INSIDE STORY OF LEADPIPES

It is possible that I can improve your sound without replacing the leadpipe with one of a different taper and bore size. The problem is that trumpet lead pipes change with age and lack of attention owing to a simple matter of hygiene. Let me tell you about my student, Odiferous Strong.

"Odie" was a very good player, and he became very discouraged with his fairly new trumpet. I had noticed that his tone was forced and lacked the warmth and beauty that he once had when he first purchased this instrument. During his lesson I decided I should play the horn and see if I made the same sounds. When I took the horn and put my mouthpiece in it, I noticed a rather peculiar odor. That gave me a clue as to what I could expect when I played on his trumpet. It was the same poor tone uncharacteristic of either his or my tone. I excused myself and took his trumpet to the restroom sink. I removed the tuning slide and sighted through the lead pipe. No wonder the sound was bad. The bore of the lead pipe was almost full from any number of pizzas, enchiladas, and lasagna he'd consumed.

I took everything apart, and with a large-size cleaning "snake," I scrubbed the inside as well as I could. Then I handed the trumpet to "Odie" and asked him to proceed with his lesson.

I have never had to clean a student's horn more than once. I made a special point to just clean their horn during their lesson without comment or lecture.

Think about it. Why talk about the importance of tone and the use of the air to produce a fine tone, if a student allows his .460 bore-size trumpet to become a .440?

THE OTHER SIDE OF THE STAND

I was a tuba player and a friend of many of JJ's students. My goal was to become a conductor, and I enrolled for private lessons rather than take a generic brass class on all the instruments. I struggled frantically to play cornet during that six-week summer session. All I proved was that JJ had the patience of Job.

Edward Alley

John always said, "Some people make fun of them now, but I will live long enough to see the return of respect for the old warhorse cornet solos." He sure was right on that one!

Gary Barrow

John instilled in me through my lessons the cornet style regarding its tonal and technical applications. This concept has carried through in my own performance and in my teaching for the last forty-plus years.

Wayne Cook

*I will always remember those Saturday lessons driving over to Denton from Shreveport. I think I had as complete a trumpet education, if not more, than I would have had by attending North Texas. We covered the **huge** amount of material and ideas from the cornet to Baroque trumpet.*

David Miller

Mr. Haynie told me, "Always work with people first, then the trumpet." Because of him, I see each student differently, with unique needs. Mr. Haynie was not in the "cookie cutter" business.

Galindo Rodriguez

A Comparison of Cornets and Trumpets and the People Who Play Them: A Two-Part Story

Part 1: The cornet is shorter than the trumpet in appearance because it has more bends.

Part II: There can be a huge difference among players.

Listen up, keep reading.

If a picture is worth a thousand words, then the previous page says a lot. Any real difference in the sound of the cornet and trumpet will occur because of the huge differences among players of either instrument. The argument over the sound or color of the cornet for use in performing organizations has gone on for at least fifty years. The makers of cornets and trumpets have been bouncing around this issue for years trying to determine what band directors and professionals want a cornet to sound like, and likewise the trumpet. All one has to do is open up the ITG *Journal* and look at the trumpet ads to see that no one can make a horn to suit everyone. Each is trying to get his share of the market. The makers have produced cornets that look like trumpets and trumpets that look like cornets. David Monette even made an instrument called the "flumpet," which has the characteristics of a trumpet and a flugelhorn. Talk is always centered on the big, fat tone of the old cornet; yet, how does one explain the full sound of my King medium-bore cornet? My thinking is that the cornet soloist is more akin to the coloratura soprano than a baritone. The truth is, hardly anyone is still living who heard live performances of any of the early soloists. The recordings we have of them define the essence of cornet playing but not the cornet tone.

Since WWII there has been another war going on among those band directors who wished to retain the tradition of three cornet parts and two trumpet parts in the scoring for band. There was and probably still is a skirmish going on between those who wish to be called a band and those who wish to be called a wind ensemble. There is a big difference in the number of players in wind ensembles compared to the large concert bands. It is interesting that a large number of bands with traditional instrumentation also call themselves a wind ensemble. I think the original idea of the wind ensemble was to have one on a part and each piece of music on a concert might use a different instrumentation. I have never observed a program of the true one-on-a-part wind ensemble that used cornets.

It seems to me that replacing cornets in wind bands with trumpets is part of an awaking and updating the wind instrument programs. In creating this new thinking of one-on-a-part music we are talking about chamber music for bands, which has unquestionably inspired composers to fill a need for a lot of music, their music.

Somewhere along the way, composers of band music stopped writing cornet parts. They write three trumpet parts instead. Publishers generally have the final say and will print "B-flat Cornet" or "B-flat Trumpet," depending on their tradition.

There has been a Renaissance of wind instrument programs at the college level. All schools of music have a full faculty of artist performers hungry for an affiliation with chamber music potential. When I arrived on the scene at North Texas in 1950, the faculty in general had lost interest in bands and band music. Many of the leaders were in fact seeking respectability, and part of that movement was to replace the cornet.

In my opinion it was not the instrument itself that had to go; it was the music the great cornetists played that did not have the intellectual strength to interest the more sophisticated practitioner. I was growing up at the end of this cornet virtuoso period and could see that I must keep pace with the times. In fact, I became a leader even though the world was not paying attention to a cornet player in Texas. Publishers of trumpet music took notice as their shelves were being emptied. I had only the French trumpet music that became my base. The French had been publishing excellent trumpet music for years, and it was interesting that much of their solo literature was written for cornet or trumpet. Later they dropped the cornet altogether and printed both

B-flat and C parts with the C trumpet preferred. Aha! That was the first sign to me that first the cornet and now the B-flat trumpet must be replaced. Today the C trumpet is the standard for virtually every orchestral player.

Mark Hindsley told me before I came to North Texas that I would be in a position to establish the duties and responsibilities of being an applied music faculty. Helping composers to get their music played and published was one of those challenges. Having several commissions for my own performances was another. For years and years North Texas had over a hundred trumpet students who bought a lot of music and played it. We printed a booklet called *Festival of Trumpet Literature,* and I sent copies to public school and college band directors and trumpet teachers everywhere. It is true that the programs attracted many trumpet students, but we did not need more students, nor did we need better ones. The purpose was to make people aware of the music for trumpet that was available.

The love of fostering new and better trumpet music was my way of saying, "Yes, I grew up as a cornet player, and I realize that the music itself is a demonstration of physical feats." The really gifted cornet player could also touch the heart of the listener as he played the melodic section—no fiery technique necessary. I never turned my back on my heritage, and at the same time, I hope that history will acknowledge the fact that North Texas has been a leader in the performance of new literature. The reason our students had little difficulty in playing the most contemporary music is because they also had the technique and musical flexibility to play any of the old cornet solos.

In 1962, I made an album called *Music for Contest,* and it was a recording of cornet solos. The school had recently purchased a whole set of Conn cornets for the band, and Conn asked me to record a demonstration album. I played a Conn cornet when I played cornet, which was not very often. I continued to play cornet when I was on display with young bands. The band directors wanted me to play cornet because they realized they were losing the battle for use of cornets on cornet parts and trumpets on trumpet parts.

Every fine player develops his own trademark and sounds pretty much the same no matter what instrument, mouthpiece, or music he performs. Several wonderful trumpet players have done their homework and recorded albums of cornet music. I do not know for sure if they actually play cornets nor do I care. They play in the proper style, and I commend their artistry.

THE OTHER SIDE OF THE STAND

Mr. Haynie made me do things with a metronome, and do them correctly so that I could demonstrate to myself that I was capable of playing the passage and improving on it. Not a method as much as a developed ability to recognize where to go from a given point.

Robert Bailey

Work on those technical passages with a metronome and prepare the recital at 110%. When the nerves set in, you can still achieve a near-perfect performance.

Gary Barrow

Scales and metronomes! I am so glad that Mr. Haynie stressed and required us to know all the scales. He would give us tests where we drew the scale name from a box and had to play it immediately with the metronome. This really required us to think and know the scale, as well as to be rhythmically accurate in our playing.

Bob Blanton

*I still have dreams that the metronome is ticking, and I am running, biking, driving, and sometimes even **flying** from West Dorm to Mr. Haynie's studio so as not to be late for an early lesson. It seems he was always typing something, and I would be sure he was paying no attention to what I might be doing, then he would have some incredibly insightful comment as he hit the carriage return (these days, it's Enter on the keyboard.) And the metronome? It was my alarm clock, and I'd overslept.*

Gary Sorensen

THE METRONOME—MY FRIEND

The metronome talked to me and sometimes I talked back. Unrelentingly my friend pushed me on and on. He was an amazing companion. Not only did he assist me in practice, he also measured my progress. He nagged at me to "Write it down. Keep a pencil handy. Get the horn off your face. You need to think and feel more. Blow the horn less. Quit looking at that clock."

When I wrote my book on fundamentals he insisted that I include a place for him. He just wanted little lines under each exercise for his presence to be recognized. Take the scales and articulation studies, for instance. On those little lines he expected me to write down the tempo I must use to play the scale and particular articulation pattern in rhythm with him, with a good tone and a good attack. OK, I got it. After the first time I play the scale I write down where I am. A quarter note=____ to ____. Each day, each week, each month, I am to move the tempo up and down from that first attempt. I get out my pencil, and he shouts, *"Hey! What are you doing? Don't erase that first number. That's how you measure your progress."* I am supposed to go slower for accuracy and musical style as if it were my favorite song. I am to go forward in tempo to develop technique. He keeps telling me that no one ever has too much technique. He says he wants me to have a reserve of technique that I will rarely use rather than always playing right on the edge of coming apart. He said that the relaxed manner with which I will play, having this reserve, will be comfortable for me. The audience, having no idea how fast I can go, will also be more comfortable and enjoy my performance. If I am on the edge, they will know I am trying to do something I cannot do.

He even told me to take him along when playing *rubato* or *cantabile* in my practice. He warned me of the fine line between playing "musically" and "being out of rhythm." The rule is this: Bend it but don't break it. "Yeah, well, OK," he says. "Go ahead and break it once in awhile for some dramatic moment in the music."

He tells me about his relatives—the battery-powered, small ones that "tick" and the old ones with sliding weights that never seem very comfortable unless they are sitting on top of a piano. But this little guy can do more than provide a steady beat. He can keep the beat and pulse duple and triple patterns, which will be good to match up the T-K and T-T-K attacks for multiple tonguing. As I said at the beginning, the metronome is an amazing friend.

He did tell me that nearly everyone has a metronome. They just don't use it!

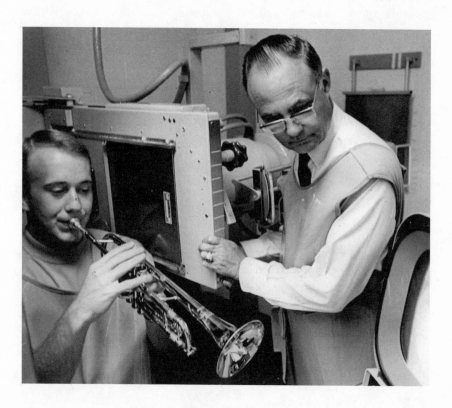

Videofluorographic research, 1968
Trumpeter Gary Dobbins and Dr. Alexander Finlay

THE OTHER SIDE OF THE STAND

Mr. Haynie always used to "blow me away" when something like this would happen: He would pick up his trumpet, blow through it and test the valves, and say, "I haven't warmed up in weeks, and I haven't played this piece for forty years . . ." Then he would play the piece, perfectly, and usually from memory!

Cynthia Thompson Carrell

I would like to thank Mr. Haynie for his logical and practical approach to warming up. My university students have affectionately referred to me as the "warm-up lady," and they know how insistent I am about this important aspect of our playing. He outlined a "flexible" plan to follow, which would include:
   1) long tones
   2) tonguing (single and multiple)
   3) technique (simple patterns to "wake up" the fingers)
   4) lip slurs
My students follow this pattern and I incorporate it daily in my own playing.

Marilynn Mocek Gibson

Mr. Haynie taught me the importance of a daily routine. This has been a mainstay in my playing and teaching. Covering the fundamentals is a matter of development and maintenance. I still practice this way today.

Dave Ritter

I recall a lesson at North Texas when Mr. Haynie became frustrated at how slowly I was slurring. He jumped out from behind the desk and grabbed a cornet off a stand next to me and proceeded to play one of the Irons exercises faster than I had believed possible. I still remember thinking, "How did he do that without even warming up?"

Ken Van Winkle

WARMING UP AND DOWN

When was the last time you dropped in on a band, orchestra, or stage band rehearsal? I feel sure the players know better, but what is usually heard is sheer bedlam. From screaming trumpets to *The Downfall of Paris* by the entire percussion section, it is not pretty.

I know of one band where the exact opposite was the case—Robert Maddox's band. He instructed his players to enter the rehearsal room quietly, take their horns from the cases, and assume a relaxed position not too unlike the army's "parade rest." Oil the valves, moisten a reed, number the measures *in pencil* of any new music in the folder, finger the difficult passages without playing, put the music in rehearsal order as observed on the bulletin board, percussion to locate all the proper equipment for the day's music, and in general "warm up" the mind, body, and attitude for the job at hand. Meanwhile, he might be returning a parent's call, preparing himself for the rehearsal, or just watching us from his office. Then, when he stood on his podium, it was he who directed the warm-up procedures. Not a lot of anything, but little bits of long tones, scales, lip slurs, fingering drills—just enough before playing a Bach chorale or some similar music, requiring the best of everything a student could produce. From note one, we were to make music.

From time to time, he would write out something new to learn on those old pull-down window shades. It was usually rhythm patterns we had never seen, and we would clap our hands and tap our feet. There was always something new to learn—maybe it was a philosophical thought or just something he wanted to thank the band for.

Now why would I tell you about this band and this director who was such a straitlaced teacher? What did his routine mean to me then and now? The word for this regimentation is *discipline*, and the hardest to do is *self-discipline*. Of such stuff is the proper warm-up and warm-down.

Let me tell you about the warm-down first. In the practice room, an individual's practice session usually ends on the hardest, highest, and loudest notes, because so much music is written that way. This is how a one- or two-hour practice period ends. By this time the lips, and even the mind, can be in a state of shock. To remedy this, I urge students to watch the clock and save at least ten minutes for warming down. On what? Warm down by doing exactly the same things you did when you warmed up. Look at runners. They don't approach the blocks trying to set a new record for the four-minute mile. They limber up their muscles first, push them to the max, and then let them relax.

If you looked in the table of contents and came into my studio on this page, go back to the beginning and read the essays about the trumpeter's version of the *Big Four*-minute mile—embouchure, breath, tongue, and fingers. Then you can tell me what a proper warm-up is. Better yet, tell yourself, and do it!

Recipe for a 1-Hour Practice Routine	
Ingredients:	
Warm up	Assortment of buzzing, long tones, lip slurs, scales
45 minutes	Familiar solos, etudes, and excerpts that stay "ready to play"
15 minutes	New material you have assigned or have been assigned
Warm down	Assortment of buzzing, long tones, lips slurs, scales
Directions:	Do not overdo the warm-up. Best if warm-up and warm-down are in addition to the practice of old and new materials

Videofluorographic research, 1968
John Haynie, video technician John Hunter, trumpeter Gary Dobbins

THE OTHER SIDE OF THE STAND

I will always remember John's straightforward approach to time management. The same method worked for the student with financial problems. The financial log exposed all the frivolous spending and found enough money for any musical need. I remember hearing John's conversation with a financially-troubled student. "Do you have a car? Sell it!!!"

Keith Amstutz

I remember a time when I was dating my future wife and not always getting in enough practice for my lessons. One week I had a Monday morning lesson just after I had brought Liz [Millender] to meet my parents. I had not practiced a single minute for my lesson that week—keep in mind, I had taught lots of lessons and played in several ensembles as a teaching assistant, but I was required to prepare a half-dozen etudes each week for my own lesson! During all eight hours of driving to and from Arkansas, I "read" the etudes, with books open in the front seat and trumpet in hand, fingering along. I got back to Denton at midnight Sunday night, and literally was not able to blow a single note of the etudes. I had no idea how I was going to play in the lesson the next day, and I was extremely stressed. But the next morning I had one of the best lessons of my life. The etudes were fresh in my mind, and they came out of my instrument beautifully (and without a single suspicious comment from Professor Haynie). I do not, however, recommend this approach as a formula for success in lessons!

*On a lighter note that wasn't so light at the time, Professor Haynie had heard that I finally got up enough nerve to propose to Liz. Keep in mind that he had taught Liz's father **and** her two sisters. At my next lesson, he said, "Congratulation, Ross. I've heard the news about your engagement to Liz. I just want to say that she and her sisters are **very** special people, and whoever marries them had **really** better take good care of them." I gulped and said I would. Boy, I had no idea what I was getting into!*

Ross Grant

Bad Habits—According to Whom?

I have encountered problems with new students, including freshmen, transfers, and graduate students, that cover just about everything you can think of that has anything to do with playing a trumpet, plus a lot of things that have nothing to do with playing a trumpet. It is necessary to deal with these problems before you can ever get around to the trumpet. Let's start with a new student who enrolled as a trumpet major and had no trumpet. He expected the university to furnish his instrument. The university didn't. I did. Then there was another student who carried a .45 automatic pistol in his trumpet case right next to his bottle of vodka. Or was it gin? I was never very critical of his lesson preparation. Anything he wanted to play was just fine with me.

Some students had money problems, spouse problems, romance problems, parent problems, and car problems, just to name a few. I always listened and tried to give them hope that everything would work out. I discovered that they just wanted to talk to someone, and students generally have a closer association with their private teacher than with anyone else on campus. It was easy to see that these youngsters in distress could accomplish very little in the practice room. In most cases, the problems went away and were replaced by new ones. Life is like that.

Trumpet-related problems were of much more interest to me. For those who did not have a good foundation, it was not too late to correct the problems and get them on the right track. Virtually every problem trumpet players have is related to embouchure, breath, tongue, and fingers. In most cases it is a combination of all four. Young players just do not spend enough time on fundamentals. I refer to these fundamentals as the *Big Four*.

Trumpet performance and pedagogy are not an exact science, so little research has been done to prove that anything you do is right or wrong. Only one of my *Big Four* components is well-researched, documented, and guaranteed. That one area is the breathing process. Naturally, it has received so much attention because breathing is a life-and-death matter. It is interesting that with all the information that can be found in the library, teachers continue to pass along questionable to absolutely incorrect information. I admit to being one of the uninformed in my first few years at North Texas. I trusted clinicians and the articles written by musicians about how we should use the air. Vocal pedagogues claimed that they were the only ones who knew how to teach breathing. They could not get away with that, so I started trying to say the same things they did. Thank goodness, most of my students ignored my lectures, and since they were practicing the right things, none that I know of suffered because of my ignorance.

In my second or third year I was giving my usual speech about how the breathing apparatus works, and I noticed my summer-only graduate student, Bob Jordan, was bothered about something. I dismissed it from my mind, but at his next lesson he did not bring his horn. "Why no horn?" I asked. He prefaced his intent by showing great respect and appreciation before he said in so many words that his father was an MD and had expected him to become a doctor as well. He went to medical school before the war, and one of his assignments was to dissect a cadaver to study the functions of the diaphragm, intercostal muscles, lungs, etc. Without hesitation, teacher became student and student became teacher. We went to the library and my "teacher" ordered up a stack of medical books and gave me one of the best lessons I ever had. How fortunate I was, and how fortunate my future students would be. It has since been my policy to tread lightly around areas of scientific concerns, remembering that a little knowledge is a dangerous thing.

Another area of imagination running amok is what goes on inside the oral cavity when playing a trumpet. Colonel Irons's *27 Groups of Exercises* had drawings that showed a flat tongue for low notes and an arched tongue for high notes. I could play the lip slurs well and honestly believed that my tongue did exactly as the Colonel described. Many of my students, however, were taught that the tongue must remain flat at all times. I discovered that a lot of brass teachers affirmed that same premise. Should I tell my students to do what I thought I did or tell them not to do as I do but to go with the flow? With the help of Dr. Alex Finlay, I could see inside the oral cavity. The Colonel was right all along. I don't hear much about the flat tongue anymore. But I am sure many fine players out there have learned to defy nature and keep their tongues from arching. Certainly the longer one can keep the tongue down, the better the tone will be. A flat tongue helps keep the throat open.

Another example of differences of opinion is the position of the tongue for attack. Many teachers tell their student that the tongue must remain behind the upper teeth for all attacks. I have some evidence that as the teeth separate and the tongue flattens for the low register, the tongue naturally goes forward and will probably touch the inside of the upper lip on the lowest notes. Ascending, the tongue arches and backs up, serving the purpose of blocking the air prior to withdrawing the tongue and releasing the air. My advice is not to try to make the tongue do anything. Just let it do whatever it wants to do.

I doubt if sufficient evidence will prove that everyone must use the same techniques in mastering an instrument. Funding is inadequate and most of us do not have the proper training to do effective and reliable research anyway.

THE OTHER SIDE OF THE STAND

Mr. Haynie was often annoyed with me because all I really cared about was playing jazz. One day, at a faculty adjudication session, I played a Charlier etude, and it was one of those "extra feel good" performances. He and Dr. George Morey, the conductor of the North Texas Symphony, looked at me wide-eyed. He said, "Okay, Bucky, you got your 'A.'"

Bucky Milam

One of Mr. Haynie's techniques was to have us keep going back to the beginning of an etude if we made a mistake. This made me concentrate even more. I found this technique very useful with my own students.

Dave Ritter

John's passion for music and his methodical approach to teaching were infectious. I remember the "practice sheets" he gave us, and that he said to practice so many minutes on lip trills, so many minutes on scales, etc. This may have seemed pedantic to some, but for young wannabes, it was just what we needed, and he knew it.

C. M. Shearer

Mr. Haynie's friendship and concern taught me so much about the "asides" in teaching. I do remember one really frustrating procedure, and I still impose it upon myself and my better students. I was playing a Charlier etude in one of my lessons. It was one of those two-page monsters, and it was going quite well until the very last line—one of those "Z double-sharps" came out instead of a note. He stopped me and said "Whoops, too bad. Well, go back to the beginning and try again." I still use that in trying to get my students to reach more perfection in their playing.

Sam Trimble

PRACTICE MAKES PERFECT, BUT WHAT *IS* PERFECT?

Always keep in mind that there is only so much time, and it's never enough, to practice. One must be selective in how to use that precious time. I have observed both extremes—the student who never plays any music because he is warming up all the time, or the student who hardly warms up at all because he is playing music all the time. This type student often ends up with some type of embouchure fatigue. Let us think about both practice and perfection.

When I began teaching my son Mark to play the trumpet, I placed a little sign in his horn case that read "Practice Makes Perfect If You Practice Perfectly." Since then I have wondered many times, what *is* perfect? If I could play like Maurice André and many others of his caliber, I would consider my playing to be perfect. But I doubt that André and those other great artists considere *themselves* perfect, so we must be flexible with the word "perfect." What is a "best performance ever" with one may be cause for further wood-shedding for another. To never be satisfied with one's own playing is unfair, demoralizing, and probably will result in giving up the trumpet in a short time. You should practice because you enjoy just holding the horn in your hands. When the mouthpiece touches your lips it should become a part of your anatomy. *You are the horn.* Horn, body, and mind all become one. That is why we practice. We are training ourselves by repetition to coordinate the embouchure, the breath, the tongue, and fingers so exactly, so perfectly, that for each note of music, the mind reacts and responds to what is on the page. The quicker the response, the more perfect the result.

During my first semester at the University of Illinois, I was preparing to take a series of proficiency exams in order to get my degree in music education in two years. I had no credits in trumpet, and I applied for senior level proficiency. I would be expected to play scales, a major solo from memory, and sight read. My solo selected for me by Haskell Sexton was Willy Brandt's *Concerto*, opus 11. I liked this solo, and it gave me every opportunity to demonstrate that I could indeed play the trumpet at senior level.

It was getting late one night in the practice room at Smith Music Hall as I was working on the final movement of my solo. It required triple tonguing, which I could do very well, but I was not as good when the notes were changing. Even then I had come to terms with the fact that far more is involved in playing these running triplets than just movement of the tongue. The changing notes required coordination of the whole body. I had devised many different ways to alter the music as a means to make the music even harder for practice purposes. First, I used just single tonguing to get the notes correct, then I practiced the entire movement T-T-K, T-T-K, and finally T-K-T, T-K-T. I used the metronome. It was during this practice period of intense concentration that tears began rolling down my cheeks. Then I recalled my voice teacher at Texas Tech, Myrtle Dunn Short, who required us to memorize a few of the sayings of *her* voice teacher, Giovanni Lamperti. The one that I remembered was this: "He who has not eaten his bread in tears does not know the meaning of work." More than knowing I had just learned how to practice, I knew that I could teach others. That confidence has manifested itself into the practice habits of my students, their students, and their students' students. So what *is* perfection? It's being as good as you can be.

Viedeofluorographic research, September 1970
Accompanist/interpreter Thomas Grubb, John Haynie,
Dr. Alexander Finlay, Maurice André

THE OTHER SIDE OF THE STAND

The University was adding more buildings and pouring new sidewalks that people didn't use. They made their own paths. Mr. Haynie made the point that it would be smarter to wait a while and see where the "trails" were being made, then pour the sidewalks where people were actually walking. That made perfect sense to me.

Ken Barker

I attended West Texas State University for my undergraduate degree in pre-med, but after two years I decided to change my major to music. I went to Denton in the summer to catch up on some required music theory classes. Naturally, I wanted to study with Mr. Haynie if he could work me into his schedule. I was very nervous about my first lesson. I arrived and played something that I had prepared. Mr. Haynie was complimentary—but he also offered many suggestions. They were: I "horn-counted" (moved too much with the beat), I rode my valves up, I did not put the initial valve down before I started playing, my attacks were not perfect, I sometimes played notes (that were not in the music) between the written slurs, and the list went on from there. This first lesson was an eye-opener. He had me get a notebook and to plan my next lesson. I mean he wanted me to write down exactly what I was going to play. You can't imagine how much I practiced to please him.

I still have that notebook.

Dick Clardy

Trumpet Jaywalking

Trumpet players often have accuracy problems when reaching for a high note in scale progression or by leap. The old adage "what goes up, must come down," holds true, so trumpet players, without realizing it, allow the embouchure and breath to get lazy. I call this "trumpet jaywalking." In other words, the embouchure and breath just do not allow the trumpeters to reach out with enough energy to secure accuracy for the top notes.

Jaywalking can become practiced behavior if the trumpet player does not use great vigilance when practicing scales and lip slurs. You must listen carefully to accomplish the goal of playing all notes in all registers evenly and with the best sound possible.

To assure that the top note is not cheated when playing scales or exercises, go for the top note as if it were the last note you will ever play, wanting it to be the best sound, attack, and release you can produce. In fact, play that top note several times and don't be in such a hurry to leave it. When practicing lip slurs, linger awhile on the top notes.

Practicing mistakes and learning how to play badly makes practice a waste of time.

Remember—jaywalking is against the law.

THE OTHER SIDE OF THE STAND

*John, it's pretty hard to sign a CD booklet when you don't know where to begin. The things are too small for any lengthy message. More than that is the very real problem of being unable to convey that which cannot be adequately expressed in words. What I **want** to say to you, what I **need** to say to you, is that your teaching and your believing in me "way back when" guided me throughout this London Symphony project. This recording has a lot of John Haynie in it. So when you see the words "With Thanks," you'll know just how much that means.*

Russell Gloyd

JJ always has a project in the works, and I have always been very impressed at how much he is able to accomplish. If he tells you he is thinking about doing something, the next time you talk to him, he will have already done it.

Anne Perry Haynie

Mr. Haynie had new ideas all the time. "Let's have five juries this semester! A scale jury that's pass/fail! And a really hard etude jury. Then a formal solo jury with coats and ties, just so we all know what a real performance is all about. And a written jury on a new book about the trumpet. Then our regular jury so everyone gets constructive comments. Yes, that will be fun!"

Clay Jenkins

Jovial	*Joyful*	*Humanity*
Organized	*Acclaimed*	*Authority*
Honest	*Moral*	*Youthful*
Nurturing	*Exceptional*	*Noteworthy*
	Sportsman	*Inspiring*
		Encouraging

Just a few of the "positives" I associate with Mr. Haynie.

Doug Laramore

THE "GO FOR IT" ATTITUDE

Recently I went to hear Ray Sasaki, professor of trumpet at the University of Texas, play and lecture. Ray said that much of his determination to accomplish his goal to be an artist both in jazz and symphonic styles was inspired by my "go for it" attitude.

Marvin Stamm has told me that every time I am in his audience, the old feeling comes back that he is on the spot; he wants my approval of his efforts since I had told him long ago to "go for it." That is to say, I supported his majoring in trumpet performance rather than in music education.

It all boils down to this: My *job* is to teach trumpet. My *goals* go far beyond that. I am not interested in tampering with specific personal things; however, I frequently have been involved in such things not of my choosing. One time a student of mine appeared at my studio door with a young lady, and I invited them in. Obviously they wanted to talk about something so I asked what I could do for them. Sheepishly, they told me they wanted to get married, and I said "Go for it," or words to that effect. I could see that my enthusiasm did not help them at all. Then my student said, "You don't understand. She's engaged to one of your other students." I said, "Sit down. You have a problem." As it turned out, I knew her family very well. I had taught the young lady's *father* when he was at North Texas, and I'd also taught her two *sisters*. I'm happy to say they're still married, and to each other!

In every lesson I taught, I tried to encourage the student to do what he or she really wanted to do, but with some caution. Some people have no sense of reality, and in their best interest, I have encouraged some students *not* to "go for it." For instance, one of my students who became a producer and conductor of international fame says the best lesson he ever had was when I told him not to expect much success playing the trumpet. Russell Gloyd is his name and he is currently Dave Brubeck's producer and conductor—has been for many years. Russell called one day and asked if he could speak to the trumpet players at their next weekly recital period as he would be between planes at the Dallas/Ft. Worth airport. "Sure, Russell," I said. "What do you want to talk about so I can put it in the program?" His answer was, "Alternatives for the Would-Be Professional Trumpet Player." He stood before the students and opened his talk by saying that I had told him that he would never make it as a professional trumpet player, which he said was correct, and he wanted to tell me publicly it was the best lesson he ever had with me. Then he went on to tell of his own career and the many ways one can be in music other than playing the trumpet. Russell is a great speaker, and the students were spellbound.

So what's the lesson here? Just this. All my life I have worked hard at everything I've ever done. *And I want my students to work the same way to be the best they can be.* It doesn't matter if they pursue something other than trumpet. The same philosophy of consistency applies across the board.

If it turns out I cannot accomplish a particular goal, I accept that and move on. Plenty of other goals are out there.

Videofluorographic research, May 1973
Gerard Schwarz, accompanied by John Haynie and fellow members of the
American Brass Quintet, sees the results of his X-rays while playing

The Other Side of the Stand

*Mr. Haynie taught me how to cope with my problems. It doesn't do much good to fix a trumpet player's problems if he or she doesn't understand the process. I believe he helped me understand this. In other words, he made me focus on "What's really going on here?" On more than one occasion, he would ask me what I thought I was doing wrong, to which I usually said something brilliant like "Playing lousy" or "Messing up." He made me be more specific and address the **real** problem. I didn't have to analyze the problem, just identify it. That has served as a basis for practice for me, as well as for instruction with my students.*

Robert Bailey

Something that always amazed me was that Mr. Haynie could talk me into overcoming some technical aspect of my playing without my ever knowing it. He was a genius in curing my mental hang-ups about playing.

Geoff Bissett

For a recurring mistake, Mr. Haynie had me make the mistake on purpose. 99% of the time I could no longer make it! Another problem spot avoided.

Ronn Cox

I remember playing an etude that had a full measure's rest at the beginning, which was odd, since there was no accompaniment. Mr. Haynie said he wished every etude began that way because such a measure can be used to set a solid tempo before beginning, to breathe correctly, to focus on what is to come, to hear ahead of time the pitch, articulation, and mood. I've often used this little trick to help students begin pieces with more confidence and control.

Michael Craddock

RHYTHMIC ENTRANCES AND JUMP ROPE

Students can have different kinds of problems with playing, and sometimes all it takes is to help them identify it. Rhythmic insecurity is one such problem. Perhaps you have observed a player who knows exactly when to come in, but for some reason he just cannot start the tone. I have had trumpet students who "swallow" the attack and can't get started. Those students who had this problem did much better when I served as a conductor and directed the entrance. But how did I help them overcome this for a successful solo performance?

A teacher has to be very careful not to be too harsh in correcting this problem of the delayed attack. Most students overcome this fear and move on in their playing. My approach to solving this problem is to have the students learn to jump rope.

First, get a piece of rope ten to twelve feet long, or if you want to be fancy, buy a nice rope with handles at any toy shop or athletic equipment store. (Boxers train with jump ropes more than any group of athletes I know.) I used to keep a piece of rope in my studio and would tie one end to a filing cabinet drawer handle. Then I would swing the rope so that I could set the tempo. Getting started is the problem for successful jump roping. If the "jumper" just stands there or jumps into the swinging rope and gets all tangled up in the rope, this is proof positive that the student's body is out of rhythm.

The Cure: Have a friend start swinging the rope. You should hold both hands up in the air, head high and flex the knees and hands, counting 1-2-3-4 over and over as your body gets in rhythm.

Keep your eyes straight ahead, not looking at the rope, but listening to the sound of the rope striking the floor. This is your metronome. You must feel that pulse throughout your body and when ready, *jump*. If it was a successful entry, you should keep on jumping because this develops the rhythmic "feel" that is the object of this lesson.

The next thing is to apply this physical activity to beginning an attack on the trumpet. With trumpet in hand but not on the lips, close your eyes and visualize your preparation for the jump, hands up, flexing knees and hands, teacher swinging the rope. When you feel the beat you should play an attack exactly with the sound of the rope touching the floor.

Now you are ready to apply these same principles to starting a piece of music by yourself. You will always have that pre-jump image in your mind, and the sound of the rope is your internal metronome. The next step is to get out any piece of music you have had trouble starting, preferably something that starts on a downbeat. Now here is the final guarantee that you will not only play a good attack, but will also be in perfect rhythm.

Imagine 32 measures of accompaniment before you enter. You need not count, just listen. You will have cues for the accompaniment as your entrance nears. Now, start exhausting air through the lips two measures before the first attack. One measure before the first attack, keep exhausting your air for three beats, and then take a breath in rhythm on the fourth beat. Attack the first note in perfect rhythm, without fear, and it will be the best sound possible. This procedure keeps you from breathing too soon and then holding the breath, which causes an insecure and tense attack.

This whole experience can be accomplished in just a few sessions. How long have you had this problem? Maybe forever. Some people have cured themselves by just going through this procedure.

The problem is in your mind. So is the cure.

John Haynie and Timofei Dokschitzer, November 1979

THE OTHER SIDE OF THE STAND

I've been able to stay pretty active as a free-lance player in my hometown of Portland, Oregon. My work includes casual engagement, show work, recordings, jazz gigs, and a few clinics. Last year, I did over 200 dates. I also take on a few students one day a week. Practice for me is mostly maintenance and re-affirming good habits. My warm-up is basically an off-shoot of John's **Development and Maintenance** *philosophy. It's very practical, addressing the fundamentals of good brass playing—tone production, lip slurs, attacks, and fingers. Then I mix Schlossberg, Earl Irons, Arban, and Clarke studies, with a little bit of Jimmy Stamp mouthpiece buzzing to get things started. Since my warm-up is often preceded by a night of hard playing, I like to play soft, relaxed, and as efficiently as possible. It just seems to set me up for the rest of the day. I think I came out of North Texas as a cleaner, more efficient player with well-rounded skills. I have no doubt it has helped keep me marketable in a sometimes tough and competitive field.*

Paul Mazzio

*In November 2002, after forty-two years, I took a lesson from John. Why? Because I have a very strong desire to continue my musical growth. I thought I would first play through the things with which I usually begin my practice and then proceed through some technical studies. I thought I might at least get past the warm-up, but—**BOY!**—was I surprised! John saw and heard various details that he felt needed to be called to my attention, things that I neither felt nor heard. His suggestions made common sense, having immediate impact. Certain issues that I had been working to master for quite a while seemed to be much more within reach. The whole lesson went that way, and we stayed with the "basics." Time seemed to slip away. It was a great experience, a marvelous lesson. This is what makes music so exciting. There is always more to learn, and it is a never-ending process. It never becomes boring or static; rather, it always retains the excitement of discovery.*

Marvin Stamm

MAN, I KNOW WHAT I NEED TO PRACTICE

Practice is practice, and for a person who is a lead player by profession with no intent to do anything else, why should he be doing the same thing that a student is doing? The student, however, had better keep the options open and prepare himself for anything that comes up.

A seasoned professional is doing exactly what he loves to do, and he knows what he has to do to prepare for the shows he has played probably a hundred times. A fine lead trumpeter did not get there by just being a high note player. Fine lead players have lots of musical tools in their bags. They can play just about anything that comes along. The rare exception is probably not going to make it anyway. I have taught some trumpeters who have the ability but not the interest in lead playing, and they are just as likely to have poor judgment in a practice routine as the lead player who simply does not want to play recital solos or etudes that have no relevance.

Much will be determined by the background of the lead player. Had he been my student, the necessity to maintain a balanced practice routine is probably so ingrained that he would not even consider changing it. The lead player who got there mostly on natural talent, little practice, and a few lessons probably has no intention of changing his ways.

Student players might become professional lead players, but it is not guaranteed any more than a youngster playing first trumpet in a concert band can expect to play first chair trumpet in the U.S. Air Force Band. A student is a student, and any number of things will have to happen before he can claim to be anything other than a student. A student should equip himself with every possible technique in preparation to play any kind of music.

THE OTHER SIDE OF THE STAND

I remember coming to lessons, thinking I knew how they would go, and always leaving surprised. Mr. Haynie was always challenging me to see things from different perspectives, and not to "lock in" to a certain way of thinking or getting into a rut.

Ken Barker

So many things I have done in rehearsing bands or techniques and illustrations I used to get a point across come from things Mr. Haynie did or said during my lessons. He had ways of making games from the music. One thing he had me do, and that I have done many, many times, is to play the last measure of a piece, then add the next to the last, etc. That's a great way to practice.

Bob Blanton

We often discussed pedagogical concepts in my lessons. It was not until much later that I found many of Mr. Haynie's specific teaching techniques, as well as the spirit of his approach, described in books and journals concerned with the acquisition of high-level psychomotor skills. For example, backward chaining, which involves learning a skill from the end point and working backward, is precisely the same technique that he used for many years without ever knowing the name for it.

Frank Campos

I remember being very impressed with Mr. Haynie's playing, particularly with the way he could pick up the horn at a moment's notice and demonstrate something. He also would present different ways to play solos or etudes by having me change the articulation or play an excerpt backward, which always made for a fresh approach and challenge.

Mike Walker

JOHN DEWEY'S SPIRIT OF CHANGE AND OTHER GUIDING PRINCIPLES

When I was a student at the University of Illinois, I took an education class that focused on the philosophies of John Dewey. Only one of his sayings stayed with me over the years, and it is this: "Without change there is no learning." There was little, if any, explanation in the classroom of this powerful and positive statement. It haunted me. Therefore, I took the following steps in trying to understand the full impact of that simple directive. To apply this quotation to various situations, let us make a checklist and find the meaning of the two key words, "change" and "learning."

Change:
✓ *To make different in some particular way*
✓ *To transform*
✓ *To give a different position, course, or direction*
✓ *To reverse*
✓ *To replace with another*
✓ *To make a shift from one to another*
✓ *To become different*
✓ *To transfer*
✓ *To alter*
✓ *To substitute*

Learning:
✓ *To gain knowledge or understanding of or skill in by study, instruction, or experience*
✓ *To come to be able*
✓ *To come to realize*
✓ *To acquire knowledge or skill or a behavioral tendency*

The first step is to develop short-range and long-range goals, which are likely different for each of us.

Long-range goals:
✓ *To become a world-class trumpet player, symphony orchestra, studio recording, recitalist, service band, jazz soloist*
✓ *To become a teacher at some level—public school or college band director, college trumpet teacher, private studio teacher*
✓ *To become a fine player and let the chips fall where they may*
✓ *To become an adequate trumpet player for the pleasure and enjoyment of music*

Short-range goals:
✓ *Improve and maintain excellent physical health*
✓ *Develop and maintain embouchure, breath, tongue, and fingers*
✓ *Work on music reading skills*
✓ *Listen to trumpet recordings and live performances regularly*
✓ *Listen in particular to your preferred venue of performance*
✓ *Listen to vocal recordings both popular and classical*
✓ *Read to understand the pedagogical beliefs of any given teacher or author*
✓ *Determine which concept is best for you through trial and error*

*   *   *

THE THEORY OF PARADOXICAL INTENT

For many years in my teaching as I tried to change a specific physical facet of performance, I would have the student go back and forth from attempting the new idea to the use of his previous habit. Some would call this doing it right and doing it wrong, with the idea that if you can do something wrong on purpose it aids in the discovery of how to do it in the newly conceived manner.

Going through this routine with a graduate student many years ago, the student mentioned that at last he understood the meaning and use of the ***theory of paradoxical intent*** he had encountered when he was a psychology major. It was good for me to know the proper terminology for a teaching technique that I had used for years, to learn by change.

An article that focused on this technique appeared in *Parade Magazine* (November 22, 1987). Written by Norman Lobsenz, it had the catchy title, "Don't Eat the Peas." In great detail Lobsenz described several examples of paradoxical therapy. I learned from reading that this concept of concentrating on a negative to create a positive was first suggested by the Viennese psychiatrist, Dr. Viktor Frankl. This technique is also called reverse psychology. I call it a trick in telling someone not to do something that you really want them to do. It works.

Relating this technique to trumpet pedagogy, it is the student who is performing the trick upon his own anatomy. My point is that if one can figure out what he is doing incorrectly and can do it on purpose, he very likely can turn it on and off at will. Now learning has happened through change as a skill, and knowledge is acquired. A behavioral tendency has been replaced. ***Change = Learning.*** Now you're ready to learn a piece of music by applying change = learning and paradoxical intent.

First, warm up the breath:
- ✓ *Select notes from music at random*
- ✓ *Play a note and hold for at least four slow beats*
- ✓ *Remove the mouthpiece from the horn*
- ✓ *Buzz the note for four beats*
- ✓ *Let the eyes focus on another note*

✓ *Continue this routine until you have played one note per line of the entire solo*

Second, warm up the embouchure:
✓ *Look through the music and find notes to slur without use of valves*
✓ *Find a natural slur (whether written slurred or not) on each line*
✓ *Repeat the two or three notes using up all the air*

Third, warm up the fingers:
✓ *By now you have located the difficult fingering problems*
✓ *Play those phrases very slowly at first, using a metronome*
✓ *Play the first two notes back and forth, over and over*
✓ *Play the first three notes as above*
✓ *Play the first four notes, etc.*
✓ *Keep adding notes until you have played the entire problem area*
✓ *As you gain accuracy and confidence, increase metronome speed*

Last, warm up the tongue:
✓ *Follow the same routine as with fingering and tongue all the notes— no slurs*
✓ *Work on a different trouble spot*

*   *   *

BACKWARD CHAINING

You should be properly warmed up by now and ready to continue the learning by change routine by incorporating backward chaining.

Begin learning a new piece from the end. Play the last measure or final note repeatedly until you are absolutely confident that you can play the final tone with good sound and good attack.

Justification: So often, when a student performs, he will miss the last note. The reason for this is that he never practices the end of the piece until he is already tired. One should learn the last phrase, which usually is the climactic point in the music, without fear of playing with abandon.

Next, practice and master the final phrase leading into the final note. It might be only a measure or two, or sometimes a more complete phrase, lasting several measures. At this point in the music, the nature of the notation characteristically has long sweeping runs into the final tone. This should be practiced slowly until each note is clearly identifiable, and played with strength and vigor.

Back up another musical phrase, play to the end. Practice slowly, and if there are no apparent problems, there will be no need to dwell on it, except for repetition and to practice continuing to the end.

Now you're ready to learn a piece of music by applying change = learning and paradoxical intent.

Sooner or later, you will encounter a difficult passage that will need special care. The problem may be fingering, embouchure and flexibility, or coordination of tongue and fingers. At this point, a new strategy may be developed.

Regardless of articulation written, tongue or make an attack on each note in question. Play very slowly with a metronome. Observe the metronomic tempo required to be able to play it perfectly at this slow tempo. Each time you practice, first play the last tempo you could play the phrase. If you can still play it at this tempo, move it up one notch until it becomes perfectly comfortable. Continue tonguing all the notes and following this identical procedure until the piece can be played at nearly the recommended tempo of the composer. Another procedure would be to play the phrase backward, sans metronome, observing the appropriate accidentals and ignoring time values (all the same length).

Justification: By now, you have looked at these same notes over and over, always looking at each note from the left. The reason I have you play the notes in reverse is to get a different view of each note from the right. The objective is learning to see distinctly each note without looking past it.

In my opinion, one should see one note at a time. We can play only one note at a time, and each note that we play requires a different setting of the embouchure, a different amount of air pressure, and the use of the correct fingerings. When reading ahead, the embouchure, tongue, breath, and fingers become confused when looking at one note and playing another.

Now return to practicing the notes of the phrase using different articulation patterns (a combination of slurring and tonguing). Play as many different patterns that come to mind, depending upon the nature of the notation. If there is a scale run in eighth, sixteenth, or thirty-second notes, use articulations like these:

☞	slur two, tongue two
☞	tongue two, slur two
☞	slur all four
☞	slur three, tongue one
☞	tongue one, slur three

Leaving notes out of a phrase, yet maintaining the proper time value, in a run of eighth, sixteenth, or thirty-second notes can help. Leave the first note out, and put a rest in its place. Next, leave the second note out.

For a real challenge, turn the music upside down and practice as if it were another piece of music using all the techniques described previously.

Justification: Typically, when one learns a piece of music from the beginning, the beginning gets the most practice. With this method of change, the note that will be practiced the most is the last one. While this may appear to take a lot of time in practice, you can be assured that the time will be well spent, because the piece will be learned thoroughly and correctly. The result will be a feeling of confidence and no special effort to memorize will be necessary.

You will know the music.

THE OTHER SIDE OF THE STAND

*A positive life lesson I learned from studying with John was that he cared deeply for us **outside** the studio. His parties, sports, and leisure outings were huge motivators for us—as valuable as the studio lessons themselves.*

Wayne Cook

*I remember that JJ always "fished" for the right metaphor or analogy to help convey a concept, and he always "caught" it. His expectations were high and he always assumed they would be met. That was very motivating. Intimidating at first, yes, but ultimately a great gift—believing in me. Who could **not** absorb that atmosphere and have it serve as model for teaching and life?*

Carole Herrick

Mr. Haynie counseled me when I had throat problems and had to give up the trumpet. Even though I was no longer a trumpet player in his studio, I remember how he had a gift made for all his trumpet students—a briefcase with their names embossed on it—and he included me. His words were, "We might do some things wrong around here, but forgetting people is not one of them!" I thank him for his inspiration and motivation.

Rick Stitzel

John Haynie is a rarity among musicians—he has the skill and patience to teach a lump of coal to play.

Matt Stock

While I was away at college, JJ would send me newspaper clippings of anecdotes or proverbs that would always arrive at just the right time. They kept me going when things were tough, and they always let me know how much he loves me. His lessons have inspired many people to reach their dreams and be the best they can be.

Rachel Zeagler

MOTIVATION

"Something as a need or desire that causes a person to act."

According to this definition, a teacher must instill in the mind of his student either a need or desire to generate a particular action. Before any action is taken, a goal must be established and the goal must be attainable and realistic. First, you need a long-range goal. Here's an example:

Long-range goal: To become a world-class trumpet player

To ultimately reach that goal, many short-range goals must be achieved along the way. These are learning conditions, responsibilities, practice habits, and even good luck. A good trumpet teacher will help motivate you every step of the way. He must approve of your long-range goal as being attainable, which will be done through an evaluation of your physical, mental, and musical capacity.

He is motivated to motivate **you** because he has a proven record of many successful former students. You have heard him play and you liked what you heard. You would like to be added to that list of successful students. This is motivation.

The teacher, after hearing you play, establishes a list of short-range goals.

Short-range goals:
- Weekly lessons
- Exercises to develop the embouchure-breath-tongue-fingers
- Textbook-type written materials to understand basic pedagogy

- Solos and etudes
- Major, minor, chromatic, and whole-tone scales
- Recordings of trumpet solos
- Recordings of symphony orchestras, wind ensembles, big bands (jazz), and vocal soloists

What has just been outlined should include some different kinds of motivations. Students not only must be evaluated, but also rewarded. The teacher should find out what other things the student enjoys. The teacher can give medals, stars, stickers, or even cash! A teacher who is alert to his students' likes and dislikes will, however, go to the trouble of selecting a fishing plug, a toy, a book, or any number of things that tell the student the teacher has an interest in him or her that goes far beyond playing the trumpet.

If a student is not **motivated** to practice, practice, and practice some more, he should re-evaluate his long-range goal of becoming a fine trumpet player. That goal is out of reach without accomplishing the short-range requirements.

Cynthia Thompson Carrell, Frank Campos, John Haynie, 1984

*This photo was taken when John Haynie received the
'Fessor Graham Award, presented annually to the faculty member
voted most outstanding by the North Texas student body*

THE OTHER SIDE OF THE STAND

Mr. Haynie once suggested that I calm my pre-performance jitters by saying a simple prayer before I went on stage. It was such profound and effective advice coming straight from his heart, and it has stayed with me ever since.

Alan Chamberlain

John said, "Peter, you play with an unusual amount of facial movement; your eyebrows and forehead jump excessively. I wonder if by cutting down on that, you could improve your accuracy." He was right. Practicing with a mirror to focus on reducing extraneous facial motion improved my playing.

Peter Ciurczak

"Don't waste facial motion. Focus your energy!" Mr. Haynie stressed not to waste motion by raising eyebrows or the forehead, because it is unnecessary for tone production. People still tell me I make trumpet playing look easy.

Marilynn Mocek Gibson

During my first year, I was to play on the Wednesday morning recital in the auditorium. I was obviously very nervous about this, and since I was afraid that my nervousness would hinder my performance, I popped a piece of gum in my mouth with the hope it would stimulate moisture. As I was playing my solo, the gum began to get very chewy, and I could not play. I took the gum out during a rest and put it on the end of my bell. Extreme laughter from the audience accompanied the rest of my performance. John had his head down on the tape recorder that was recording my performance, shaking his head in disbelief. I finished the solo, went off stage, and was very slow coming back out to the audience because I didn't want to face John. The next day, 'Fessor Graham, who was in charge of the Wednesday morning recitals, asked me to repeat my gum performance the next day for his music appreciation class. Everyone enjoyed the activity, except for John, who was absolutely disgusted that my bad behavior had been encouraged.

Joe Harness

STRESS

I once heard that a well-known symphonic band director would tell his trumpet players, "No cracked or missed attacks will be allowed." The consequences for doing the forbidden were not spelled out, but this command is the same as a coach telling his quarterback and running backs, "There will be no turnovers due to interceptions and fumbles." The obvious reason for these rules by directors and coaches is in the nature of positive thinking, "Just don't miss." It sometimes works, but let's try to understand why these mistakes are made. Unquestionably, the problem is stress, anxiety, and just plain old fear.

To remedy, or at least reduce, anxiety in performance there are at least two schools of thought. The more common solution is to treat the condition by encouraging positive thinking. In extreme cases of stage fright, many performers use a beta blocker prescription drug.

Let me suggest another: *Practice learning how to be nervous, then practice playing in that condition.*

Often it is difficult to do a task poorly, on purpose. So how can you be nervous on purpose? In the practice room it is difficult to mentally conjure up recital or concert conditions, so let's create physical conditions where you can handicap yourself for practice purposes. Practice the trumpet in the physical postures listed below:

1. Stand on one foot and practice away. Now stand on the other.
2. Sit in a straight-back chair and extend one leg straight out. Now extend the other leg.

In each posture it will not take long to become uncomfortable, and you will begin to notice tension traveling to all parts of the body. That tension likely will cause you to miss notes as you lose control of the embouchure, breath, tongue, and fingers.

The point of creating discomfort or a handicap in the practice room is to develop control over all parts of the anatomy, leaving nothing to chance. As you gain this control you will gain confidence. With this confidence and assurance you will at last look forward not only to rehearsals but also to playing before an audience.

Stress exacts a toll in many ways that can ruin a performance. To avoid this, I recommend that each student develop his or her own body language characteristics—mannerisms that can be turned on or off. Some body language during performance is good, because a relaxed posture helps the audience enjoy the music and the resulting emotion. But other mannerisms can creep into a performance just when you have other things to worry about. If you work on this ahead of time, you will recognize what's happening and avoid it. Practice rocking from side to side, changing position of the feet, flexing the knees, raising and lowering the horn, and even ripping the horn off the lips after the final note.

One very obvious performance mannerism is "horn counting," where some almost violently conduct with the horn, thus ruining the direction of tone. Vibrato can disappear or, even worse, become magnified. Some performers show their stress by lifting the eyebrows and wrinkling the forehead. This could be real trouble because a connection exists between this movement and anything that interrupts the coordination of the *Big Four*: embouchure, breath, tongue, and fingers.

By all means, practice in front of a mirror and videotape your rehearsals. Don't put this off. The dress rehearsal is a poor time to find out which mannerisms are acceptable and which ones are not. Learn your tendencies and eliminate the unacceptable ones well in advance of the performance.

Students sometimes take their playing too seriously to the point of a nervous breakdown. Before getting anywhere near this point, I suggest you take a blank sheet of paper and write down every bad thing you think will happen to you as the result of a poor performance. The thoughts may include the following:

1. I will fail trumpet.
2. My scholarship will be taken away.
3. I will be kicked out of school.
4. I will be too embarrassed to remain in school.
5. The audience will "boo" me.
6. People will laugh at me.
7. My friends will not speak to me.
8. My parents will disown me.
9. My sweetheart will break our engagement.
10. My puppy will run away.

None of these things will happen. Just read this book of essays over and over. You will find suggestions to help solve any problem you might have. Use your practice time with more imagination and take responsibility for your performance.

THE OTHER SIDE OF THE STAND

Mr. Haynie did a lot of modeling where he would play a phrase and have me repeat it. I think the fact that he could always demonstrate style was one of the most valuable things about my lessons. I learned a great deal from that practice of trying to copy or repeat what he played. It was also an inspiration to hear him play. I think that playing duets was a great aid in learning to sight read and in developing an awareness of pitch and precision.

Bob Blanton

John's insistence on our learning scales and chords to the point of frustration was perhaps the most helpful in my career. The fact that knowing these and recognizing them on a page was invaluable as a sight reading tool. I soon realized that sight reading is nothing more than seeing patterns you already have in memory and playing them.

Bob Ferguson

I played occasionally in the North Texas Orchestra and Opera Orchestra. This was yet another learning opportunity—to play a B-flat instrument and transpose the music as it changed to other keys. I had never done that before. But my mentor, Mr. Haynie, was there to help.

Judie Barker Goodwin

*John once played a dirty trick on me when he had me sight read **and** transpose Caffarelli on my jury. Stepped all over myself!*

Ron Modell

Transposition was a key element in my lessons and later helped me as a performer. As a band director, being able to quickly transpose has helped me in score reading and rehearsals.

Mike Olson

SIGHT READING AND TRANSPOSITION

Without headlines or fanfare, learning to sight read and to transpose was built into the North Texas Course of Study through the requirements of scale exams, technique development, and specific etude books. Sight reading means playing a piece of music you have never seen before. Transposition means to play a piece of music in a different key; in other words, you look at one note and play another. Success in both areas requires perfection in knowing and playing scales in every major key and at least three of their related minor keys.

Using my book, *How to Play High Notes, Low Notes and All Those In Between*, you are confronted with learning to play in all twelve tonalities, with many variations, all designed to reduce the amount of note and time combinations you have not seen before. If the Practice Guides are followed as prescribed there will be few note patterns you will not have seen. The more patterns you practice, the more patterns you will recognize immediately and sight read without error.

The basic principle in transposition is that you are learning a different set of fingerings for each scale or modality. Many systems are designed to help eliminate fear of transposition. Any system will work if you know scales and chords so well that your reading of them is simply a reaction. To get started, I suggest using the *Vingt-Quatre Vocalises* by Bordogni, published by Leduc. Each study has been transposed to a different key that, when played without transposing each phrase correctly, makes no musical sense at all. All studies are very tuneful, and it is possible to avoid some errors because the easier tunes can be played "by ear" to compensate for lack of experience in transposition.

Some would say this is cheating, but I think it is better to play the correct note because it's a good musical choice rather than to play the wrong note and never hear the problem. Long before this point in time the student should ask the question, "Why must I go through this transposition training? Why not just get started using the real thing, orchestral excerpts?" My objection to choosing this route is that it is slow, and you may get bored to death with the music by the time you can finally play it. And there is a good chance that you will have learned the excerpt by ear rather than by sight. Learn to sight read and transpose and all that orchestral literature will be yours for the playing in real life, not just from an excerpt book in somebody's studio—even mine.

Suggested Rhythm and Sight Reading Books

Bordogni	*Vingt-Quatre Vocalises*	Leduc
Caffarelli	*100 Melodic Studies*	Ricordi
Dufresne	*Develop Sight Reading*	Colin
Nagel	*Trumpet Studies in Contemporary Music*	Belwin Mills
Stevens	*Changing Meter Studies*	Editions BIM
Stevens	*Contemporary Trumpet Studies*	Billaudot

John Haynie, February 13, 1986

All smiles after his performance of the Carnival of Venice *with the*
North Texas Wind Ensemble at the TMEA Convention

THE OTHER SIDE OF THE STAND

Mr. Haynie devised a program of study that was organized to a degree I had not encountered before I attended North Texas. It took an incredible amount of work and careful thought to build that program, from the technique and scales exam to the terms tests, from the weekly recitals to the book exams. I have never seen or heard of a more comprehensive and well thought-out program of study.

Frank Campos

Another thing I took with me from my lessons with Mr. Haynie was the study of trumpet solo literature. Not only was I armed with an unmatched collection of music from the standard repertoire, but every time he taught me how a solo should be played, it was also a lesson in how an ensemble piece should be rehearsed, whether it was for concert band, brass ensemble, or choir. He let me borrow no fewer than one hundred recordings to hear different interpretations.

Ross Grant

John Haynie introduced me to French recital literature. The etude and recital material was vast and did much to change the emphasis on teaching at my university, where the focus had been on German literature. When the faculty began to hear the improvement in technique, tone, flexibility, pitch, and control of their trumpet players, they began to add French literature to their course of study for applied music. This addition created a more lyrical and musical performance in recital and ensemble playing.

Purris Williams

John Haynie is the most generous man I have ever known. He seems to always put everyone else's desires and needs ahead of his own. He unselfishly gives of his time, energy, resources, and talents. I have received so much trumpet music from JJ that I could go into business. If you can't find what you need at your local music store, give me a call!

David Zeagler

Developing a Trumpet Library

This specific selection of methods, etudes, and texts was used in the University of North Texas Course of Study featured in the February 1983 ITG *Journal.* Leonard Candelaria collaborated with me in structuring these materials. If I were still active in the music world I am sure this would be a different list now. Nevertheless, these materials have stood the test of time, and anyone who owns all these books will have an excellent library.

The Course of Study is not a perfect document and must be adjusted regularly. I allowed flexibility to the point anyone could play and study whatever his or her playing level deserved. But everybody wanted to start with the Jolivet or Tomasi *Concerti.* No wonder they would have problems with range and endurance! The Course of Study was designed to keep about seventy-five percent of the load as music the students needed to know and could play comfortably, with work. Save the other twenty-five percent for top-of-the-line goals for the future. So many students want to do the opposite. The Course of Study kept more students on the right track. The music we can play well, not what our ego wants to play, controls much of the success we enjoy.

The Course of Study requires the use of orchestral studies at the upper levels with emphasis in the early years on transposition studies. Too often the students and their teachers go directly to memorizing orchestral excerpts. I maintain that there is no rush about learning orchestral music, because it is highly unlikely that a student right out of college is going to be qualified to even play an audition with the hundreds of outstanding trumpet players seeking the few positions that are available. Therefore, the college student should use every minute of his practice in learning skills so that when the time comes he will have no problem playing the notes, including the required transposition.

Level 1

Category	Title	Publisher
Pedagogy		
Haynie	Pedagogical Concepts for Development and Maintenance of Technique for Brass Instruments	NTSU
Technique		
Haynie	Development and Maintenance with Practice Guides	Colin
Embouchure		
Little	Embouchure Builder	Pro Art
Rhythm		
Barker	Sight-Reading and Technique	Moorcroft
Transposition		
Caffarelli	100 Melodic Studies	Ricordi
Jazz		
Haerle	Scales for Jazz Improvisation	Studio P/R
Musical Terms		
Haynie/Candelaria/ Herrick	A Glossary of Musical Terms from Trumpet Literature	NTSU

Additional materials selected at the discretion of the teacher

Arban	Complete Conservatory Method	Carl Fischer
Balasanian	18 Intermediate Etudes	MCA Music
Concone/Sawyer	Lyrical Studies for Trumpet	The Brass Press
Decker	Intermediate Serial Studies	Kendor
Gates	Odd Meter Studies	Gornston
Getchell	Practical Studies Books 1 and 2	Belwin Mills
Hering	32 Etudes	Carl Fischer
Pottag	Preparatory Melodies	Belwin Mills
Small	27 Melodious and Rhythmical Exercises	Carl Fischer

Level 2

Category	Title	Publisher
Pedagogy		
Farkas	The Art of Musicianship	Musical Publications
Technique		
Haynie	Development and Maintenance with Practice Guides	Colin
Embouchure		
Irons	27 Groups of Exercises	Southern
Rhythm		
Barker	Sight-Reading and Technique	Moorcroft
Transposition		
Caffarelli	100 Melodic Studies	Ricordi
Jazz		
McNeil	Jazz Trumpet Techniques	Studio P/R
Musical Terms		
Haynie/Candelaria/ Herrick	A Glossary of Musical Terms from Trumpet Literature	NTSU

Additional materials selected at the discretion of the teacher

Arban	Complete Conservatory Method	Carl Fischer
Bousquet-Goldman	36 Celebrated Studies	Carl Fischer
Brandt	34 Studies	International
Collins	In the Singing Style	Queen City Brass
Goldman	Practical Studies	Carl Fischer
Hering	Etudes in All the Major and Minor Keys	Carl Fischer
Klosé	209 Tone and Finger Exercises	Gornston
Vanntelbosch	Vingt Études Mélodiques et Techniques	Leduc
Voxman	Selected Studies	Rubank

Level 3

Category	Title	Publisher
Pedagogy		
Johnson	The Art of Trumpet Playing	U of Iowa Press
Technique		
Haynie	Development and Maintenance with Practice Guides	Colin
Embouchure		
Smith	Lip Flexibility on the Trumpet	Carl Fischer
Rhythm		
Nagel	Trumpet Studies in Contemporary Music	Belwin Mills
Transposition		
Bordogni/Porret	Vingt-Quatre Vocalises	Leduc
Jazz		
Matteson/Peterson	Training Aids for Flexibility and Improvisation	Matteson
Musical Terms		
Haynie/Candelaria/Herrick	A Glossary of Musical Terms from Trumpet Literature	NTSU

Additional materials selected at the discretion of the teacher

Balasanyan	20 Studies	International
Berdiev	17 Studies	King
Bozza	16 Etudes	Leduc
Broiles	Trumpet Studies and Duets: Book 1	McGinnis
Clarke	Technical Studies	Carl Fischer
Gisondi	Bach for the Trumpet	McGinnis
Hickman	The Piccolo Trumpet	Tromba
Kase	21 Studies in Style and Interpretation	Southern
Longinotti	Studies in Classical and Modern Style	International

Level 4

Category	Title	Publisher
Pedagogy		
Altenburg/Tarr	Trumpeters' and Kettledrummers' Art	The Brass Press
Technique		
Haynie	Development and Maintenance with Practice Guides	Colin
Embouchure		
Nagel	Trumpet Skills (Lip Flexibility)	Mentor
Rhythm		
Stevens	Changing Meter Studies	Editions BIM
Transposition		
Various	Selected orchestral excerpts	See excerpts
Jazz		
Ricker	Pentatonic Scales for Jazz Improvisation	Studio P/R
Musical Terms		
Haynie/Candelaria/ Herrick	A Glossary of Musical Terms from Trumpet Literature	NTSU

Additional materials selected at the discretion of the teacher

Bodet	Seize Études de Virtuosité d'Après J.S. Bach	Leduc
Broiles	Trumpet Studies and Duets, Book II	McGinnis and Max
Charlier	Trente-Six Études Transcendantes	Leduc
Falk	Vingt Études Atonales	Leduc
Sabarich	Dix Études	Editions Selmer
Smith	Top Tones	Carl Fischer
Tull	Eight Profiles	Boosey & Hawkes
Vizzutti	Advanced Etudes for Trumpet	The Brass Press
Webster	Method for Piccolo Trumpet	The Brass Press

Level 5

Category	Title	Publisher
Pedagogy		
Baines	The Brass Instruments	Chas. Scribner's Sons
Technique		
Haynie	Development and Maintenance with Practice Guides	Colin
Embouchure		
Schlossberg	Daily Drills and Technical Studies	Baron
Rhythm		
Stevens	Contemporary Trumpet Studies	Billaudot
Transposition		
Various	Selected orchestral excerpts	See excerpts
Jazz		
Slone/Aebersold	28 Modern Jazz Trumpet Solos	Studio P/R
Musical Terms		
Haynie/Candelaria/ Herrick	A Glossary of Musical Terms from Trumpet Literature	NTSU

Additional materials selected at the discretion of the teacher

André	12 Études-Caprices dans le Style Baroque	Billaudot
Arban	Célèbre Méthode Complete, Vol. 3	Leduc
Bitsch	Vingt Études	Leduc
Boutry	Douze Études de Virtuosité	Leduc
Broiles	Trumpet Baroque (piccolo trumpet)	Queen City Brass
Caffarelli	Seize Études de Perfectionnement	Leduc
Chaynes	Quinze Études	Leduc
Nagel	Speed Studies	Mentor
Reynolds	48 Etudes for Trumpet	Schirmer
Ruggiero	Huit Études Atonales	Leduc

Orchestral Excerpts

Composer	Title	Publisher
Bach/Güttler	Complete Trumpet Repertoire, Volumes 1, 2, 3	Musica Rara
Bartold	Orchestral Excerpts, Volumes 1, 2, 3, 4, 5	International
Farr [Hardin]	A Trumpeter's Guide to Orchestral Excerpts	Camden House, 2nd edition
Handel/Minter	Complete Trumpet Repertoire, Volumes 1, 2, 3, 4	Musica Rara
Johnson	20th Century Orchestra Studies	Schirmer
Neuhaus	Orchesterstudien für Trompete	Musikverlag Hans Gerig
Pietsch	Die Trompete	University Music Press
Purcell/King	Complete Trumpet Repertoire	Musica Rara
Strauss	Orchestral Studies	International
Voisin	Orchestral Excerpts, Volumes 6, 7, 8, 9, 10	International
Wagner	Orchestral Studies, Volumes 1 and 2	International

THE OTHER SIDE OF THE STAND

I am so pleased to have Mr. Haynie's records. My students still play all these songs and listen to his renditions. **Mont St. Michel** *is my favorite.*

Rick Bogard

Mr. Haynie's utilization of daily drills such as **Development and Maintenance** *stands out. Even a professional performer does not have to use all the required techniques every day. But when any tool or technique is needed, we also know that we better have that skill ready and operable.*

Lyman Brodie

I had the entire trumpet section of **42nd Street** *doing Mr. Haynie's coordination studies. I first showed them to my friend, Joe Mosello, after he suffered a stroke, thinking they would be great for helping him get his chops back together. He loves them, and when the other guys heard him practicing, they all went crazy for them.*

Elaine Burt

Mr. Haynie's idea of **Development and Maintenance** *is at the heart of every accomplished trumpet player's soul. Trumpeters have used this concept for 150 years, but his putting a name on it must be a milestone in trumpet history.*

Max Morley

As I listen to Mr. Haynie's recordings, I realize once again that music is more about soul and emotion than it is about "eating concrete" like you find in the politics of everyday life.

Remus Morosan

The first solo Mr. Haynie gave me to play as a 6th grader was **Mark 1-0.** *I knew this was written for his son Mark, and this meant a lot to me.*

Debra Millender Widdig

WRITINGS, RECORDINGS, COMPOSERS

·

Unlike Anne Hardin's friend, Ray Bradbury, who has written every day of his life, my plunge into the world of writing short stories has been a recent development. My earliest efforts at writing were of a practical nature. I wrote about how to play the cornet and trumpet, both for my students and also to use as handouts at my clinics. It should come as no surprise that the first one I wrote was a twelve-page booklet, typed and hand-stapled, entitled "So You Want to Play Cornet." Since I was mostly self-taught about how to manage the fundamentals, it was fairly simple to write about where I placed the mouthpiece, etc. As I look back, my early attempts were very average and middle-of-the-road. I improved with effort, and I had a number of articles and reviews appear in magazines such as *Music Educators Journal, ConnChord,* and *The Instrumentalist.* One article I wrote for *The Instrumentalist* was called "How to Play the Carnival of Venice in Four Easy Lessons" (May 1967). The four easy lessons later became what I called my **Big Four**.

My work in the more sophisticated area of fluoroscopic research produced a more sophisticated booklet, *A Videofluorographic Presentation of the Physiological Phenomena Influencing Trumpet Performance.* This was a write-up of a presentation I did with Dr. Alex Finlay, and my interest in the research, quite simply, was to discover what happened inside the oral cavity during tonguing and slurring. The uniqueness of the project sparked a lot of interest from the press with headlines like "Skeleton Blows Hot Notes for TV Special" and "Skull Session Is Held." I made many presentations about my findings, one being at the National Trumpet Symposium at the University of Denver, August 12–16, 1968. I had no burning desires to set the world straight nor did I wish to get into conflict over special concerns of other teachers.

My friend, Phil Farkas, had written his wonderful book, *The Art of Brass Playing*, and I referred to it often to describe what I believed. Writing a book to compete with the Farkas book made no sense to me. What ***did*** make sense was to expand concepts already out there to reinforce what I taught in my studio, and this is how the three trumpet method books I put together came into being.

The first was *Development and Maintenance of Techniques*, published by Charles Colin around 1972—it's undated. My students called it the "*D & M* book." The book was my idea, but not my material. Haskell Sexton introduced me to a great book called *The Secret of Technique Preservation* by Ernest Williams. With every phase of the book, Williams said in his preface to play in all keys. Of course, no one ever does that. Charles Colin, who held publishing rights to all Williams's publications, gave me his permission to revise, interpret, and extend *Secrets*, and he would publish it. There were obvious areas that *Secrets* did not address. In my version of the book, concepts are stated in such a way that there should be no doubt about why we practice these studies and how to do them.

My second book, *Twelve Study Groups*, was published by Alphonse Leduc (Paris) in 1972. This was a revision of the French work, *La Semaine du Virtuose*, by Alexandre Petit. The original Petit book was not well-organized and included no exercises with minor scales. I asked Leduc for permission to rewrite it for my students. Their response was the same as that of Charles Colin: "Do it and we will publish it." Both this book and *D & M* covered the same kind of materials with the same intent. So, why two books that do the same thing? For variety. Some students preferred one book over the other. Some students hated both books because if you have a weakness, these exercises will find it. Having everything written out in every key has a way of finding the problems.

The third method, *How to Play High Notes, Low Notes and All Those In Between*, was an extended and revised version of the studies in *D & M*. It was published by Charles Colin, and undated. The foreword says it was published in my "37th year," which would be 1987. Charles Colin published this version when all copies of *D & M* had been sold. He timed the publication and presentation to concur with the ITG Conference at the University of North Texas in 1987. The coordination studies, 5A and 5B, found in each tonality, when properly used, are the most beneficial of any exercises in a daily routine. I went through the text with every student and played through at least one tonality so there would be no doubt about why and how to approach it. Playing the chromatic scales five different ways in one breath was something few ever accomplished. My goal with this book was to encourage students to think and be flexible, to be imaginative and take chances.

Recordings

When I arrived in Denton at North Texas State College in the summer of 1950, I did not own a single LP recording of trumpet solos. I had heard one 78 rpm recording of Leonard B. Smith playing *Spanish Caprice* and *My Heaven of Love* ten years earlier when I was a high school student. The next 78 rpm trumpet recording I heard was during the summer of 1947 when I ran across the George Eksdale recording of the Haydn *Trumpet Concerto*. Other professional recordings were probably available, but the solo recording market was certainly not what it is now. The orchestral players were the ones who could have done it, but they had to keep up with their own job requirements. Some big-name soloists were in the "public ear" in every juke box that could drop a 45 rpm record on a spindle—people like Glenn Miller, Tommy Dorsey, Benny Goodman, and Harry James. Harry adapted his outstanding technical facility to a jazz style. Someone wrote virtuoso pieces for him, and his name became a household word. Harry's son, Harry Jeffrey James, was a student of mine for several years. Then along came another colorful trumpet player, Rafael Mendez, whose recordings overlapped the 78 rpm to LPs.

Still, trumpet players were slow to take advantage of this opportunity to be heard by the masses. I recall buying every recording released during the 1950s. Roger Voisin introduced us to early music with his recordings. Cornetist Jimmy Burke made some recordings, then Leonard Smith and George Reynolds took a chance and recorded music we saw on many contest lists, still mostly the cornet virtuoso pieces. In my early years at North Texas, I found and bought a recording of Helmut Wobisch playing the Haydn *Concerto*. As other recordings became available, I became familiar with interpretations other than my own.

In December 1958, I appeared as guest soloist for the CBDNA convention that was held at the University of Illinois. Marilyn and I remained in Urbana over the Christmas holidays to prepare for a recital at the School of Music. Mark Hindsley recorded our entire program during these practice sessions, and they were later produced as an LP recording by Golden Crest Records called *John Haynie, Trumpet* (RE7008).

Since all the concerts with the Illinois Band were recorded, Mr. Hindsley put my performances from the first evening—the Haydn *Concerto* and Robert Russell Bennett's *Rose Variations*—on the University of Illinois Concert Band LP #23. The *Suite for Trumpet* by William P. Latham, which was performed the following evening, appears on LP #24. In the months and years that followed, *Rose Variations* was requested and performed more than any other solo in my repertoire. Not only was it an exciting addition to new trumpet literature, it also greatly enhanced the quality of compositions for trumpet and band.

I recorded my second solo album on the Austin Record's Southwest Artist Series, and it was called *John Haynie Plays Music for Contest*, featuring cornet and trumpet solos on the Texas Contest List. Obviously, there was no such thing as dubbing a missed note. If you didn't like what you heard, you had to start over. The Tomasi and Jolivet *Concertos*, written in 1949 and 1954, were not yet staples in the professional repertoire, much less anything that would appear on a state contest list. But what some of these solos lack in technique, they make up in beauty of sound, interpretation, and expression.

I knew how important it could be to a young player to have access to recordings of trumpet music, and these two albums were a good variety for the time.

Composers

I have been fortunate all my life to have been surrounded by talented composer/colleagues, many of whom honored me by adding works to the pool of trumpet literature. All six composers highlighted here had some kind of Texas connection to me as a friend, student, or colleague.

Larry Austin

I first met Larry Austin when he attended a band camp at Texas Tech when he was in high school, and he became one of my trumpet students in the early 1950s. Larry's skills as a composer were amazing, and choosing that direction for his music was a great decision.

Larry's youngest daughter, Aurora, was a cornet player, and in 1975, she asked him to write a solo for her state solo contest in Florida. How can a father say no? Larry was very involved with the music of Charles Ives at the time, and extremely talented in the electronic music field, so he used a sound patch (in electronic music terms) from an Ives manuscript to begin and end Aurora's solo. The rest he wrote himself. He named the piece *Charlie's Cornet*, as a tribute to the cornet bequeathed to Ives by his father, and he dedicated the solo to me. Larry Austin taught on the North Texas faculty from 1978 until his retirement in 1996.

Rule Beasley

Rule Beasley is the multi-talented husband of my multi-talented student, Lida Oliver. Composer, bassoonist—you name it, he can do it. We met in 1956 when the North Texas band was on tour in Rosenberg, Texas. In 1961 or 1962, I asked him to write a piece for me to play on C trumpet. Rule was on the faculty of Centenary College in Shreveport, Louisiana, at the time. He agreed, and the result was *Fanfare and Scherzo*. Marilyn and I premiered this in 1963 for the Ft. Worth Composer's League. Rule was a member of the North Texas faculty from 1966–1973.

Merrill Ellis

Merrill wrote a delightful solo *8771-W and Trumpet Piece*. It was a happy little piece that was fun to play. I liked it so much that I commissioned him to write a piece for C trumpet. He named this work *Einyah Festival*. He composed two scorings— one for C trumpet, piano, and drum set, and the other for C trumpet and band. I played both versions many times. The middle section is the most extensive lyrical playing I had ever done, and with only drum set as an accompaniment. He wrote a song for my son Mark. It had another clever title that defined the song perfectly. He called it *Mark 1-0*, because the entire melody used only first valve or open trumpet notes. This is a Class III solo on the Texas UIL list and is published by Gore Music. Merrill taught theory and composition at North Texas from 1962 until his death in 1981.

William P. Latham

In the early 1950s, there was a void in quality trumpet compositions written by Americans. Bill Latham entered this arena with his *Suite for Trumpet* (1951). He did three scorings—the first was scored for trumpet and strings, and in my view is the most elegant of the three. The second scoring, also published in 1951, was for trumpet with a piano reduction. I liked the *Suite* so much, that I asked Bill to write a new piece for trumpet and band. He quickly responded that he wouldn't have time to write a completely new composition, but he had always wanted to do a wind ensemble version of his *Suite*. So it was agreed that he would score the work for trumpet and band, and I would premiere it as soloist with the University of Illinois Band on December 19, 1958, for the College Band Directors National Association convention in Urbana. Dean Kenneth Cuthbert, ever looking to add to his renowned faculty, hired Bill in 1965 as Professor of Music/Coordinator of Composition at North Texas.

Near the end of my performance career, he wrote another piece for me called *Fantasy for Trumpet*. This was a difficult contemporary piece for trumpet and wind ensemble. I premiered *Fantasy for Trumpet* at the University of South Alabama at Mobile.

Grant Sharman

Grant Sharman was my classmate at Texas Tech for a year-and-a-half following my military service. In the spring of 1947, I asked him to write a solo for me with band accompaniment. He wrote a waltz with variations, and called it *A Day in June*. It was published in 1950 by Charles A. Wiley, Austin, Texas. I am pictured on the cover wearing my University of Illinois band uniform, holding my cornet.

Fisher "Mickey" Tull

When Mickey Tull arrived on the North Texas campus in the fall of 1952, he was already a fine trumpet player and budding dance band arranger. Mickey was equally at home with both jazz and traditional trumpet styles. It was in his third year that I introduced him to *Dix Études*, written by Raymond Sabarich, published by Leduc. This music would change the direction of his career to composition and become the model for his composition *Eight Profiles* twenty-five years later in 1980. Each profile bears the initials of individuals with whom he formed life-long friendships.

In 1975, Mickey was commissioned by a group of my past and present students to compose a work for trumpet and piano "honoring John James Haynie in appreciation of his 25 years of outstanding service to North Texas State University." The work, *Three Bagatelles*, was premiered on May 1, 1975, by my former student, Tom Parriott, then professor of trumpet at Sam Houston State University, and accompanied by Charlotte Tull, Mickey's wife.

Note: Most of these compositions were recorded by John Holt, professor of trumpet at North Texas, and Natalia Bolshakova, piano, between February 7, 2004, and May 18–19, 2004, at the Mesquite Arts Center in Mesquite, Texas. The CD is called *UNconventional Trumpet: Music by University of North Texas composers Ellis, Beasley, McTee, Mailman, Austin, Latham, and Tull*, Crystal Records CD763.

John Haynie, Trumpet
Golden Crest Recital Series

Aria con Variazioni	Handel/Fitzgerald
*"Polly Oliver"**	arr. Fitzgerald
*"Rule Britannia"**	arr. Firzgerald
Black is the Color of My True Love's Hair	John Jacob Niles
Concert Etude	Alexander Goedicke
Lament	John Klein
Étude de Concert	Marcel Poot
Aria	Tenaglia & Krieger/Fitzgerald
Allegro	Tenaglia & Krieger/Fitzgerald
*"My Lovely Celia"**	arr. Fitzgerald
*"Begone Dull Care"**	arr. Fitzgerald
Serenade	Alexander Bakaleinikoff
Rustiques	Eugène Bozza
Mont Saint-Michel	Geoffrey Robbins
Boutade	Pierre Gabaye

*from *English Suite*

John Haynie Plays Music for Contest
Austin Records Southwest Artist Series

Carnival of Venice	Del Staigers
Sonata VIII	Corelli, arr. Fitzgerald
Stars in a Velvety Sky	Herbert L. Clarke
Andante and Allegro	J. Guy Ropartz
Song of the Pines	Earl Irons
Grand Russian Fantasia	Levy, arr. Buchtel
Prayer of Saint Gregory	Alan Hovhaness
Capriccioso	Paul Jeanjean
Fox Hunt	R. M. Endresen
Norine	Herbert L. Clarke
A Trumpeter's Lullaby	Leroy Anderson
Mitene	Ernest Williams
Conversation for Cornet	Clare Grundman

THE OTHER SIDE OF THE STAND

*I was on my way to class when I saw a notice that an Opryland USA team would be doing auditions at North Texas **that day**. The only thing I had ready was something I was working up for my lesson with Mr. Haynie, so that's what I played an hour after reading the audition notice. Afterward, the auditioner said sarcastically, "Wow, couldn't you find anything hard? How would you like to move to Nashville?" And I said in true John Haynie style, "How's the fishing?" He said, "Great." I was offered the job a month later, and I've been in Nashville ever since.*

Scott Ducaj

I was awarded a teaching assistantship without ever having studied with John Haynie, so it was quite clear that I had much catching up to do. Quickly, after what I recall as being a rigorous and extensive interview and audition, he said, "Well, you can play the trumpet, and you know a lot of excerpts. We have some work to do, and I have strong ideas about how it is going to be done. Also, I have a little more than a year to expose you to the body of literature for the trumpet, so let's get started." (I have looked back many times at the assignment dates in my personal library and get weak in the knees.) Those were the most wonderful months of my professional life!

Don Owen

*I was offered a job at Midwestern State University if I completed a perform-ance degree instead of a music education degree, so I had a lot riding on my audition. It was my worst performance ever. I shook through all three move-ments of the Haydn **Trumpet Concerto**. I am looking at the worn and faded evaluation at this moment. In the "Remarks" section of the evalua-tion, Mr. Haynie wrote: "The audition was a disappointment, but not Ken Van Winkle, the person. I believe in you with all my heart." I can't tell you how many times his confidence has carried me through my career.*

Ken Van Winkle

THE AUDITION FOR A SCHOLARSHIP

Here's my routine in hearing a potential student for the first time. Boy or girl, it doesn't matter.

- I ask him to warm up in my presence just as if I weren't there. I am looking for evidence of what he thinks is a proper warm-up—a big clue about what to expect.
- I then ask him to tell me the name of the last solo he worked on. It is amazing that he has been working on the solo for three months and does not know the name, much less the composer.
- I ask if he can play it from memory. No. Does he have the music? He lost it, or the band director took it back.
- Well now, what did he come prepared to play for scholarship audition and admittance? Nothing.
- So, I guess you will just have to play some scales. Let me hear your written pitch scale of E-flat major. What note does it start on?
- OK, take a look at this little song and let me hear the nicest tone you can play. Finally I hear him play. Just what you might expect from a youngster who has no imagination or expectation of what it takes to learn how to play. His total interest has been playing in bands and jazz bands with virtually no individual practice.

(This scenario happened over and over even if the student had taken private lessons. Obviously this student should not pass the audition or be admitted.)

Seldom is anyone refused admission, since I believe a state school should give everyone a chance to prove themselves. After the audition, a weak, unprepared student is classified as "Development," and a strong, more capable player will be classified as "Maintenance." These classifications designate the purpose for which each student will be using the Course of Study I put together, particularly their trumpet technique book, *How to Play High Notes, Low Notes and All Those In Between.*

Regarding the prescribed Course of Study, students must show a working knowledge of all materials; however, the student classified as "Maintenance" will be permitted to move rapidly through the early materials until he reaches the appropriate level for his age, training, and ability.

Auditions are a fact of life in the music business. This testing is invaluable to show how he ranks with others and how the standard of trumpet playing continually improves. For placement in performing groups, there is no more appropriate and fair method of selecting personnel.

The Haynie Family, August 2001

Jordan, Mark, and Anne Haynie; John and Marilyn; Katie, Melinda, Rachel, Dave, and Cole Zeagler. Photo taken in Crested Butte, Colorado, to commemorate John and Marilyn's 50th wedding anniversary

THE OTHER SIDE OF THE STAND

At one of our "get acquainted meetings," Mr. Haynie questioned me about what I wanted to do with my interest in music. I assured him that my interest was mainly limited to playing the trumpet, but that I would probably major in music education in order to have something to "fall back on." Even though our meeting went on for another twenty or twenty-five minutes, I quickly realized that with my last "wisdom-filled comment," my portion of our conversation had come to an end. With his gentle, but firm, manner, Mr. Haynie imparted to me that music education was not exactly the most logical field to "fall back on"—in fact, there was hardly anything worse than a teacher who really didn't want to teach. When I had an opportunity to teach, I always felt honored to be part of such an important, challenging, and noble profession.

Gary Dobbins

One of the things I took with me from my lessons with Professor Haynie was, first and foremost, "how to teach." His incredibly organized and methodical system of administering the North Texas brass department left no stone unturned. Even I could learn how to teach students to play, and I was armed with an arsenal of materials. I applied what I learned in trumpet lessons to the conductor's podium of concert, marching, and jazz bands, and to beginner classes on all instruments.

Ross Grant

I have a wonderful memory of Mr. Haynie's terrific organizational skills. I was always so impressed with them. Watching him helped me develop those skills myself. He consistently exhibited a strong, positive influence on his students and very cleverly convinced us that we were capable of greatness, whether or not we were really at that level at that particular moment in time.

Scott McAdow

WHY TEACH?

A very wise professor of music always told his students to stay out of music, music education in particular. Teaching is only for those whose passion is to share knowledge or skill with those who wish to learn. If you happen to be a fine player on any instrument playing professionally (part time) is very possible. Your dedication to teaching must not be altered in any way by accepting jobs that conflict with this. Do not allow yourself to hold on to a teaching job so you can play gigs. This same professor said that no matter what job you start, work at that job as if it were a lifetime appointment.

During my entire career I wanted my students to work at the trumpet or whatever they played as if they were in training to be a professional performer. Even though a degree might read Bachelor of Music in Music Education, this does not eliminate the holder from competing for a professional appointment. This was so understood by my students that they never stopped their lessons just because they had completed their trumpet requirements. In fact, many of my music education majors were far better performers than some who were trumpet performance majors.

In my counseling with students and parents, I would sometimes suggest that the student not go to college at all if he or she had no intention of teaching. Why not put your money where your mouth is? Set up an educational account for the student to equal the cost of a four-year teaching degree. Send that student to New York, Chicago, Los Angeles, or Boston to study with a high-profile teacher. Just think. No PE requirement, no education courses and other such to sleep through or not attend. All that time could be spent practicing and taking lessons and doing what you really want to do. If you find you are not the teacher's "delight," without assurance you will find your way in a performance career, you could renegotiate your plans and go to a college for an education degree or enroll in a completely different program. Then play the horn for fun.

Somewhere along the way, however, students got the message that I did not want to hear they were getting the music education degree to have something to fall back on. This assumption was bad for the whole program in music education. One of the big problems in our school systems today is that there are a lot of people teaching who hate to be there. Now, in some ways the music education people lower the bar by not expecting their students to be "as good as they can be as musicians." Their attitude is that you have to pass a "proficiency exam," then take no more lessons. In my opinion, the music education students should be the finest players. A trumpet performance major who becomes a professional musician will be responsible only for himself. Whether he is a huge success or total failure, he is the only one affected. But it is almost guaranteed that a music teacher who is a poor musician will limit countless students' lives. Of course, there are exceptions both ways.

The degrees my students chose to pursue were their business, and I did not try to talk them into becoming a teacher. It was my intention to give them my best effort to help them become musicians. The higher their performance level, the higher their students' performance level. I was always proud of their successes in teaching.

Who *was* that very wise professor of music, you might ask. Well, since you asked—it was I, and hundreds of others like me.

Keith Johnson and John Haynie, 2004

Regents Professor of Music, Keith Johnson, was hired in 1986
upon John's retirement from active teaching

THE OTHER SIDE OF THE STAND

When I was about fourteen, I got upset because playing the trumpet made a ring on my lips. I started to cry and told Mr. Haynie that I didn't like it, and he said, "Well, we can take care of that! Sell your trumpet!" I was not expecting that! We never discussed it again. I've been telling the girl trumpet players in my band the same thing for almost twenty-five years.

Marsha Millender Adams

I looked forward to seeing what clothes John wore. I especially was intrigued by those Argyle socks that Marilyn knitted for him.

Lida Oliver Beasley

Mr. Haynie was my father away from home. He made sure that I took care of the basics of life. He even told me to take a typing class—and I did!

Elizabeth Pollard Bowen

*One day, I had dressed up to be videotaped for a conducting exam, and when Mr. Haynie saw me in the hall, he asked me why I was so dressed up. When I told him, he commented, "Why don't you dress up for your lessons with me like that?" I dressed up for **every** lesson from that point on!*

Cynthia Thompson Carrell

In 1950, Mr. McAdow added girls to several ranks in the center of the marching band block so that our skirted uniforms were lined up together. Virginia Walberg, Anna Jean Hale, and I played a trio with the band on our concert tours.

Judie Barker Goodwin

John afforded opportunities to perform with excellent musicians. The resulting confidence in my abilities provided a base for future leadership skills.

Pat Bode Saunders

GIRLS AND TRUMPETS

This essay may get me into lots of hot water with today's generation of young women, but there was a time when few girls played the trumpet. From my observation, parents may have felt it was unladylike for a girl to play a trumpet and fit in the same profile of proper wearing apparel. Little girls were supposed to wear dresses, not pants. It was a part of a protective mechanism that fortunately all parents did not participate in.

It is true that excessive mouthpiece pressure may leave a ring on *any* player's lips, and I've seen players who've played the same number of years and practiced the same number of hours with and without that telltale ring. But back to the girls. If she continues to play past high school, chances are she is not concerned about the ring other than wishing she could use less pressure and avoid having the mouthpiece ring on her lips in the first place.

When I was growing up in Cisco, Texas, girls just did not play cornet or trumpet. In Mexia, I recall only one girl who played cornet. Her name was Mary Ann Stubbs, and she was a good player. She could always play her part in our cornet trio. Two of the finest cornet players in the state of Texas were Fay Moser of Waco and Jennings McLean of Caldwell. They became acquaintances of mine though the All-State band when I was in high school.

When I attended Texas Tech and the University of Illinois there were no girls playing cornet or trumpet. But when I got to North Texas I had music major girl trumpet players who were always wonderful students. Among my first students that I inherited from Maurice McAdow were Virginia Walberg Frey, Judie Barker Goodwin, and Gene Iles Jacob (horn). Soon to follow were Nona Beth Barker, Lida Oliver Beasley (baritone), Nancy Meyers Childress, Anna Jean Hale, and Pat Deemer Kimbell.*

Others I was fortunate enough to teach, whether they were in junior high, senior high, or at the university, were Marsha Millender Adams, Elizabeth Pollard Bowen, Elaine Burt, Cynthia Thompson Carrell, Erin Crossen, Marnie Duke, Cathy Edwards, Marilyn Glass Ellison (horn), Holly Fuson, Marilynn Mocek Gibson,* Lauren Haskins, Bonnie Heron, Carole Herrick,* Nancy Hockett, Ruth Jane Holmes, Cathy Myer Kliebenstein,* E. Diane Lyle-Smith, Mandy McCasland, Ann McMahon,* Cindy Mikel, Chris Minear, Kate Morey, Eunice Morrison, Jane Parker, Trish Rooney, Virginia Ruffin, Pat Bode Saunders, Alice Schmid, Charlotte Taylor, and Debra Millender Widdig.

These young ladies were all excellent trumpet players. They were all good sports, and I was always pleased by their spirit and serious lesson preparation. Years later, several mentioned that their lessons were important events on their schedules and they dressed accordingly. I noticed their finery, and they noticed mine!

*served as teaching assistant

John Haynie and Anne Hardin, February 2006

THE OTHER SIDE OF THE STAND

The Two O'Clock Lab Band was preparing some music for a major concert that was particularly challenging from a technical standpoint. The director, Leon Breeden, told us he wanted some "outside help" to prepare this music, and he arranged for Mr. Haynie to conduct a special brass sectional. There was quite a buzz about this at the time. A lot of other players, jazz and legit, came to observe. The sectional was very successful. During the sectional, the great Dallas-based lead-trumpet player, George Cherb, walked in. He had no idea this special rehearsal was taking place. Mr. Haynie saw him and stopped the rehearsal. George came forward and these two great masters in their own realm engaged in a few minutes of shop/trumpet talk. I'll never forget being struck by the obvious respect these two virtuosi had for each other. I would like to thank them for presenting a perfect "picture-is-worth-a-thousand-words" model that, though we must live with categories, we still should all realize that at the highest level of musical accomplishment, the categories are meaningless. No one represents this better than John James Haynie, as brought home by that "duologue" on that day long ago.

Bob Morgan

Mr. Haynie taught me more about trumpet playing, teaching trumpet playing, trumpet performance, and classical music interpretation, than any other tutor in my career. I would not be where I am today without his help and guidance.

Jay Saunders

*Mr. Haynie made sure that I knew of a great trumpet soloist who had come to town to play solos with the One O'Clock Lab Band in the fall of 1963. He said I should **not** miss it. So it was during my seventh grade year that I got to hear Maynard Ferguson play **Maria** and other unbelievable pieces with that fantastic band. Talk about an epiphany!*

Richard Waddell

The Non-Jazzer, Found Out

After all these years it has been discovered that I, the non-jazzer, did play in a dance band at the University of Illinois. In fact, I played in several. Here is the story.

I arrived in Champaign-Urbana with nine dollars in my pocket. I was a member of the marching band, which was preparing for a trip to New York for the Illinois—Army football game. I needed money.

During a rest period, a fellow walked by a group of us and into the band building. He retraced his steps a few minutes later. One of those sitting on the steps said, "Hey Bill, I hear Tom won't be back in school this fall." Bill answered that he would sure miss Tom because he was the best lead player on campus. As Bill Shelton walked away I followed after him, and asked if I could try out. He said, "Sure, man. Bring your axe and join the hackers over at such-and-such church tonight." I worried the rest of the afternoon about where I could get an axe. I showed up anyway, and not one single person had brought an axe.

Bill didn't ask, and I didn't tell him I had never played in a so-called big band. But what the heck? I could play high and loud, and I was a good reader. In fact, these guys were not worth a hoot. They played dirty tones, scooped notes, and couldn't play four or more eighth notes evenly. What they all did was play the eighth notes like triplets, or maybe like dotted-eighths and sixteenths. I decided to go along with them, since they definitely were pretty lousy readers of music who didn't know any better.

They called it a gig. I got it. I was so hungry and so glad to have a job that if they wanted to mess up basic rhythm patterns, so what? I quietly told the second player they'd better get that problem worked out before they played for A. A. Harding and Mark Hindsley.

THE OTHER SIDE OF THE STAND

I still have that fishing lure Mr. Haynie gave me when I was about thirteen. It is on a shelf in a place of honor in my living room.

Marsha Millender Adams

A book about John Haynie would not be complete without a fishing story or two. The fishing part of his life certainly influenced his strength of character, as well as the patient side of his personality. A university President always likes to hear from faculty members first-hand. John called one spring day simply to see if I would care to go fishing on Lake Texoma. Having heard of his prowess as a fisherman, I joyfully replied, "Yes!" We arrived at the dock early one Saturday morning. Clouds were overhead, and an occasional mist fell about us. Our guide was the dean of fishing guides on the lake, Max Eggleston, who took one look at the clouds and said something good would come in with the weather. "Be sure to follow the gulls. They know where the fish are." And that's just what we did. The fish hit almost as fast as the lures could touch the water, and by that time I matched John fish for fish. I think he was ready to throw me overboard! Max said he seldom had experienced a day of fishing like we'd had. I learned about the gulls and finding fish. I learned how to use a Garcia 5000 reel and how to select a lure that will appeal to both a striped bass and a black bass on the same day. I learned about the joy of fishing from a master teacher outside his class-room, but a master teacher just the same.

C. C. "Jitter" Nolen

My fondest memory of Mr. Haynie was our discussions about fishing in Northern New Mexico. He knew all the best spots for good trout fish-ing. When I wasn't ready for a lesson, I would engage him in conversation about fishing. That worked a few times, but soon his comment was, "What's the matter, Pancho, didn't you practice this week?"

Frank "Pancho" Romero

TRY FLY FISHING—IT IS EASY

Unlike other types of fishing, fly fishing is backlash free. In fact, you don't even need a reel or a lot of the things most of us buy. I have boxes and boxes of stuff I never used, or if it *was* used, it didn't help catch trout! You can catch all kinds of things when fly fishing, and Dr. Alex Finlay topped the list. He was a student of mine, but not on trumpet. I taught him how to fly *fish*, but on the Firehole River in Yellowstone National Park, Alex Finlay caught a moose. Now picture this. Alex was just minding his own business, smoking his pipe, and having a grand old time when a moose ambled up to the stream from behind and watched Alex beat the water. Alex was casting away with his line, going as far behind as with his forward cast. He snagged something on his back cast and, thinking it was a rock or stump, turned to see the moose standing there with an Adams #12 hook in its nose. So the first rule of fly fishing is: Always know what's behind you. It might even be an IRS agent who wants to investigate your tax return.

In trumpet-speak, we would say that trumpet players must stay on high alert and be discriminate in their purchases of musical equipment. I mentioned that a fly fisherman does not have to use a reel; nor does a trumpet player have to have a case for his horn. A fly fisherman does need a good fly rod and the best line made. It is the line one casts, and the cast must be accurate. A trumpet player must also be accurate or he likely will not be asked to play another gig.

A trumpet and mouthpiece equal a rod and line (or a reel and line for regular casting). I daresay that a good trumpet player will also be a good fly fisherman. Tied to the fly line is a nine to twelve-foot tapered leader, and tied to the leader is a fly. Don't ask me why it's called a fly. Just stretch your imagination and call the bait "a fly."

The Haynie School of Dry Fly Fishing started back in the 1960s. All those eligible for a certificate had to have their first exposure to fly fishing with me as their teacher. To earn a certificate, they must have hooked, landed, and released at least one fish. There have been no failures at graduating, though some were close.

Learning a piece of music on trumpet is much like looking at a stretch of stream. You see the notes first but probably not the music. That comes later. With streams, you see the water first, and you have to hope that the fish come later. What do you do? Exactly what jazz players do when they see an unadorned melody. You improvise! All fly fishermen must learn to improvise or they should go to the truck, have a Coke, then take a nap.

The jazz player should know where he is in the music at all times; with fishing we will say that he has caught his fish if he returns to the tune at the right time. The fisherman starts changing flies, making longer tippets, and casting the fly at the unlikely place to find fish. Remember that fish are caught in the most unlikely looking places. No hatch equals no rising fish. See that little willow tree growing right at water's edge? It is in the sun and the water barely covers the rocks. See that big ***brown***? You don't? You had better get some non-glare sunglasses, because I know there is a fish there. (I will not mention how I know a fish is there, but I caught one there last week!) Anyway, cast just the right amount of line to lay the fly about six feet above the spot where you expect to catch fish. No, no, no—not over the water where the fish is. Cast off to the side so you will not spook it. After several false casts you will be laying your fly down like a butterfly with sore feet. To accomplish that, imagine that the water is at eye level so the fly never leaves your sight, and it settles on the water without a splash. Now keep up with the line as it floats toward you.

With your left hand take the slack out of the line. Bang, you got a strike, but when you set the hook by lifting the rod tip, the fish didn't touch the fly, so you must do the whole routine again. Maybe this time you will get him. What did you say? You are as nervous as when you played your first jury exam for me. Oh yes, I remember your mistakes there, too. You learned from those mistakes, didn't you? Make one more cast. Good. If you see any movement in the water set the hook. Hey! You got him. Release the fish, and you'll get your certificate. Too bad about that jury exam. You just keep fishing and apply the same effort in the practice room. Who knows, you just might become a trumpet player.

And what happened to the moose? Alex cut the line, and got out of there as fast as he could.

THE OTHER SIDE OF THE STAND

*I often think of all the golf analogies applied to playing the trumpet John used. In particular, he compared the manner of breathing to that of a relaxed golf backswing and follow-through. I don't even play golf; however, that worked with me and **still** works with my students.*

Craig Hurst

John and I played golf on several occasions over several years. With golf, he demonstrated the same dedication as with his music. On one afternoon, I arrived at his home to find out that, because of an accident, John had seriously injured one of his eyes. A large bandage covered his eye and part of his face. Nevertheless, he insisted on keeping our golf date and proceeded to shoot 72 on a difficult course. Vintage John Haynie.

Bill Nugent

Mr. Haynie was a very self-deprecating man, not at all averse to telling stories showing himself in far less than the awesome light in which we all viewed him. One tale he related to us was the time when, as a guest golfer of some note, he wound up for a huge drive off the first tee, and with all the dignitaries who had so chosen to honor him watching, Mr. Haynie topped the ball!

Gary Sorensen

Mr. Haynie's comparisons of trumpet performance to golf have made a lasting impression on me. After I started playing golf, I realized that concentration and thinking makes for better ball hitting and more right notes.

Mike Walker

GOLF—
A GAME FOR TRUMPET PLAYERS

Golf is a game. It doesn't make any difference what score you shoot. Just go out to the course for exercise. Enjoy being with friends. Be thankful to be outdoors, take a deep breath, and smell the fresh-cut fairways. So you can't hit the ball as far as you once could. So what? Oh, you hit shots like a beginner? Go to the practice range and work it out.

OK, so golf is *not* a game. It is a passion, and the score I shoot does make a difference. For exercise I can ride my Airdyne bicycle, and I can enjoy being with friends everyday. Yes, I am thankful to be outdoors, and I can do that when I fish and hunt. It is a given that I can't hit the ball as far as I did at one time, and I miss the joy and thrill of a big solid hit. I hit shots now that would be an embarrassment to a beginner, and that's with regular practice on the driving range. I love the game so much that I can't quit. It was easier to stop playing the trumpet than it is to quit golf.

Golf and trumpet playing are built on fundamentals. Let's examine the parallels. The fundamentals of golf and trumpet performance require extreme concentration and keeping all aspects of the game in focus. The basics of a golf grip relate to how to hold the trumpet; the stance is posture; the take-away is like taking a breath; hitting the ball is exhaling the air when blowing the trumpet. Golf professionals refer to the point of impact; trumpet players call it the attack. The follow-through of the swing suggests playing notes full value. A golfer must have a feel for how far he can hit each club in his bag; the trumpet player must develop the feel for hitting each note in the chromatic range of his instrument. And on command, the embouchure, breath, tongue, and fingers must respond perfectly.

Tempo and rhythm are common to golf and trumpet performance, and most missed golf shots and most missed trumpet tones are in some way related. Musicians have used a metronome forever, and more and more golf professionals are now requiring their students to practice with a metronome.

The mental game of golf's good shots is the direct result of practicing and developing confidence to carry the lake, to avoid shanking the ball, to loft the ball from a bunker—better yet, avoiding the bunker in the first place! Sam Snead once said that practice puts brains in his muscles. He also said the more he practices, the luckier he gets

The parallels go on and on. You get the idea. In fact, I am leaving for the practice range right now with my metronome that once talked to me about my trumpet practice. Maybe he will come to my rescue once again. I hate the way I play golf, in spite of all the excuses I have.

I can do better.

I think I can, I think I can, I think I can.

*John posing here for fishing guide Max Eggleston, in the East River
headwaters near Crested Butte, Colorado, summer, 1980*

Taking a golf lesson, January 2006

John James Haynie, 1934

I was so small the school would not buy my uniform, so my parents bought it. It hangs in my closet to this day.

John Haynie

Our maternal grandmother Nannie helped our family immensely in further-ing John James's career. We always kidded John that he was Nannie's fa-vorite, but we knew in our hearts that she simply recognized that God had something very special in store for him, and she was merely helping the cause by giving of her resources. My husband Bill reminds me occasionally, "Your brother doesn't walk on water, he goes at least ankle deep."

Patty Haynie Wendell

A BOY AND HIS HORN

When my parents were working out of town, I always stayed with my grandparents, Nannie and Papa—Jessie and John Benedict. Papa was a janitor for the Humble Oil Company district offices, and I would follow him around and help out, mostly running errands.

One of these times that I was staying in Humbletown, we had a visitor on a Saturday afternoon. He was a friend of Papa's, but this day he wanted to see me. I followed him out to his truck and saw that he had a little puppy he wanted to give me. I had never had a dog before and had always wanted one. After I heard the requirements for owning a dog, I agreed to them all.

Before leaving, our guest said he had something else for me. I had seen this shiny object in the car seat and wondered what the thing was. He said it was a cornet. He took it out of the car, held it in his hands, and put it to his lips and blew. A beautiful sound came out. I asked him to do it again and this time he played a song. At that moment I knew I must learn to make these same beautiful sounds.

He handed the cornet to me, and I gently held the cornet the same way he had, placed it against my lips and blew. It sounded different from the sound my grandfather's friend played, but in that instant I became a cornet player. To this day I have never changed my embouchure.

I played the horn on and off all day, every day. Harsh sounds became decent sounds. I could play high notes and low notes and a few in between. (Does this ring a bell?) The only music I ever heard was church music, and it wasn't long until I could pick out some hymn tunes. Nannie saw how interested I was in blowing on the cornet and said she wanted the local band director, Mr. G. C. Collum, to hear me. Arrangements were made for me to take lessons at ten cents per lesson. In an old hymn book he would write numbers under each note to indicate which valve or valves to push down to play the note. It was not necessary at this point to give each note a name.

Back in these days there was no air conditioning, so everyone sat outside in the evenings waiting for the house to cool off a few degrees. Hoping someone would listen, I would play my cornet. I could pick out several hymns, and others would sing along with me. Mother's next door friend asked if I would play at her church in the community across the railroad tracks. "Of course he will be glad to play," said my mother. And so it happened that I played my first concert in the black church in Cisco, Texas. I remember that one of the hymns I played was *In the Sweet By and By.*

In 1934 or 1935, Mr. Collum left Cisco to become the Eastland, Texas, band director. At the same time, Robert Maddox, the band director in Ranger, Texas, became the director at Cisco. Mr. Maddox was a remarkable band director and teacher. He did not do a lot of talking; rather, he led by example. In 1936, the Cisco band received a first division rating in spite of our less-than-standard instrumentation. The band had no French horns, no oboe, and no bassoon. This was a great beginning for the Cisco band, and under the direction of Robert Maddox, it had an excellent future.

But when I was fourteen, Mr. Maddox announced his resignation as Cisco band director to become the band director in Mexia, Texas. At Mexia Mr. Maddox encountered an unusual situation for band directors. J. K. Hughes, one of the oil barons of Texas, was the self-appointed benefactor of the Mexia Black Cat Band. Mr. Maddox would have no equipment shortages and would at last have a complete band instrumentation of his choice. Each year Mr. Hughes would supply the band with whatever was needed, and each fall he would take the band to Dallas for a day at the State Fair. Mr. Hughes took special pride in having the band parade into a large bank in downtown Dallas, form a circle, play a couple of songs, and head back outside, resume parade formation, and move on to the next bank.

This was a wonderful opportunity for Mr. Maddox, but it was a bitter disappointment for me, and for the first time since I started playing, I lost interest in the cornet and was undecided about playing in the band.

Then a miracle happened.

Soon after Mr. Maddox was settled into his new job in Mexia, he asked my parents if young John James could be allowed to live with his family in Mexia. It was all decided; all I had to do was to say yes. Excited, I said yes, knowing that my dreams of being a band director would come true.

What happened to the puppy? He ran off chasing a rabbit one day and I never saw him again.

Margaret and Robert Maddox, 1944

Daddy was happy to have John James share in his music world, and we were happy to have him join our family in Mexia. Daddy teased him a lot. John James had a taste for pepper on his food, and it worried Mother and Daddy a great deal. At one meal Daddy had loosened the top on the pepper shaker, and out it came—didn't faze John James in the least. They even consulted a doctor to see if so much pepper was harmful to him and were told "not a bit." That ended their concern—for the time-being anyway!

Virginia Maddox Hankins

MY LIFE WITH ROBERT MADDOX

When I think about what my life might have been without Robert Maddox, I really cannot imagine what I would have become. I was just a little boy when he came to town as the Cisco Public Schools band director. My older sister Jessie Lee played flute in the high school band, and she came home every day talking about this wonderful, no-nonsense band director. She told the story of how, at the first rehearsal, Mr. Maddox kicked out of the band a bunch of potential trouble makers who had pulled some kind of prank. Some of these boys were the band's best players. Mr. Maddox immediately offered to reinstate them, but they first must apologize to the band for wasting its time. Some did, some did not. Jessie Lee was very impressed that this man showed compassion and, at the same time, let everyone know that the Cisco Lobo Band would be a disciplined group.

I was in grade school, so I had not met this strict man who had such a big heart. My mother set up a time for Mr. Maddox to hear me play. After hearing me, he arranged things so that I could walk from my elementary school to the high school daily to practice with the high school band. Cisco was not a big town, and we did a lot of walking in those days.

I do not remember much about those first practices, but I discovered quickly that those little black spots on the music had names. I caught on right away that the note on the first line was called "E," when before I knew it as only "first and second valves down." I went home saying to myself that there sure was a lot to learn about this music. I just knew that Jack Lauderdale was the best cornet player I had ever heard, and I was thrilled that I got to sit beside him and play the same notes. Mr. Maddox knew that Jack would teach me far more than he could do from the podium.

I was improving remarkably well, and was introduced to "Mr. Arban." Jack graduated, and my new standmate was Glenn Tableman, two years older than I. Glenn and I spent untold hours practicing together. Of course, we avoided the keys with all those sharps and flats since we had no private teacher to make us practice the things we didn't play very well. But could we fly on double and triple-tongued exercises!

I will always remember Glenn's beautiful tone. One year he played *Birth of Dawn* by Herbert L. Clarke, and I can still hear that natural vibrato. I had long ago noticed that when he played songs, his lips and jaw went up and down like saying "ya-ya-ya." I could not make the sound like Glenn did, but I found that if I rocked my right hand and arm back and forth I could make that pretty sound. Neither of us knew we had learned how to produce a vibrato.

Along the way Colonel Irons came to town, and we were introduced to lip slurs. I could do these really well right off. When Glenn discovered girls, our practice sessions were reduced. Being younger, I was still more interested in cornet solos, contest preparation, competitions, playing solos in church, and realizing that I wanted to become a band director like Robert Maddox. All this time I watched, listened, and learned from Robert Maddox the administration of bands, teaching beginners, conducting skills, and most of all, human relationships.

He served as an example of honor, integrity, courage, wisdom, generosity, determination, toughness, softness, discipline, punctuality, respect, and a belief in a greater power than our own.

Regional Contest, Lubbock, Texas, 1937

*I loved being around Mr. Maddox and would hang around him and ask
questions just so he'd talk to me. I was twelve years old. What was I asking
Mr. Maddox? I can only guess that I wanted him to hear my solo one more
time.*

John Haynie

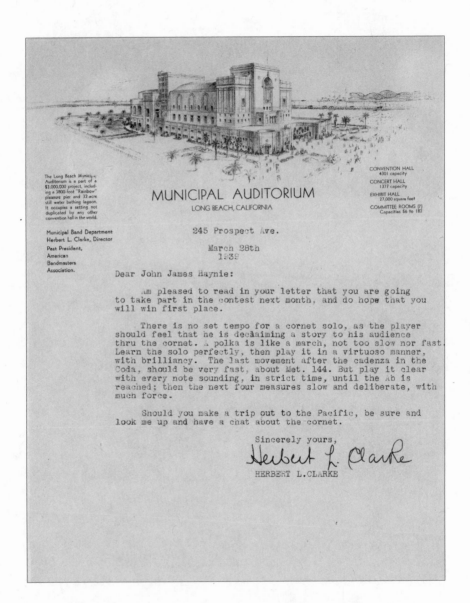

MUNICIPAL AUDITORIUM
LONG BEACH, CALIFORNIA

The Long Beach Municipal Auditorium is a part of a $3,000,000 project, including a 3800-foot "Rainbow" pleasure pier and 32-acre still water bathing lagoon. It occupies a setting not duplicated by any other convention hall in the world.

CONVENTION HALL
4301 capacity
CONCERT HALL
1377 capacity
EXHIBIT HALL
27,000 square feet
COMMITTEE ROOMS (7)
Capacities 56 to 182

Municipal Band Department
Herbert L. Clarke, Director

Past President,
American
Bandmasters
Association.

245 Prospect Ave.

March 28th
1939

Dear John James Haynie:

    Am pleased to read in your letter that you are going to take part in the contest next month, and do hope that you will win first place.

    There is no set tempo for a cornet solo, as the player should feel that he is declaiming a story to his audience thru the cornet. A polka is like a march, not too slow nor fast. Learn the solo perfectly, then play it in a virtuoso manner, with brilliancy. The last movement after the cadenza in the Coda, should be very fast, about Met. 144. But play it clear with every note sounding, in strict time, until the Ab is reached; then the next four measures slow and deliberate, with much force.

    Should you make a trip out to the Pacific, be sure and look me up and have a chat about the cornet.

Sincerely yours,

Herbert L. Clarke

HERBERT L.CLARKE

Herbert L. Clarke's "Lesson-in-a-Letter," 1939

ALL-STATE BANDS AND CONTESTS

In 1937, I attended my first All-State band clinic in Fort Worth. The guest conductor for the All-State Band in 1937 was Mark Hindsley from the University of Illinois. It was beyond my imagination to ever think he would later become my father-in-law.

In those days the All-State bands were made up of students their band directors brought to the Texas State Band Directors Convention. I sat where Mr. Maddox told me to sit, usually starting out on the 3rd parts. Conductors moved us around without challenges or formal auditions. The year the convention was in Mineral Wells, auditions were held after we got there, and it was a three-way tie: Jennings McLean, Fay Moser, and me. Would you have guessed that Jennings was a girl? She and Fay were both terrific and much better than I. Since the All-State bands were used to acquaint band directors with literature for contest consideration, it was decided that the first chair player would change according to the band's classification and the music we were playing. So, for Class A band compositions, Fay Moser was first chair cornet. For Class B compositions, I sat first chair. And for Class C band pieces, Jennings McLean sat at the top. When we changed seats, it was done with great drama.

I participated in numerous contests during my public school years. A "National Contest," in which one winner was declared, had existed for years. But when I participated, the National Contests were regional, and divisional ratings were awarded. Regionals were held in February and March; Nationals were held in April or May. One must receive a First Division rating at the Regional level to perform at the National Contest.

I do not have any memory of that first 1936 contest when I was eleven years old. The unsigned rating sheet indicates a grade of 94% and a "one" rating. I do remember that the solo Mr. Maddox picked for me was *Morning Glory Polka* by H. A. VanderCook. At a band camp the following summer, I even had a lesson with Mr. VanderCook on his solo. Judge Ralph Smith wrote on my comment sheet: "Fine player, could play more difficult number. Keep the good tone going."

Even though Mr. Smith thought I could play something harder, my "one" allowed me to advance to the National Competition. It was held in Oklahoma City in 1937. The judge? None other than Dr. William D. Revelli. (I had the opportunity to show him his rating sheet of my performance of VanderCook's *Morning Glory Polka* many years later.) Revelli was quite a personality. He rated my performance as a Division II and wrote, "The tone is sweet and solid, the delivery quite good. Avoid running out of breath at the end of the phrase. Breath control is your big job. When making a crescendo on rapid passages reduce the weight of the tongue. Your tongue is too heavy in those passages. Hold still with your lips between rests. Take more breath and be more consumptive with it. A fine beginning. Outstanding strong points: tone quality, style, phrasing, an excellent teacher. Outstanding weak points: breath control and tonguing. Memory." [Signed] Wm D. Revelli

The next year, 1938, Colonel Irons judged my National performance in Abilene, and he awarded me a Division 2+ rating. I played Llewellyn's *Premier Polka*. Again, my choice of music was not good. The Colonel wrote, "Triple tonguing is hard to perfect. Work and keep working. Get all kinds of lip slurs for daily practice, ten to twenty minutes each day. You just almost made first division. I believe with a better solo you could do it. Outstanding strong points: technique." [Signed] Earl D. Irons.

You'd better believe that the next year, when I was an 8th grader, I took no chances with my music selection. I chose *Bride of the Waves* by Herbert L. Clarke, and I even wrote to Mr. Clarke asking if there were any special things to watch out for. Maybe that was an unusual letter for an 8th grader to write to someone so famous. I'll never know. But Mr. Clarke answered my letter: "There is no set tempo for a cornet solo, as the player should feel that he is declaiming a story to his audience through the cornet. A polka is like a march; not too slow or fast. Learn the solo perfectly, then play it in a virtuoso manner, with brilliancy."

Colonel Irons was my judge again at this National Contest, and this time he awarded me a First Division. He listed tone and tonguing as outstanding strong points. He specifically noted the absence of any "outstanding bad points" by writing the word "Missing" in that section.

In 1940, the Nationals were in Waco. I played Colonel Irons's *Emerald Isle*. My score sheet was positive but I still couldn't shake the criticism about my style. Judge R. B. Watson wrote, "Your cadenza was a little hurried in places. The notes do not all come through. Someone has taught you to play the <u>an-dante</u> frame with less style. The <u>polka</u> strain is done a bit fast to give it the musical value it is entitled to. The trio strain seems a bit hurried. Congratulations on the splendid recovery after missing your high 'F'." [Signed] R. B. Watson. Missing that high F was of more concern to me than playing andante with less style!

By my junior year in high school, I seemed to have hit my stride. My performance of Clarke's *Shores of the Mighty Pacific* earned me a Division I and these comments from judge Winston Lynes: "A very artistic performance. A very brilliant start and very tasteful playing. Your technique is very, very good."

In many ways, the best was yet to come. Mr. Maddox, my band director, bought a recording of Leonard B. Smith playing *Spanish Caprice* and *My Heaven of Love*. I wore the record out. The solo was not on the Texas Contest List, but Mr. Maddox got special permission for me to play it. Mr. Maddox did everything in his power (and sometimes out of his power!) to challenge me to the highest level I could achieve. It was a testament to his encouragement that of my final performance, Mr. Weldon Covington wrote only "Very fine", and the rating 1+. I felt like I'd proven that Mr. Maddox's faith in me was justified, because none of this ever would have happened if it hadn't been for him.

Contests

Year	Location	Judge	Solo	Score
1936 Prelims	Abilene	(unknown)	*Morning Glory Polka*	I
1937 Regional	Lubbock	Ralph Smith	*Morning Glory Polka*	I
		Ralph Smith	*My Buddy* (duet)	I
1937 National	Okla City	Wm. D. Revelli	*Morning Glory Polka*	II
1938 Regional	Abilene	(unknown)	*Premier Polka*	I
		D. O. Wiley	*When You and I Were Young* (sextet)	I
1938 National	Abilene	Earl D. Irons	*Premier Polka*	II+
		(unknown)	*When You and I Were Young* (sextet)	I
1939 Regional	Abilene	Dean Shank	*Bride of the Waves*	I+
1939 National	Abilene	Earl D. Irons	*Bride of the Waves*	I
1940 Regional	Waco	(unknown)	*Emerald Isle*	I
		C. R. Hackney	*Sails on a Silvery Sea* (trio)	I
1940 National	Waco	R. B. Watson	*Emerald Isle*	I
		Lewis Moffatt	*Sails on a Silvery Sea* (trio)	II+
1941 Regional	Waco	(unknown)	*Shores of the Mighty Pacific*	I
		(unknown)	*Crusaders* (student conductor)	I+
1941 National	Waco	W. E. Lynes	*Shores of the Mighty Pacific*	I
1942 Regional	Marlin	Weldon Covington (both)	*Spanish Caprice*	I+
			Annie Laurie a la Moderne	I
1942		No National Contest held		

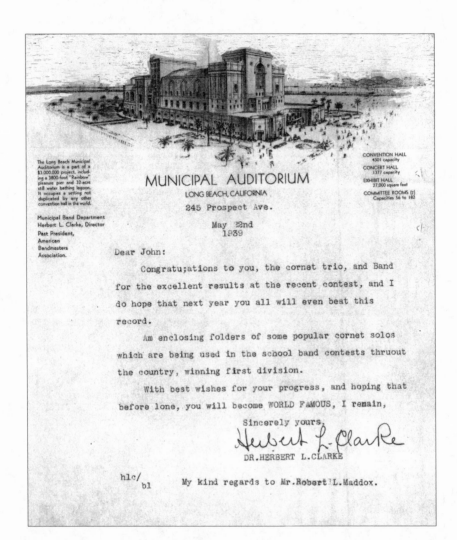

The Long Beach Municipal Auditorium is a part of a $3,000,000 project, including a 3800-foot "Rainbow" pleasure pier and 32-acre still water bathing lagoon. It occupies a setting not duplicated by any other convention hall in the world.

Municipal Band Department
Herbert L. Clarke, Director
Past President,
American
Bandmasters
Association.

CONVENTION HALL
4301 capacity
CONCERT HALL
1377 capacity
EXHIBIT HALL
27,000 square feet
COMMITTEE ROOMS (7)
Capacities 56 to 182

MUNICIPAL AUDITORIUM
LONG BEACH, CALIFORNIA
245 Prospect Ave.

May 22nd
1939

Dear John:

Congratu;ations to you, the cornet trio, and Band for the excellent results at the recent contest, and I do hope that next year you all will even beat this record.

Am enclosing folders of some popular cornet solos which are being used in the school band contests thruout the country, winning first division.

With best wishes for your progress, and hoping that before lone, you will become WORLD FAMOUS, I remain,

Sincerely yours,

Herbert L. Clarke

DR.HERBERT L.CLARKE

hlc/
    bl   My kind regards to Mr.Robert L.Maddox.

*I wrote to Mr. Clarke a second time to give him the results of the National Contest and to thank him for his help. His "lesson in a letter" helped me earn my first division rating. The more important lesson I learned had nothing to do with my rating or winning another medal. It was that if someday I became world famous as he predicted, I should never fail to help someone who might take the time to write **me** a letter asking for advice.*

John Haynie

John Haynie and Colonel Earl D. Irons, 1939

In terms of both solo literature and teaching materials, options were quite limited during the first half of the twentieth century. Clarke's **Technical Studies**, *the Arban* **Celebrated Method**, *and his own* **27 Groups of Exercises** *were the three books most often recommended by Colonel Irons. The Arban book was expensive, and some students were reluctant to make the purchase. The Colonel saved one of his most famous lines for them. "A cornet player without an Arban's is like a preacher without a Bible!"*

Gary Barrow

John and I talked about trumpet players and trumpet teachers one day. I asked him, "Is Colonel Irons considered the old school now?" He replied, "I try not to describe anyone as being of the 'old school.' If we live long enough, we will both be of the 'old school.'" Very true!

Charles Millender

COLONEL EARL D. IRONS—
MY CHILDHOOD HERO

I was in grammar school when I first heard Colonel Irons play lip slurs. His Arlington State Concert Band was on tour and played in Cisco. He had his King cornet with him, and of course he played lip slurs from his book, *27 Groups of Exercises*. I'd never heard anything like that, and I could hardly wait to get home from the concert to get my cornet out to see if I could play those wonderful sounds—so many notes on any fingering combination. You know what? I could do it. I could make those sounds, having no idea how the lips, tongue arch, and air functioned. From then on, I became a lip slur fanatic and sought opportunities that required lip slurs. If the music did not contain lip slurs, I would put them in anyway!

I never had regular lessons with the Colonel. The closest I ever came to lessons was when I went to the Texas Tech summer band camps in 1938 and 1939 as a high school student. The camps were two weeks of intense music-making and fun, and the Colonel would conduct the band and teach the cornet classes. He would often single me out to demonstrate how he wanted his lip slurs to be played. On other occasions he would hear me play at clinics like the Texas Music Educators Association meetings, when he would again have me play lip slurs and high notes. As I recall, I had no idea what those high notes were. He also judged me at the regional-level National Solo Contest twice, giving me a Second Division rating in 1938 for my performance of *Premier Polka* by Llewellyn and a First Division rating in 1939 for Clarke's *Bride of the Waves*. Just prior to the outbreak of World War II, the Colonel made arrangements to take a couple of other Texas boys and me to Long Beach, California, to take lessons with Herbert L. Clarke the summer following my high school graduation. I've always regretted that it never happened—by then we were at war, and all my friends were enlisting or waiting for their draft notice.

During my first year of teaching at North Texas, Colonel Irons retired, and he asked me to play one of his solos with the Arlington State Band on the concert that honored his retirement. Having no car, I took the bus to Arlington, played *Song of the Pines* on the concert, and got back on the highway, still wearing my white dinner jacket, carrying my suitcase in one hand and my cornet case in the other, planning to hitchhike to Dallas. As luck would have it, a doctor from Dallas, who had attended the concert, picked me up and took me to the train station. I then caught a train to Austin, where I rehearsed the Haydn *Trumpet Concerto* with the Austin High School Orchestra the next day.

I was not offered any pay for playing at the Colonel's retirement concert, and wouldn't have taken it if it'd been offered, but the Colonel wanted to do something for me to show his appreciation. A few weeks after the concert, I received a call from Heinrich Roth, president of the Reynolds Band Instrument Co., telling me that Colonel Irons had called him to tell him about me, and that I was the new trumpet teacher at North Texas. The Colonel had suggested that Roth offer me a set of Reynolds horns, which I accepted. Soon after I received the horns, it didn't take long to realize that I liked them very much. This was 1952, and my father-in-law Mark Hindsley, who was the Director of Bands at the University of Illinois, had recently developed a spring-operated trigger that moved the trumpet tuning slide either way, which he called the **T**une **A**s **Y**ou **P**lay mechanism. Mr. Roth also agreed to add this device to my horns, providing I could borrow a set of horns from the University of Illinois Band for his designer to copy. Not only did he offer to add them to my horns, he would put them on any of my students' horns. For all these years, including my military duty, I'd used the King cornet my grandmother bought me back when I was in high school. Except for special occasions when the cornet was the more appropriate instrument to play, I now owned and played my first real trumpet. Not only that, but the following year I added one of their first C trumpets to my arsenal of horns. It was ***excellent***—the whole horn was scaled down, which made it a true C trumpet, not like the others at the time that were just B-flat trumpets with a set of shorter C slides.

While I did not take any lessons with Colonel Irons, he was my idol, and I'll always believe he considered me as one of his boys. In his last years after he retired to his beloved golf course at the Arlington Country Club (he designed the first hole), he would take me around the course coaching me in how to hit the ball. We would sprinkle ant poison around and move on to the next hole. Come to think of it, he told me a lot more about hitting the golf ball than he did about how to play the trumpet.

Corporal T/5 John Haynie, 1944

While still in Germany after WWII, I decided I would no longer wear my silver ID bracelet you see here. I found a kindly old silversmith who maintained his skills and trade during the war in a little town that seemed not to know or care about the war. He spoke no English but understood perfectly what I wanted. He melted down the bracelet and made a medallion in the shape of "LVH" for my mother, Lelia Virginia Haynie.

John Haynie

WAR AND DUTY

December 7, 1941, was just another Sunday and the Maddox family and I had gone to church. It was only later that day that we all heard of the attack on Pearl Harbor. War was not something I had ever expected to be part of my life, and even if it was, I thought it would all be over in a couple of weeks. I couldn't imagine how a kid just out of high school would be much of a soldier. If they wanted me, they would let me know. I was a high school senior, and I could hardly wait to play my solo, *Spanish Caprice*, at the solo contest. It had taken nearly three years to learn, and it was beginning to sound pretty good.

I was thinking and talking about going to college. No member of my family had ever gone to college, so I would be the first. The Texas Tech catalogue listed the costs, and I knew there was no way I could earn that much money. I had been away from my family, living with Mr. and Mrs. Maddox and their family for three years, but I'd never had a job. Mr. Maddox would give me a dollar a week, and my parents and Nannie would send a few dollars once in a while whenever they could, which was not very often.

I graduated from high school without much fanfare. Mother, Nannie, and sister Patty came down for the event, and I went back to Cisco with them. After the collapse of my dad's decorating business, he went from town to town building army facilities. Dad took me with him that first summer to Amarillo. He was a fine carpenter, and I became a carpenter's helper. I made twenty-five cents an hour for an eight-hour day, time-and-a-half for working an extra two hours, and double time when working for twelve hours a day. I was allowed to keep all I made, and my parents gave me my meals and lodging. Many nights when I got home, I was so tired I didn't take my clothes off—I just fell into bed. Rarely did I get as tired when I was in the Army Infantry. It was a dull and boring summer and there was no time or place to practice my horn.

It was the end of the summer of '42, and my job was winding down. I had saved enough money to pay my fees at Texas Tech, so after I put in my last week at work in Amarillo, I took the bus to Lubbock, about one hundred miles away. I met some people in the Tech band who would become life-long friends. There were not many of us left. The band had been a fine organization, but it had been devastated by the war-time draft. At each rehearsal there would be a few more empty chairs; some guys never returned to claim their place.

Mert Starnes, a Lubbock boy, invited me to move out of the dormitory to his house to avoid the hazing, which was pretty tough. We freshmen living in the dorm got worked over by the upperclassmen daily. Mert and I had a great time. Mert's Uncle Rhea was his legal guardian, and Mert was the first friend I ever had who owned a car. I am still impressed that his uncle sent him off to California to take lessons with the famous Herbert L. Clarke. He was a little young to get much out of it. I never heard Mert practice at all—not once!

The first semester ended in early December, and I was off to a good start with my classes. My eighteenth birthday rolled around on December 14th, and I got my notice that I was scheduled to be inducted within thirty days, so I packed up and went to my family home in Cisco. I was lucky to have more than thirty days; I was called into service on May 23, 1943. I reported to Camp Wolters, just out of Mineral Wells, Texas, and I was there for several weeks before being sent out by myself to Washington, DC. My assignment was to the 76th Infantry Division Band stationed at Fort Meade, Maryland.

I was able to bypass basic training because I was sent in as a replacement for direct overseas duty. I was told that I would go to Fort A. P. Hill, Virginia, for war-games training and then on to the Pacific combat zone. After completing this training camp, I was sent home for a fifteen-day leave. I was glad to get home to say goodbye to my family.

Once back at A. P. Hill, it was announced that only front-line troops from the 76th Division were to be sent to the Pacific theater. Those in the rear echelons would be sent to Camp McCoy, Wisconsin, to form a new division that would test winter equipment.

While at Camp McCoy, the Army Special Services created a show band to tour Wisconsin to help sell war bonds. I was assigned to this unit as trumpet soloist in the summer of 1944; we played for standing-room-only crowds for a month. Once, in Milwaukee, we played a five-night stand for 20,000 people. What an experience *that* was. A special arrangement was made from the piano accompaniment of *Spanish Caprice*, and it was a great hit with the appreciative audiences across the state.

After the bond tour we returned to Camp McCoy, and again the function of the 76th Division had been changed. We now had been activated as a battlefield division to enter the Battle of the Bulge. We would go in to replace a division that had been wiped out by the German counterattack. After we crossed the Atlantic and arrived in Germany, we moved rapidly. The 76th Division was assigned to Patton's 3rd Army, and my unit was assigned temporary duty as Military Police. We should have had three trucks to move our gear, but only one was available. The truck was piled so high with barracks bags that it couldn't get under the telephone lines. Someone came up with the bright idea for a couple of GIs to ride on top of all the duffle bags and, with forked sticks, to lift the telephone wires while the truck passed under. You guessed it—it was my idea, so I was given the opportunity to defeat the enemy by clearing telephone lines out of the way. This had gone well all day, but I was about to have a "close encounter of the worst kind." I made the mistake of not facing forward in order to dodge the tree limbs. Sure enough, when I did face forward, a tree limb struck me right across my mouth, sweeping me from atop the truck. I awoke in an army field hospital.

If you're squeamish, read no further. My teeth were hanging loose, and the attending dentist hadn't had a dental patient in weeks. He told me that he intended to remove all my front teeth. For a trumpet player this was a fatal blow, but it seems that band directors were always rescuing me. As soon as the dentist left, CWO John Sandidge, my band director, came after me and took me out of there. He not only saved my teeth, but also probably saved my life, as well. The usual duty assigned the injured after recovering was a transfer to a rifle company. Instead, I was returned to the band, and after my mouth healed I began to learn how to play again. For many years my front teeth were loose; in time there proved to be no permanent damage.

Less than three months later, on November 13, 1945, I was honorably discharged. I returned to Cisco, Texas, and my immediate plans were to return to Texas Tech.

I survived the war, and I did my duty to serve my country. I proudly display my campaign medals of Good Conduct in Battle, the World War II Victory Medal, the American Theater medal, and the most prized of all—the European Theater Medal with three battle stars. Accompanying it is a citation that reads "Certificate of Merit for Conspicuously Meritorious and Outstanding Performance of Military Duty against an Armed Enemy of the United States from February 15 to May 8, 1945, in Luxemburg and Germany."

Sergeant T/4 John Haynie, 1945

*My skill at hunting helped put food on our table when I was a boy, so a buddy and I decided to supplement our company's Easter rations with a chicken, a duck, a goose, anything. We had a bit of success, but getting our prizes back to camp turned out to be somewhat of an experience. Bob Snook, the Division Chaplain's assistant, had a jeep. So he and I went out to find where we'd left our two geese. We were OK until Bob decided to take a shortcut back to our quarters. We drove through a little town, all boarded up, with not a person around. A mile or so out of the village, we met a company of GIs coming our way. The captain stopped us and wanted to know where we got the jeep, what were a chaplain's assistant and an MP doing in that location, and why we had two dead geese in the back. We told our story, and we knew we were dismissed, fortunately, when the Captain said, "You were lucky soldiers, because we haven't secured that town yet. Now! Forward, **harch**." After all this, the geese were too tough to eat!*

John Haynie

Grace and Haskell Sexton, 1950

I had the pleasure of studying with Haskell Sexton for two years at the University of Illinois. He was a warm, supportive teacher and a really beautiful player. He was perhaps the best kind of teacher in that one learned from him both by what he did as well as by what he said. He was a kind and gentle man, generous in spirit and with a ready sense of humor. He had a deep understanding of human nature, and he always seemed to know the right response for every situation. I remember only too well my very first lesson with him. I was so nervous I could hardly play. After a couple of minutes of listening to me attempt to play through a bad case of the shakes, he put his hand on my shoulder and said, "You will be fine. Why don't you put the trumpet in the case, and let's go have a beer." It worked wonderfully. He taught me much about how to play the trumpet, more than a little about good beer, and most importantly, that we teach people, not the trumpet.

Keith Johnson

HASKELL SEXTON—
MY TEACHER

It was during the fall semester of 1947 that I first met Haskell Sexton. He insisted that everyone call him by his first name, which seemed unusual to me, steeped as I was in the tradition of Mr., Mrs., Yes Sir, and No Ma'am. What was OK with Haskell was OK with me. I quickly discovered that informality was a clue to knowing the real Haskell Sexton. I was treated as an equal, and in reality we were not too far apart in age. He respected my talents and seemed very pleased that I had come to Illinois and would be his student. At the time, our private lessons were for a mere thirty minutes per week, but Haskell gave me far more time than that. Our lessons always ran overtime. He had me come in for extra help, and often I would go to his home. Haskell's wife Grace would play my accompaniments.

I cannot recall a single conversation with Haskell in which he brought up a pedagogical concept. One time I did mention to Haskell that both he and Leroy Kirsch (the best player on campus in 1947) had different embouchures from mine. I cannot remember his exact words, but they meant "So what?" I didn't ask again, but I continued to study them, and I determined that they played "pucker system" and I played "smile system." I had never heard of either one. So I watched Leroy and Haskell and found that in a short time my embouchure looked more like theirs. It is interesting to note that both Leroy and Haskell were students of Joseph Gustat of the St. Louis Symphony Orchestra. Leroy was a power player, and with the same type of embouchure. Haskell was all finesse, with a delicate, clean, and beautiful tone. I was somewhere in the middle, without either Leroy's big, powerful sound or Haskell's purity. On the other hand, I had more flexibility and range. We were quite a team. Haskell sat between Leroy and me for three years in the University of Illinois Concert Band. The little things Haskell would say made so much sense as he continually coached us in proper ensemble perform- ance, routine, and habits. When Haskell was a student, he had played for our director, A. A. Harding. Haskell always knew what Mr. Harding wanted to hear. Rarely did we have to suffer the Harding stare. When anyone messed up, all Mr. Harding had to do was look over his spectacles and say, "John, reading?" When Mark Hindsley replaced A. A. Harding, Hindsley added a new dimension, which was his requiring the band to play with greater precision of attack, more careful intonation, and with more attention to detail of every aspect of the music and com- posers' intentions. In a nutshell, the Harding bands played with more abandon, which was exciting and lots of fun. The Hindsley bands played the music more accurately and better in tune, which provided an even greater sense of accomplishment.

My lessons with Haskell were always a musical experience since I played mostly solo literature and with piano. Sometimes when an accompanist was not available we would play from the Charlier book. He would play so elegantly that I could hear things that were just not there when I played the same thing. I would like to think that I have had some of that same influence on my students.

Haskell introduced me to the best of trumpet literature with special emphasis on the French trumpet conservatory contest pieces. What a sharp contrast to the limited repertoire of virtu- oso pieces I knew. As mentioned before, I had little knowledge of anything other than the virtuoso cornet solos I had played as a teen. I could play from memory a large number of the tradi- tional cornet solos, but with little regard to the musical possibili- ties even in this kind of solo repertoire. Haskell did not want me to give up what I could do; he simply wanted me to do more in making music with those pieces.

In my opinion, the major difference between the French music and the cornet solos I knew was the fact that the cornet solos were all written to be played with band accompaniment. The French solos were all conceived as pieces for trumpet and piano. The cornet solos were an exhibition of physical feats much like a vaudeville act, while the French pieces demanded a more subtle technique. A French solo played without the piano part makes no sense at all, but a cornet solo can stand alone without any accompaniment.

Haskell Sexton also helped me discover the latest and best of the American compositions for trumpet. Just after World War II, the National Association of Schools of Music commissioned solo works for all wind instruments that included both sonatas and concertos by leading American composers. Ernest Williams wrote six *Concerti* for trumpet, the second being my favorite, which were still of the cornet-type but yet in a more extended concerto form. Certainly this was a step forward and a link with what was to come.

In one of my early lessons with Haskell, he showed me a newly published trumpet sonata by Paul Hindemith. I played right through it without much difficulty and when finished I looked at Haskell, he looked at me and asked what I thought of it. I said it was the worst piece I'd ever played. He laughed. I laughed, too. Then he said, "You have a right to whatever honest opinion you may have, but I want to know **why** you think it is such a bad piece of music?" Without hesitation I told him that there was no opening cadenza featuring lip slurs, no double or triple tonguing to speak of, no singable theme, and no high F at the end. Haskell thoughtfully mused in his kind way, "John, that says more about you than it does about Hindemith and his music."

In time, and well before I came to North Texas as a teacher, I developed a real and sincere appreciation for all those things that Haskell taught me about style, finesse, use of dynamics, nuance, and doing it all with a mastery of playing the notes. As a footnote, the Hindemith *Sonate* is one of my top five works ever written for trumpet. This does not mean one should never again play a Clarke-type solo. It does mean that, even when playing a virtuoso cornet solo, one should play it with the same musical intensity as any other piece of music.

Haskell never discussed or made assignments in orchestral excerpts for me even though I played principal trumpet in the orchestra for three years. He did require some transposition. He knew my ambition was not to play in an orchestra as a career; in fact, my ambition did not hold even the thought of ever teaching in a college. I played the trumpet because I always played the trumpet. It was a big part of my life. Haskell treated and taught me accordingly.

During my first year at North Texas I kept a little notebook on my desk in which I wrote down every student problem I encountered. Knowing that Marilyn and I would be going to Urbana sooner or later, I wanted to discuss these problems with Haskell. Sure enough the following year we spent an evening with Haskell and Grace, and after dinner I got out my little notebook of questions and handed him the notebook. He thumbed through it and finally said, "John, you will figure all that out. Let's play ping-pong." He was correct; I did. I discovered that Haskell was teaching me a very important lesson. I had an unusual talent and did not have the same problems as other students. He had the answers for those who had the problems, but he wanted me to take the initiative to work out my own pedagogical concepts.

Even though I studied only three years with Haskell, he brought out in me a passion for artistic performance that became evident in the performance of my students. Make no mistake about it. Without Haskell I would have had no foundation for my teaching philosophy. His background and excellence have become a part of my heritage, but his finest quality had nothing to do with the trumpet. That human quality of caring for me, guiding me, and having high expectations for me was a lot more important than learning solo literature. Haskell was a great teacher and just what I needed at that time in my life.

Leroy Kirsch and Haskell Sexton, 1950

Haskell Sexton was a wonderful teacher, a true gentleman, and extremely gracious. He treated me as a family member. I spent many evenings at his home, listening to cornet solos, discussing music and musicians, and drinking coffee prepared by his wife Grace. Once, John was playing for the "Ice Show," for pay(!), and they needed another trumpet player. John asked me to play. I had made a commitment to play a "gratis" job. Along came Haskell, who said, "You take the paying job, and I'll play the free one for you." We students were always on a tight budget, and Haskell was always concerned for our welfare. A stickler for detail, Haskell always said,

> *"Be sure all attacks are clean and precise."*
> *"Don't be satisfied with sloppy playing."*
> *"Listen for clean, clear tone."*

His lessons were tailor-made for the needs of each student. These were the things that kept me working in the right direction.

Leroy Kirsch

LEROY KIRSCH—MY ILLINOIS STANDMATE

Leroy Kirsch was a celebrity in the School of Music and Band at the University of Illinois when I arrived in the fall of 1947. He was the best of the best, and he was my standmate in the band and orchestra. We were co-principals in the band, and I was principal and he was second in the orchestra. Our teamwork did not go unnoticed. In our last band rehearsal together, Mark Hindsley said to us, "In the spirit of cooperation you two have demonstrated I hereby declare you 'Cornetists Emeritus.'"

Leroy was a powerful player, and it was good for me to have the experience of having to play up to someone else's volume. My *"forte"* was technique and range, so we were fine complements of each other. In almost every rehearsal and concert, Haskell Sexton sat between us, coaching us all the way. Leroy and I sat side-by-side in the orchestra, and we had the opportunity to play under Igor Stravinsky, Georges Enesco, and Aaron Copland.

I can't remember everything we played under Stravinsky's direction, but I have a wonderful memory of performing his *Pergolesi Suite*. It has a great C trumpet part with lots of double tonguing and high C's. I was playing my King cornet, the only horn I had. I played well but never short and crisp enough to satisfy Stravinsky. He expected to hear the French C trumpet sound and concept. The *staccato* he expected was a great challenge for me, and I later taught it as a style.

Georges Enesco was quite frail, but he had an enormous energy. One of those unexpected life-lessons happened when he gave me a lecture on entrances, responsibility, and attention. He was conducting Beethoven's *Symphony No. 6*, which has many long rests. I studied for another class during these rests. I could count on Leroy to help me out, and he would nudge me right before my entrance on a sustained concert A. I would pick up my horn, play the note, and then return to the books. Enesco was dissatisfied with the way I played that one sustained note. Very kindly, he said something like this: "Young man, the one note you are to play is quite essential in the structure of this movement. While you may not think it is of any importance, rest assured it is heard and felt by the entire orchestra and the audience. Please look at me, and I will bring you in as I have tried to do. Thank you. Let us commence again." What an humbling experience *that* was. Since then, I have tried to make every note count, not only in my own playing, but also in that of my students. To continue the story, from then on I was ready, on the edge of my chair, eyes on the Maestro. He looked at me, and like he was playing for me, he drew my sound into the equation of notes and harmony. He smiled as I entered in perfect rhythm. From then on, I loved playing that one note. And to think all my life I had been under the impression that to be great it took an electrifying technique to have a satisfying musical experience.

Aaron Copland was very demanding and not the delicate, soft-spoken person as was Enesco. We played *Rodeo*, and I never did please him with the big trumpet solo. I could never play it loud enough and rough enough for his expectation. Again, the importance of having the right horn for the job became my learning experience for the Copland concerts.

During my first year at North Texas, conductor George Morey asked me to gather the troops for a performance of *Fanfare for the Common Man*. By now I had a trumpet that I think would have pleased Copland. Believe me, the building shook as we gave it our all. I was asking in my heart, "Mr. Copland, is that what you wanted?" His answer was probably, "Very well done, *but not loud enough*."

If Leroy had been there, we might have had a chance!

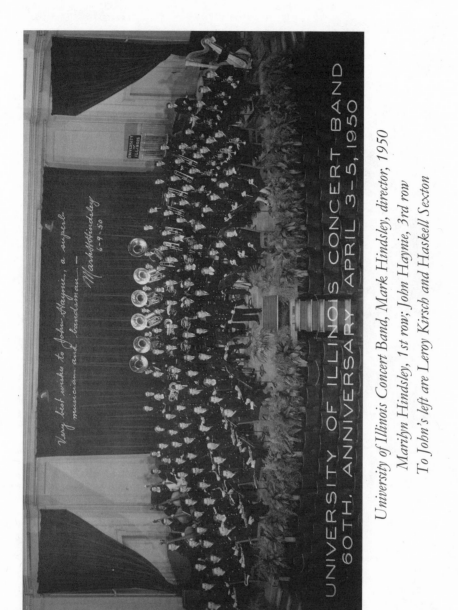

Very best wishes to John Haynie, a superb
musician and bandsman —

Mark H. Hindsley
6-9-50

UNIVERSITY OF ILLINOIS CONCERT BAND
60TH. ANNIVERSARY APRIL 3–5, 1950

University of Illinois Concert Band, Mark Hindsley, director, 1950
Marilyn Hindsley, 1st row; John Haynie, 3rd row
To John's left are Leroy Kirsch and Haskell Sexton

PROGRAM

Brandenburg Concerto No. 2 in F Major for Trumpet,
Flute, Oboe, Solo Violin, Strings, and Continuo   *J. S. Bach*

    Allegro

    Andante

    Allegro assai

  Trumpet: John Haynie

  Flute: Alexander Lesueur

  Oboe: Donna Miller

  Violin: Larry Bishop

Scheherazade Suite   *N. Rimsky-Korsakov*

    Allegro non troppo

    Andantino; Tempo giusto

    Andantino quasi Allegretto

  Violin Solo: Louann Hardy

Tales From the Vienna Woods   *Johann Strauss*

It looks like an ordinary program, but it became my contract for life.
August 8, 1950

A SIX-WEEK AUDITION

During the spring semester while I completed my master's degree, I began searching for a band directing job in some of the nearby communities in Illinois. Also, I kept in touch with my former high school band director, Robert L. Maddox, who had developed the Odessa Public School Music Program into a fitting parallel to its athletic stature. I interviewed during the summer of 1949, between undergraduate graduation and beginning my master's degree, which Uncle Sam would still pay for. There had been no guarantee that I would be offered a job.

My ego suffered a jolt at one of my interviews in a community which shall remain nameless. The superintendent of this little town in Illinois conducted the interview, and I thought I had made an impressive appearance and just might have accepted the position had it been offered. Confident as I was, the Superintendent congratulated me on my musical and academic achievements. Then he added, "I seldom hire 'A' students and performers of your ability. We are just a small school in this farming community." I was stunned to be told that my efforts to be the best I could be as a performer, to have graduated with Highest Honors, and achieve straight A's in graduate school would not qualify me for a job as a small town band director in this particular school system. With this revelation, I asked the Superintendent if the students were graded on their scholastic efforts, and he assured me that they were. I asked one final question. "Do you encourage everyone to make C's?" No answer.

So much for my search for a job near the University of Illinois. Besides, I knew I must return to Texas. My good friend from Texas Tech days, Charles Senning, wrote that he was leaving a band job in Ozona, Texas, and that he had recommended me to replace him. I filed an application, but several months went by, and I had no response.

Time was moving along and still no job, but what I did not know was that things were happening in Denton, Texas. Dean Walter Hodgson had approval to hire a complete faculty of wind-instrument teachers. Lee Gibson, woodwinds; George Morey, flute and orchestra conductor; and Leon Brown, lower brass, already had been hired and were on the job at North Texas. Dr. Hodgson called Haskell Sexton and offered him the position of Professor of Trumpet. Haskell did not wish to leave Illinois to teach at this small, unheard-of School of Music, but he told Dr. Hodgson, "I have a Texas boy you might want to look at," and I was sent an application form. I completed and returned the application reluctantly because my goal was to be a band director—still.

Weeks went by until on the very same day I received two contracts, one from Ozona, Texas, for the following 1950–1951 academic year with a salary of $4500.00. The other contract was to teach all brass for a six-week summer term as a "Temporary Instructor of Music." The contract stipulated $3200.00 for the academic year 1950–1951. This simply meant that I would have a six-week audition with no strings attached for North Texas or me at the end of the term.

At last I would have a job, but I needed help in making a decision as both were interesting offers, but only one seemed career-oriented. Haskell obviously liked his job of teaching trumpet, so I thought he might advise me as what to do. In typical Haskell Sexton style, he wouldn't tell me what to do, but he had recommended me and that fact alone gave me much encouragement. Next, I took both contracts to Mark Hindsley for his evaluation. Much to my surprise he advised me to take the North Texas job to teach brass. In his wisdom he was prophetic in saying a major change was about to explode in the makeup of college teaching staffs. He told me I would be on the ground floor and would have the opportunity to shape not only the trumpet program at North Texas, but also shape the administration of, the literature for, and build the foundation for the development of pedagogical musical information unknown at that time. In other words, there were no rules that would limit making my program the best it could be. I took his advice and moved to Denton.

When I arrived to begin my duties, Dean Walter Hodgson was out of town; however, he left several messages with this secretary and Manuel Meyer, who was acting property master. I was assigned a teaching studio, introduced to the faculty, toured the campus, and I settled in to teach. I got a quick lesson in university paperwork because my first order of business was to read through the stack of memos sitting where my solos should have been. One memo in particular made all the others of little concern. It was a memo from the Dean, and it went something like this. "Dear Mr. Haynie: On August 8th I will be conducting the college orchestra in a performance of the Brandenburg Concerto No. 2, which will feature you on the solo trumpet part. I understand that the school has a Trumpet in F, though how it became a part of our inventory is somewhat of a mystery. Please check this instrument out because rehearsals will begin when I return. Yours truly, Walter Hodgson, Dean."

Before I could even get used to the idea I would be performing the *Brandenburg*, I had a call from the Director of Bands, Maurice McAdow. Right off the bat, Mr. McAdow asked if I would like to play a solo with the band for the outdoor concert at the Union building. When? Thursday evening. Of course, I'd be happy to. Then he invited me to sit in and play regularly with the band, and this continued for the next nine years.

I had a band accompaniment to Tommy Dorsey's beautiful song, *Dawes Melody*. The tessitura was high and ended on a high F. The crowd was gracious, Mr. McAdow was delighted, and the brass students were pleased with their new teacher.

Now on to the *Brandenburg*. I checked the inventory, and sure enough, there was a Bach F trumpet—with no mouthpiece. This F trumpet, however, had a cornet-sized mouthpiece shank. I had my own King M5 mouthpiece, but it didn't work well on this little horn. I got in touch with Vincent Bach, and he sent me a 10½CW. This was a better match, but I didn't like the sound. I had a hunch. I noted that his mouthpiece catalogue stopped with a number 20 diameter rim, so I had him send me a 20C cornet mouthpiece. Ahoy there, trumpet world! After a few days practicing on that mouthpiece, I could play so high a dog might not hear it. I had found my Bach "F trumpet" mouthpiece. Since I was playing cornet in band everyday, I used the 20C all the time, increasing my accuracy with each rehearsal.

I had never practiced the *Brandenburg* in any lesson with Haskell. You must remember that my concentration was solo literature, but I had heard the piece on a 78 rpm record in a music history class. I liked it so much that I used it as a model for a concerto assignment in music theory.

I discovered that you either have the basic ability to play the *Brandenburg* or you don't. Thank goodness, I had it. The rehearsals were good, and the concert went well. So well, in fact, that Dean Hodgson called the following morning and invited me to accompany him to the President's office to remove the word "Temporary" from my contract. Little did I know that at that meeting, they simply could have marked it out and written in the word "Permanent."

I could turn my attention to my personal life now, with plans for a visitor at the end of my six-week audition. Her name was Marilyn Hindsley, and I had a ring in my pocket I hoped she would accept.

ORCHESTRA PERSONNEL

FIRST VIOLIN
Louann Hardy
　Concertmaster
Chris Xeros
Larry Bishop
Robert Cretsinger
*Joseph Kirshbaum
Rosemary Bruce

SECOND VIOLIN
Jerome Guilbeau
　Principal
Nina Reed
Winifred Gunn
Paul Kelly
Bob Payne
Mathilde Gardner
Charlene Rosenthal

VIOLA
*Olga Eitner
　Principal
*Thomas Harllee
Ruth Gibson
Colin Fisher

CELLO
*Alan Richardson
　Principal
Marjorie Bounds
Mary Jane Sullivan

BASS VIOL
Bob McLain
　Principal
George Minter
Ann Sealy
George Dawson

FLUTE
Alex Lesueur
Billy Perry

PICCOLO
Jervis Underwood

OBOE
Donna Miller
Gladys Crisler

ENGLISH HORN
Janet Smith

CLARINET
*Lee Gibson
Charles Titsworth
N. A. Lee

BASSOON
Ray Bostick
Gilbert Johnson

HORN
Allen Myers
Richard Moore
Ben Branch
Ivan Goodwin

TRUMPET
John Haynie
Doug Wiehe
Euel Box

TROMBONE
*Leon Brown
Paul Elliott
James Knighten

TUBA
James Bledsoe

TYMPANI
Jack Rumbley

PERCUSSION
Don Childress
Glenn Cunningham
Elaine Taylor

HARP
Anita Harvey

**ZITHER
Glenn Cunningham

HARPSICHORD
Clifford Shipp

MANAGER and LIBRARIAN
Jervis Unde____

*Faculty Members
**Zither through courtesy Lawhon Music Co.

The missing asterisk by my name was simply an oversight by the secretary. I was considered full-time faculty, even if just for six weeks!

THE OTHER SIDE OF THE STAND

When any of us were ill, John sent us to his doctor. Going to his home for parties was not only fun, but inspiring because of the caring way he treated his family. I remember that we all wanted to be on his bus for band tours. He would sometimes have the driver stop, get out, and buy oranges or some other treat for the whole group.

Lida Oliver Beasley

What a great feeling it was to be at North Texas during those first years.

Pat Deemer Kimbell

A constant factor during my North Texas years was the example John set for all of us, personally as well as musically. Those evenings at his home charcoaling or winding down from someone's senior recital helped form that "Haynie bunch" bond, which for me has been rarely equaled and never sur-passed.

Leon "Ned" Nedbalek

*When I entered North Texas, I was an unneeded baritone player who was converted to be a horn player. I was in the doldrums, and I suspected that my horn teacher wished that I would go away. I didn't go away, but he did. Mr. Haynie accepted me as his student probably out of the goodness of his heart. At my first lesson with him, everything was turned around in rapid order. His opening remark was, "Now it's time to get you moving, young man." He challenged me, and we covered so much material that when I left, I felt like a horn player for the first time. It felt good just to **be** something.*

James Schell

It was never as important to me that John didn't play the trombone as was the fact that he was such a fine musician.

Tom Wright

LISTENING AND LEARNING
IN THE 1950s

My greatest challenge as a first-year teacher was to gain the respect of my students. With the exposure I was getting while performing with the band, orchestra, and brass choir, they had no doubt that I could play. My playing ability carried me through periods when I didn't have all the answers to my students' problems. Having taken lessons in college on each brass instrument served me well, and the students themselves were advanced enough that they were more interested in interpreting music than how to hold the horn. As it turned out, some of my proudest results came from the early horn, trombone, and baritone students I taught. Some embouchure changes had to be made occasionally, even though I lacked experience in this area. I researched everything written, talked with fine players, and used much imagination, but mostly counted on the student himself to find something that would work. Happily, the embouchures I changed or modified resulted in improved playing for those students.

While I was filling up my teaching load with lower brass students, the halls became crowded with trumpet students. At this point, I was not allowed to take on additional lower brass players, but I kept some I had started like Lida Oliver Beasley, Tom Wright, Bobby Knight, Gene Iles Jacob, and Phil Elliott. Once they graduated I never taught lower brass again.

An important event in 1950–1951 was Leon Brown's brass choir appearance at the TMEA convention in Galveston. In that All-State Band was Howard Kennedy, the band's first-chair trumpeter. I played a couple of solos with piano as part of the brass choir concert, and Howard Kennedy became my first

"first-chair All-State Band player" to enter North Texas in the fall of 1951.

1952 was a banner year for the School of Music as enrollment of freshmen, not only trumpet students, but also the other wind and percussion instruments soared. It is important to know that Dr. Gene Hall was hot news because of his earned doctorate even though his field was jazz. It was a happy situation for me and the jazz program. No longer was there ever a shortage of fine trumpet players, and in those years students wanted to play in all ensembles.

In the later 1950s, Marilyn and I did a two-week tour of Texas, performing everything on the state contest list. I wrote up a brief statement/analysis of each solo—what the demands were, the range, the difficulty of the accompaniment, whatever. We were gone for fourteen days, and we gave nineteen different clinics in that period of time. Sometimes we did two a day. Some clinics were all day; some of them were half a day; some of them were just an hour or two, depending upon the region. I'd go to Edinburg, Texas, and they would have maybe 200 to 250 cornet players and their band directors come in from the whole region, and I just played requests. Whatever they wanted to hear from the Contest List, I'd play. What those kids would do! They'd go through that list and see which one required the highest notes. They were out to kill me! Sometimes those requests came from kids that I knew could never play that piece. They just wanted to see if I could do it. So, I finally got smart, and I had the band directors make the requests of pieces they felt the kids could use. Then I had a certain number that I played anyway, even if no one requested them, because I thought they ought to know about them. There was one particular piece with a very difficult piano interlude, and I didn't want Marilyn to spend time she needed for other things just to learn that part. So we worked out a plan that if this particular piece were ever requested (and it was one time), we would play to the beginning of the first interlude and I would stop and say, "Well, you get the general idea," or "We're running out of time. Is there another request?"

I never had a group of students with the same curiosity and spirit as those of the 1950s. They were highly competitive and very imaginative, which kept me on my toes trying to stay a step ahead of them. A long list could be made of "firsts" that this class of trumpet players accomplished. They were energetic about everything that I expected and went even further in creating other opportunities for learning.

In 1990, about eighty former students had a reunion at my home, and again in 1995, 2000, 2003 (during the ITG Conference), and 2005 as part of the North Texas Homecoming festivities. Without question, this class of students made a tremendous impact on the School of Music. Students from other years have created their own reunions and have similar accomplishment, but those post-World War II years were different for all of us.

Of our reunions, former student Bob Ferguson said it best, "It feels like we all just returned to school after a summer vacation."

Marilyn, Melinda, Mark, and John
Christmas 1962

MARILYN, MELINDA, MARK

When I first saw her working in a record shop in Champaign-Urbana, Illinois, I had no idea how we could get acquainted. If I'd had any money, I would have bought a record for an excuse to start the conversation. But I didn't have a record player either! So I just watched her smile and charm the customers. I did go by again, just to see that smile, but it wasn't until a year later that I saw her in Smith Music Hall at the University of Illinois, and everyone seemed to know her except me. When I was told that she was Mr. Hindsley's daughter Marilyn, I assumed she would not be allowed to date an ex-GI, but as they say, "Hope springs eternal." Her brother, "Huck" Hindsley, marched in the rank ahead of me in the "Marching Illini." This was just the break I needed, so I asked if he could he fix me up with a date with her. He was noncommittal—"Maybe so, maybe not." The "maybe so" is what happened, and by the next marching band rehearsal our first date was set. Now since you know what Paul Harvey calls "the rest of the story," here are some things you may not know about Marilyn.

She was born in Cleveland, Ohio, and the family moved as her father's career developed. The Hindsleys lived in Ft. Worth, Texas, for two years while Mark was in the Army Air Corps Special Services, in charge of bands during World War II. Marilyn attended McLean Junior High School and enjoyed the school and large city. She played flute in the school orchestra and continued playing piano in church—something she'd done since the fourth grade.

When the family moved back to Urbana at the end of Mr. Hindsley's military service, he resumed his duties as A. A. Harding's assistant. Marilyn played flute in the Urbana High School Band, but her first love was the piano, for which I am grateful.

She graduated from Urbana High School in 1948 as co-valedictorian of her class, and she enrolled at the University of Illinois. During that first year, she was so motivated by her flute teacher, Mary Frances James, that she changed her major from piano to flute. She graduated from the University of Illinois in 1951, and her name is engraved on the Bronze Tablet for Academic Excellence.

It wasn't long after that first date that we started talking about getting married. We figured out that she could graduate from college in three years and two summers, and Mr. Hindsley was in on that conversation. The engagement was not a surprise to anyone because she had been wearing my music fraternity pin during her sophomore year when I was a graduate student.

I taught at North Texas for a year while she finished her coursework. We wrote lots of letters to each other every day. Telephone calls were too expensive. I went to Urbana seven times during that year to visit her, and she took the train several times to visit me in Denton. During one visit, I met her in Dallas, and on the way to Denton I stopped by Bachman Lake Park, asked her to marry me and took that ring out of my pocket. The wedding date was set—August 26, 1951; this would also be the twenty-fifth anniversary of Mark and Helene Hindsley.

August 26 finally arrived, and we were married in the First Methodist Church in Urbana, Illinois. I still had no car, so we borrowed Nannie's Chevrolet (yes, the same Nannie who bought my three cornets) so we could drive to Colorado. We spent three days at the Broadmoor Hotel Resort in Colorado Springs. The "honeymoon special" was a three-day package for seventy-five dollars that included all meals!

Interestingly, Marilyn began her career as a band director, the same profession for which I had originally trained. Soon after her arrival in Denton following our marriage, she accepted a position as band and choral director in a consolidated school district about twenty miles from Denton. Marilyn took the job at mid-term, and the situation at first was less than desirable. The small ensemble they called the band consisted of fewer than twenty students. The weekend before Marilyn's teaching began I went with her to look at the equipment and music that the school owned. We found instruments lying all around on the floor and out of their cases. Many were in bad condition. The music library consisted of the *Bennett Band Book*, and many of the pages were strewn about. We put together what we could, but she didn't sleep very well before her first day of teaching.

Fortunately, the administration was behind its young music teacher. Some known trouble-makers (those who chewed tobacco and spit it into their horns, for instance) were immediately removed from the band and the already-small group was reduced to about twelve. And there were no flutes! For a while I had two jobs—the one at North Texas and the one of helping her get started at her school.

Marilyn got to know my students and they loved her. For years she celebrated Mother's Day by having the trumpet students in our yard for their end-of-the-year party.

Soon we became parents to two children: Melinda was born in 1954 and Mark in 1956. Even with two small children at home, Marilyn was convinced by friends and faculty members that she needed to teach piano in her home. Soon she added flute students and juggled home responsibilities with her teaching. Additionally she was very active as a piano accompanist primarily to me. She remembers learning the accompaniments for the entire Texas State Contest List while our two young children played together in an adjoining room. When the Dean of Women from North Texas came to call, she almost couldn't get into the house for all the toys in the living room.

As the children grew, Marilyn and I became their strong supporters and cheerleaders. Both Melinda and Mark were excellent students in such different ways: Melinda always came home with a stack of books to study, and Mark's homework consisted of a piece of paper stuck in his back pocket. Melinda was the social one, resisting going on family vacations for fear of missing out on something; Mark became an Eagle Scout and enjoyed fishing and golfing with me. While Melinda cherished her first chair flute position in band, she was more proud of being a Student Council officer and Valentine Queen. Mark, besides being first chair trumpet in band, was Band President and became a member of the All-State Band, as well as being designated as Outstanding Trumpet Soloist by the University Interscholastic League at the Texas State Solo and Ensemble Contest.

Melinda attended the University of North Texas, and graduated from the University of Houston in 1978 with a bachelor's degree in education. She married David Zeagler on December 27, 1974, in Denton. She now serves as librarian at Barbara Bush Elementary School in Houston. Mark graduated from Texas Tech in 1978 and earned his law degree from the University of Texas in 1981. He married Anne Perry on April 30, 1983. He is a Dallas attorney and has been legal counsel for the International Trumpet Guild for several years. He plays his trumpet regularly.

Marilyn kept a piano and flute studio in our home until I retired and we wanted to become more independent. Besides being an active church member and a community volunteer, she accompanied all her flute students in regional and state contests, and gave innumerable student piano recitals. Also she accompanied my private trumpet students in their contests. Marilyn put her accompanying skills to work again, this time for our grandchildren. One of her greatest joys was to accompany all four of our grandchildren for their high school contests. In Melinda and

Dave's family, Rachel played flute, grandson Cole played the trumpet, and Katie broke the tradition and played horn. Mark and Anne's daughter Jordan also played the flute. Marilyn already knew most of the flute and trumpet accompaniments on the Texas Contest List, but she had to get busy and learn the horn accompaniments for Katie.

The family surprised us on our 50th wedding anniversary with a musical serenade entitled, "This Is Your Life: A Tribute to Fifty Years of Marriage." The instrumentation of the "Hollywood movie score" was a bit heavy on the melody side, but everyone played—Rachel on flute, David and Cole on trumpet, Katie on horn, Mark on baritone, Jordan on piano, Anne on triangle, and Melinda was the narrator and conductor. Mark had the arrangements composed for this instrumentation, following my own advice to students: "If it's worth doing, it's worth overdoing." It was quite a production, and we loved it.

As I look back at our marriage of over fifty years, blessed with two wonderful children and four grandchildren, I am reminded daily that I couldn't have chosen a finer human being, a finer performer, or a more loving wife to share my life. My own career has been full of so many achievements, but marrying Marilyn is the best thing I ever did.

Mark Hubert Hindsley
Director of Bands, University of Illinois, 1950

Who could have imagined when I played in his Texas All-State Band in 1937, that fifteen years later he would become my father-in-law?

John Haynie

MARK HINDSLEY—
MY FATHER-IN-LAW

Even though Mark Hindsley is better known today as a conductor, transcriber for band music, scholar, educator, innovator and gentleman, he was first and foremost my father-in-law. I have already written of his "Three C's" of a musical performance. In the case of Mark Hindsley as my father-in-law, I would add a fourth "C"—that of "Consistency." I observed this trait first-hand as a band member, then a family member.

He was raised on a farm in eastern Indiana, playing the cornet in his family orchestra, the Sunday School orchestra, and the city band. His talent came from his mother, a self-taught pianist. He entered Indiana University when he was fifteen and graduated at age nineteen with a Bachelor of Arts degree "with highest distinction" in chemistry and was a member of the Phi Beta Kappa Society. As fate would have it, just as he was ready to start his master's and doctoral degrees in chemistry, he was offered the band position at Indiana University. He went on to earn a Master of Arts in Music and never looked back. This consistency to be the best he could be served as a beacon for my own ambitions.

After two years as Director of Bands at Indiana University, Mr. Hindsley accepted the job as supervisor of instrumental music in Cleveland Heights, Ohio. He directed the bands and orchestras at Cleveland Heights High School, where after only four years his band won superior ratings at the national competition. This is especially amazing since he inherited a struggling music program with an enrollment of eighteen students. Not surprisingly, *The School Musician* magazine selected him as one of the nation's ten top music directors in 1934.

This was a big year for Mr. Hindsley. Albert Austin Harding, known as the father of the modern concert band, asked Mark Hindsley to come to the University of Illinois and assist with all phases of the Illinois band program. His football bands became legendary and some of his traditional "Marching Illini" routines are still used today. He also taught instrumental classes in the School of Music. Marilyn remembers one summer when he concentrated on learning how to play the oboe. When she saw him practicing, she thought he had swallowed the mouthpiece!

In 1942, he was commissioned as a Captain in the Army Air Corps Flying Training Command and supervised more than 150 bands. Then in 1945 he was assigned to head the music faculty at Biarritz American University in France, with a student body population of two thousand United States military personnel, and he advanced to the rank of Lieutenant Colonel. Again, his consistency is demonstrated by his voluntary enlistment.

In the fall of 1947, I arrived at the University of Illinois expecting to play in A. A. Harding's band. I will never forget the first rehearsal of the Illinois Band, which had convened for a marching band trip to New York City to cheer on our football team when they played against Army in Yankee Stadium. That very day I auditioned for Haskell Sexton, who called in Mr. Hindsley, who then called in Mr. Harding to hear me play and sight read. I was more unnerved in this audition than I had been during the Battle of the Bulge a couple of years earlier. I cannot remember a single thing they asked me to play other than my signature solo, *Spanish Caprice*. I do recall reading a manuscript that was a transcription for band by Mr. Harding. I must have done well enough, for I was told I would sit beside Leroy Kirsch, the best trumpet player on campus.

Then we went to the marching band rehearsal. Mr. Hindsley was the marching band director, and this was his rehearsal. We started with a Bach chorale. Never had I heard anything like this. Even with a marching band instrumentation, it was little different from the concert band. The sound of the brass was enhanced by the fantastic sound of the woodwinds. I just stopped playing, put my horn in my lap and sat there listening. The local Cisco paper had this to report about that magnificent band: "In presenting its formations, the Illinois band keeps music foremost. No pistol shots or whistle blasts are used. Every movement is synchronized to the music, no matter how intricate the maneuver."

After the retirement of Mr. Harding, Mr. Hindsley became the Director of Bands. At the same time he was elected president of the College Band Directors National Association after developing its now-famous Declaration of Principles. In 1957, he was elected president of the American Bandmasters Association and in March of that year hosted its annual convention. This convention celebrated the dedication of the new Harding Band Building on the campus of the University of Illinois that Mark Hindsley helped design.

Beginning in the early fifties, he inaugurated a series of fifty-nine LP recordings of music for Concert Band, which received distribution and acceptance worldwide. Records number 23 and 24 feature live performances with me as guest soloist for the concurrent CBDNA convention and the January 1959 series of concerts played by the Illinois bands. These performances are still remembered as the most significant of my early career. The years were rolling by for both of us, and Dad—I could finally utter the word—retired in 1970 to his transcriptions and publishing company. We shared the stage one last time for my own retirement concert, with other luminaries in the band world—Robert Winslow, William D. Revelli, and Frederick Fennell. The occasion was a concert featuring these four conductors for the

Texas Music Educators Association convention, and you'll read about that special concert in the last essay.

It was a fitting tribute that James Keene, current Director of Bands at the University of Illinois, produced a three-CD package of recordings of Mr. Hindsley's transcriptions, played by the Illinois Band, and conducted by Mr. Hindsley.

As an author, Mr. Hindsley wrote eight books on bands and instrumental music education, such as *School Band and Orchestra Administration* (1940), *Tuning the School Band* (with Ralph Potter, 1960, 1961, and 1970), and *Hindsley on Bands: The Gospel According to Mark* (1979), and contributed to several others. He also wrote over forty articles for a dozen magazines. His original compositions and transcriptions have been printed by thirty publishers worldwide.

Mark Hindsley was a pioneer, an innovator, and a musician for whom I had the most profound respect. But he was also my father-in-law, Granddad to my children and Great-Granddad to their children. When our oldest grandchild Rachel was growing up and participating in band, she had band directors who referred reverently to Mark Hindsley. I'll never forget the phone call she made to Marilyn one day to ask, "Just who *is* Great-Granddad?"

Now she knows.

Captain Mark H. Hindsley, 1943

My dad was very proud of his Army career. He was stationed in the Texas Pacific Building in downtown Ft. Worth with just enough fuel on his gasoline ration card to get him there and back home, no more. He once organized six of his bands into one big band to perform at Farrington Field in 1944. They marched in a parade downtown, followed by an inspection by the Commanding General of the Army Air Forces Training Command, Lieutenant General Barton K. Yount. Keeping physically fit in the Army set a pattern he followed all his life. He took walks everyday, and at age 75 climbed up to the high podium to conduct the massed bands at a University of Illinois football game. The announcer proclaimed that it was his 75th birthday, and the band played **Happy Birthday** *while the fans sang to him.*

Marilyn Hindsley Haynie

THE
SYMPHONIC
WIND
ENSEMBLE

Robert A. Winslow, Director
Dennis W. Fisher, Assistant Director

Guest Conductors:

Mark H. Hindsley
Frederick Fennell
William D. Revelli

Soloist   John J. Haynie

Announcer   Edward A. Baird

Choral Students of Northeast ISD, San Antonio, Texas

Texas Music Educators' Association
Thursday, February 13, 1986 8:00 p.m.
Theatre for the Performing Arts
San Antonio Convention Center
San Antonio, Texas

*I was principal trumpet in the wind ensemble for this TMEA concert, and I
still remember marveling at how I came to be there at that moment, playing
in the band accompanying Mr. Haynie, with Granddad and Mother listening in the audience. I had always been conscious of the connection between
Mr. Haynie and my family; how Granddad, Robert Maddox, Sr., was his
teacher, how Mr. Haynie was the teacher of my uncle, Robert Maddox, Jr.,
and now he was my teacher, too! I felt honored to be part of this tradition.*

Paul Hankins

THE GRAND PERFORMANCE

One essay in this book is called "On Stage—the Reason for Being." I wrote the essay for students to know how I prepared for the most important solo performance of my life. Here's the background for that performance and why I would accept the challenge. By 1985, I had not performed publicly for several years, but each time I picked up my horn and played for or with a student, I considered it to be the most important performance at the time. Then came the real invitation, issued by Dr. Robert Winslow, to appear as a soloist with the North Texas Wind Ensemble for their upcoming concert at the 1986 TMEA Convention in San Antonio. He had also invited, and they'd accepted, three of the most famous band conductors of our time to share this concert—Mark Hindsley, William D. Revelli, and Frederick Fennell. I accepted his invitation without hesitation. Even though it was a spur-of-the-moment decision, it took on more meaning as we prepared for this concert.

My first decision was to ask Bob Winslow to conduct the band accompaniment himself, which would assure ample rehearsal time. It became clear that this performance would be my farewell to the university, because I would move from full-time teaching to a period of modified service. My first solo performance on the North Texas campus was with Maurice McAdow's summer band in 1950, so it would be very appropriate to make my last performance with the North Texas Wind Ensemble. Furthermore, a solo performance as a guest of the Texas Music Educators Association would be a farewell and tribute to the TMEA for their dedication to ever-improving public school music in Texas. The stage was set for the performance of my life.

What would I play? My repertoire included just about everything written for trumpet, but I wanted a piece that would "say it all" about my life and career. In keeping with the historical significance with the guest conductors, I decided that only a cornet solo would be appropriate. Not just any cornet solo. It had to be the Staigers *Carnival of Venice*. And not just performed on any cornet—I would play the high school cornet Nannie bought me. This one solo would demonstrate everything I had ever taught—embouchure, breath, tongue, fingers, style, vibrato, rubato, intonation, and a little bit of show business for good measure.

February 13, 1986 was there before I knew it. Backstage were these great musicians with whom I chatted, reminding Bill Revelli that he had judged me at the Regional-level National Contest in 1937, listening to Fred Fennell reminisce about shared experiences, and recalling my University of Illinois days with my father-in-law, Mark Hindsley. Ed Baird, the announcer, brought me on stage, "the reason for being," and Bob Winslow struck up the band. Suddenly I was playing away—high notes, low notes and all those in between. I poured my heart into the theme. My friend, the metronome, talked to me all the while. "First variation, pretty good considering your fingers are older and a bit arthritic. Second variation better, but not perfect. Save the perfect for the triple-tongued variation." I did as ordered. For a touch of show business I let the cornet fly from my lips with a touch of abandon after the last note. It was my finest moment. The audience burst into applause, I bowed to the crowd and the band, and Bob and I left the stage. "John, the last variation one more time for an encore?" "That's fine, just faster." We played our brief encore, and this time, before I even played the last note, the applause began. It seemed to say, "John James Haynie, your years at North Texas will be appreciated and never forgotten."

The sound of the applause lingers still.

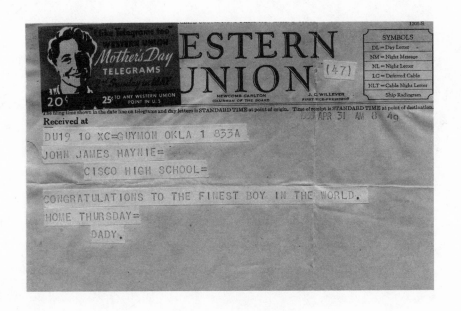

Telegram from James Haynie, dated April 31 [instead of May 1], 1939

My dad was on the road a lot, but he always managed to keep in touch. I don't know how he found out about my First Division rating at the National Contest, but he sent this telegram to me c/o Cisco High School. It reads: "Congratulations to the finest boy in the world. Home Thursday=Dady." I have never forgotten how proud he was of me.

John Haynie

AFTERWORD

With forty years of teaching behind him, even considering the five-year period of modified service, I wondered how John Haynie handled the transition from "leaving the office on Friday afternoon" to "I'm retired on Monday morning." His explanation was characteristically candid. "For one thing, teaching has never been a nine-to-five job. I'd like to meet the person who thinks it is. There is a routine, certainly, but the flexibility in this profession is what keeps it fresh. Recitals to give and attend, new music to learn and teach, the responsibilities of new students, and the joy of former students' successes. It takes about fifteen minutes to get from the College of Music building to my home, and by the time I got home that Friday, I was retired. I donated my studio music to the North Texas library, the solos with band accompaniments were given to Texas Tech, the church music stayed with my church where Michael Steinel uses it and keeps it organized, and the recordings are part of Keith Johnson's studio materials to use and lend as he sees fit. I wanted students to have access to all that. Forty years and it was done. I loved it, but that part of my life was over."

He added, "When I entered modified service, I started playing more, especially at my church. I started my career by performing in a church, and I ended it the same way. On my 74th birthday, I performed at church—the prelude and all the hymns, complete with Doug Smith's descants. I did a special offertory, and at the end of the service I played a very festive postlude. It was probably the most mistake-free performance I've ever given—the one I always knew I could give. I saved the best for last and put the trumpet away for good."

In some ways, John's retirement is no different from his forty years at North Texas. He still enjoys a good game of golf;

unsuspecting fish are still in danger, as are ducks, quail, and anything else in season. His enthusiastic support of his beloved University of Illinois football and basketball teams is stronger than ever. He enjoys cooking, though Marilyn says with most recipes he's more imaginative than talented. I can attest that his version of chicken and dumplings is one of the best comfort foods around. And when he dips out a cup of the *roux* and hands it to you to taste—well, move over, Campbell's.

Always a bit of a "gadget man," his interest in technology has kept up with the times. He transfers his digital photographs to disks, adds music, and deals with a steady batch of email. You know he's telling the truth when he says, "It's more challenging if you never read the manuals." He finally bought a drill press, a table saw, and a radial cross-cut saw, and reorganized the thousands of odds and ends in his shop. He builds boxes. More discriminating people would call them pieces of furniture. No matter what he builds, he calls it a box.

His first career goal was to become a band director like Robert Maddox, and he retraces that path a bit when, every year since 1990, he has judged middle school/junior high bands at the Sandy Lake FunFest near Denton. He writes, "I never look much at the score. I just listen to the sounds and write about the physical stuff in a down-to-earth way. At the end of a day, my three C's have become several complete alphabets."

For many years, John and Marilyn have spent the summers in Colorado, usually in Crested Butte. This is the home of The MoUNTain Institute, which began in 1998 as a summer opportunity for University of North Texas students to study and perform in casual indoor and outdoor settings. The Haynies are two of the institute's sponsors. They enjoy attending concerts and John coaches trumpet players in master classes. Afterward, the group usually finds its way to the Haynie home for a cookout or get-together.

Generous in the studio and at home, the Haynies joined the University of North Texas President's Council and established the John and Marilyn Haynie Trumpet Scholarship, as well as the John and Marilyn Haynie Endowment for Trumpet Projects. The endowment was established to support the trumpet faculty—for guest artists, clinicians, travel for faculty or students, computers, whatever the need. John's royalties from this book go to the endowment fund. John said, "It was especially important for us to set this up so that other young people can have the same chances I had. I had all sorts of talents and tried to be the best I could be at everything I did. I had a lot of luck in being at the right place at the right time. Every door I've ever opened has been a winner. Sometimes I opened the door. Sometimes it was opened for me. That's all I've tried to do for every student who came through my own door."

Projects like this are often called a "labor of love"; too many times they just become a "labor." This adventure has stayed fresh and fun from the beginning. John invited me to come inside his virtual studio, and he made a certificate proclaiming me to be an honorary student. But just as the word "temporary" was removed from his six-week contract in 1950, he's long since removed the word "honorary" from my certificate. He and Marilyn have made me feel like a member of their family—a feeling I treasure.

John has so enjoyed writing about and relating his studio strategies that he's picked up his old mouthpiece and is practicing buzzing, while encouraging me to dig out my own and to do the same. Mark has given him a trumpet, and I'll bet it won't be too long before the house smells like homemade valve oil again.

Anne Hardin

CONTRIBUTORS

Marsha Millender Adams, *Bachelor of Arts/Music, Cameron University, 1983; Master of Music, Southwestern Oklahoma State University, 1990.* Band director, Tom Bean, TX, 1983–84; Central HS, Marlow, OK, 1984–90; Lawton Public Schools, OK, 1990–present.

Edward Alley, *Bachelor of Music Education and Master of Music, UNT, 1957.* Conductor/Administrator. Positions include conductor, 7th Army Symphony Orchestra, Goldovsky Opera Theater; vice-president, Affiliate Artists, Inc.; director, Rockefeller Fund for Music, NY; orchestra manager, New York Philharmonic; associate director, Juilliard Opera Center; married to mezzo-soprano Nancy Williams.

Keith Amstutz, *Bachelor of Music, Michigan State University, 1963; Master of Music, Michigan State University, 1964; DME, University of Oklahoma, 1970.* Brass instructor, University of Texas at Arlington, 1964–67; trumpet instructor, UNT, 1967–70; professor of trumpet, University of Kansas, 1970–1973; professor of trumpet, University of South Carolina, 1973–present. Developed and patented "Braceguard," the orthodontic shield for instrumentalists with braces. President, AKMS, Inc.

Larry Austin, *Bachelor of Music Education, UNT, 1951; Master of Music, UNT, 1952.* Composer. Works have been performed and recorded by the New York Philharmonic, Boston Symphony, National Symphony orchestras, as well as other major ensembles in North America and Europe. Awarded the *Magistère* prize in the 23rd International Electroacoustic Music Competition, Bourges, France, 1996. Faculty member, UC, Davis, 1958–72; University of South Florida, 1972–78; UNT, 1978–96.

Robert Bailey, *Bachelor of Music, East Central State University, Ada, OK, 1969; Master of Music Education, UNT, 1979; Ph.D. Music Education, UNT, 1989.* Trumpet instructor, Northeastern State University, Tahlequah, OK, 1980–present; Ft. Smith Symphony, Bartlesville Symphony, Tulsa Philharmonic, Breckenridge Music Institute, CO.

Ken Barker, *Bachelor of Music Education, West Texas A&M University, 1977; Master of Music Education, UNT, 1978*; Assistant music editor, 1979–93; senior editorial director, 1993–present, Word Music, Nashville, TN. Gospel Music Association Award for Choral Collection of the Year, 2002. Ken, wife Brenda, and their seven internationally adopted children were selected as

Tennessee's 1997 Adoptive Family of the Year by Davidson County Family Services.

Gary Barrow, *Bachelor of Music Education, UNT, 1969; Master of Music, Catholic University of America, 1973; Ph.D., UNT, 1981.* Professor of trumpet, Arkansas Tech University, Russellville, 1981–present.

Conrad Bauschka, *Bachelor of Music Education, University of Wisconsin, 1957; Master of Music/Trumpet Performance, UNT, 1958.* Principal trumpet, West Point Band, 1958–61; professor of music, University of Florida, 1961–64; professor of trumpet, Texas A & M University at Commerce, 1964–present.

Lida Oliver Beasley, *Bachelor of Music Education, UNT, 1956; Master of Music Education, University of Illinois, 1957.* Faculty, Santa Monica College, 1985–93; Emmy Award, on-camera performance as conductor of *Faust*, Santa Monica College Orchestra/Opera Workshop, 1991.

Geoff Bissett, *Bachelor of Music Education, UNT, 1976.* Band director, Brownfield MS, 1976–1985. District manager, Franklin Life Insurance, 1985–93; ranked number 33 in company sales, 1988, winner of the Centurian Award. Employed at Frenship Schools in Wolfforth, Texas, 1997, associate high school director since 1998; consistent UIL sweepstakes award winner with second band.

Bob Blanton, *Bachelor of Music Education, UNT, 1964; Master of Arts, West Texas State University, 1970; Faculty of Fine Arts Certificate in Conducting and Wind Literature, University of Calgary, 1987.* Band director, Richardson West JHS, 1965–69; Richardson HS, 1969–72; director, music education and bands, Klein ISD, 1974–82; director of bands, associate professor of music education, Texas Christian University, 1982–92; director of fine arts, Klein ISD, 1992–present; elected to American Bandmasters Association, 1987.

Rick Bogard, *Bachelor of Music Education, University of Central Arkansas, 1977; Master of Music/Trumpet Performance, Baylor University, 1978; DMA/Trumpet Performance, UNT, 1994.* Professor of trumpet, University of Texas at Arlington, 1990–present; member, Dallas Opera Orchestra, 1989–present. Author: *Daily Warm-Ups and Skills Studies for Trumpet*, Gore Publishing Co.

Elizabeth Pollard Bowen, *Bachelor of Music, UNT, 1987.* Junior high band director, 1988–92, 2003–present; proud mom, 1992–present.

Lyman Brodie, *Bachelor of Music Education, University of South Florida, 1969; Master of Music, UNT, 1972.* Associate professor of music, associate dean for student, alumni, and community affairs, University of Central Florida, 1990–present; principal trumpet, Dallas Wind Symphony, 1985–present, Orlando Philharmonic, 1992–present.

Duncan Brown, *Bachelor of Music/Trumpet Performance, West Texas State University, 1979; Master of Music/Trumpet Performance, West Texas State University, 1981.* Band director, 1981–present; Memphis HS, Memphis, TX, 2001–present; MHS Band was state finalist, Outstanding Small School Bands, 2005; Who's Who Among American Teachers, 2005, 2006; CD (with wife Cindy), *Amazing Grace.*

Elaine Burt, *Bachelor of Music/Jazz Studies, UNT, 1988; Master of Music/Jazz Studies, UNT, 1991.* Free-lance performer, New York, 1993–present. Shows include *Annie Get Your Gun* with Bernadette Peters and Reba McEntyre, *Two Gentlemen of Verona*, and *Peter Pan.* Appearances with various artists on *Today* and *Rosie O'Donnell* shows.

Frank Campos, *Bachelor of Music/Trumpet Performance, California State University at Fresno, 1977; California Teaching Credential, 1979; Master of Music/Trumpet Performance, UNT, 1984*; professor of trumpet, Ithaca College, NY, 1986–present. Author, *Trumpet Technique*, Oxford UP, 2005.

Cynthia Thompson Carrell, *Bachelor of Music Education, UNT, 1986; Master of Science/Music Education, University of Illinois, 1987; DMA/Trumpet Performance, University of Illinois, 1997.* Presser Scholar, UNT, 1986; Winner, ITG Mock Orchestra Competition, 1987. Assistant professor of music, Harding University, Searcy, AR, 1998–present.

Alan Chamberlain, *Bachelor of Business Administration, UNT, 1982; Master of Business Administration, UNT, 1995.* Owner/President of Denton Trinity Roofing, 1980–present.

Peter Ciurczak, *Bachelor of Music Education, Oberlin Conservatory, 1955; Master of Arts, Columbia University, 1959; Ph.D./Musicology, UNT, 1974.* Professor of trumpet, Emporia State University, 1963–1972; chair, Departments of Music, Emporia State University, 1972–1979, and University of New Mexico, 1979–88; director, School of Music, University of Southern Mississippi, 1988–99.

Dick Clardy, *Bachelor of Music Education, West Texas State University, 1972; Master of Music/Applied Trumpet, Catholic University of America, 1975.* Band director, The Colony HS, 1986–2001; John Philip Sousa Foundation Sudler Flag of Honor, 1994; TMEA Class 5A Honor Band, 1997; Midwest Band Clinic performances, 1994, 1998; American Bandmasters Association Convention, 2000; Carnegie Hall, 2001, 2006; band director, Klein HS, Klein ISD, 2001–present; president, TMEA, 1998–2000; American Bandmasters Association; TBA Meritorious Service Award, 2005.

Wayne Cook, *Bachelor of Music, UNT, 1962; Master of Science/Music Education, University of Illinois, 1964.* Professor of trumpet, Indiana State University, 1964–1966, and University of Wisconsin at Milwaukee, 1966–99, *Emeritus*, 1999; trumpet faculty, Wisconsin Conservatory of Music, 2002–present; CD, *Epifania: Five Pieces of Leonard Salzedo with Tuned Gongs*, Albany Troy Records (DDD), 2002.

Bud Cothern, *D.D.S., University of Illinois Dental School, 1951.* Practiced dentistry, Denton, TX, 1951–87. Took up the trumpet again at age 65.

Anna Cox, *Graduate, Flower Mound Marcus HS, 1996.* Performed at the Montreaux International Jazz Festival, Vermont Jazz Festival; has performed with artists such as Steve Weist, Randy Brecker, Denis DiBlasio, Gregg Bissonette, Mike Vax, Timi Ishii, Randy Hamm, Glenn Kostur, Ed Peterson, Frank Mantooth, and Kris Berg. Free-lance performer, Dallas/Ft. Worth. Daughter of Ronn Cox.

Ronn Cox, *Bachelor of Music, UNT, 1970; Master of Music/Composition, UNT, 1976.* Band director, TX, 1977–2001. Pender's Music Co., 2001–2003. Private trumpet teacher, Lewisville, TX, 2003–present. Father of Anna Cox.

Michael Craddock, *Bachelor of Music, UNT, 1975; Master of Music Education, UNT, 1977; DMA/Guitar, UNT, 1983; lute study, Schola Cantorum Basiliensis, Switzerland.* Assistant professor of guitar, University of North Carolina at Greensboro, 1980–87, private teacher (guitar and lute), Basel, Switzerland, 1990–present. CD, *Tablatures de Guiterne* (Cantus Records), 2005.

Gary Dobbins, *Bachelor of Music, UNT, 1970; Master of Music, Michigan State University, 1972; DMA/Trumpet and Conducting, University of Northern Colorado, 1988.* Trumpet/brass teacher, Texas State University, 1972–77; University of Louisiana, 1977–84; member, Baton Rouge Symphony, 1978–89;

orchestra director, Richardson ISD, 1996–2003; member, Dallas Wind Symphony, 1989–present; instrumental teacher, Dallas ISD, 2004–present.

Scott Ducaj, *Bachelor of Music, New Mexico State University, 1982; Master of Music Education, UNT, 1985.* Musician, Opryland USA, 1985–90. Author, *20 Modern Jazz Duets,* 1985; *Cool Tunes,* 2002. Studio player and teacher, 1990–present. CD, *Desert Home,* 2001.

Larry Engstrom, *Bachelor of Arts/Music Education, California State University at Fresno, 1981; Master of Music/Trumpet Performance, UNT, 1983; DMA/Trumpet Performance, UNT, 1991.* Assistant professor of trumpet, University of Nevada at Reno, 1987–2001; chair, Department of Music and Dance, 2001–2003 and director, School of the Arts, University of Nevada, Reno, 2003–present; principal trumpet, Reno Philharmonic Orchestra, 1988–2001. Four jazz quintet CDs, *Balance, Boats, North,* and *Contemplation.*

Bob Ferguson, *Bachelor of Music Education, UNT, 1956.* United States Army Band, Washington, DC, 1957–85.

Marilynn Mocek Gibson, *Bachelor of Music Education, Texas Tech University, 1977; Master of Music Education, UNT, 1979.* Assistant professor of music, University of Louisiana at Monroe, 1979–present; commissioned works for trumpet and bassoon by Keith Gates, Roger Jones, Walter Ross, and Gwyneth Walker.

Russell Gloyd, *Bachelor of Music, UNT, 1971.* Conductor/producer, Dave Brubeck Quartet, 1971–present. Guest orchestra conductor, Washington, DC, Atlanta, Dallas, San Francisco, Russia, Italy, and Poland. CDs, as conductor, DBQ: *To Hope! A Celebration* (Telarc CD-80430), live performance at the National Cathedral, Washington, DC, and *Beloved Son; Pange lingua Variations; Voice of the Holy Spirit (Tongues of Fire); Regret* (Telarc 2CD-80621).

Ivan Goodwin, *Bachelor of Music Education, UNT, 1952; Master of Music Education, UNT, 1954.* Band director, Ennis, TX, ISD, 1952–74. Awards: Ennis HS Band won eleven UIL Sweepstakes and Division I marching ratings 1955–74. Assistant superintendent, Ennis ISD, 1974–85. Member, TBA Hall of Fame. Husband of Judie Barker Goodwin.

Judie Barker Goodwin, *Bachelor of Music Education, UNT, 1952.* Taught elementary grades, 1953–60; elementary music, 1960–74, assistant band director, Ennis, TX, ISD, 1974–91. Wife of Ivan Goodwin.

Ross Grant, *Bachelor of Music Education, Ouachita Baptist University, 1977; Master of Music Education, UNT, 1979; Ph.D./Music Education, 1989, UNT.* Band director, DeSoto HS, TX, 1982–2001; assistant professor of music education, Texas Christian University, 2001–2003, band director, Azle HS, Azle, TX, 2003–present, seven-time UIL State Marching Contest finalist, Tournament of Roses Parade 1992, 2002.

Paul Hankins, *Bachelor of Music Education, West Texas A&M University, 1982; Master of Music Education, UNT, 1986; DMA/Trumpet Performance, University of Illinois, 1999.* Professor of trumpet, Delta State University, MS, 1999–present. Son of Virginia Hankins; grandson of Robert Maddox, Sr.

Virginia Maddox Hankins, private flute teacher in El Paso, TX, 28 years. Mother of Paul Hankins; daughter of Robert Maddox, Sr.

John Harbaugh, *Bachelor of Arts, University of Northern Iowa, 1975; Master of Music Education, UNT, 1977.* Professor of music, University of Alaska at Fairbanks, 1988–2002; professor of trumpet, Central Washington University, 2002–present; board of directors, National Trumpet Competition, 1998–present; clinician, United Musical Instrument/Conn Corporation.

Anne Hardin, *Bachelor of Music, Georgia State University, 1976; Master of Music Education/Performance Certificate, University of South Carolina, 1978; Ph.D./Music Education, University of South Carolina, 1990.* Editor, International Trumpet Guild *Journal*, 1978–96; band director, 1978–2004; Beaufort County [SC] Teacher of the Year, 2002–2003. Author, *A Trumpeter's Guide to Orchestral Excerpts* (W. R. Welch, 1977; Camden House, 1986); *Yamaha Band Student Teacher's Resource Guide, Yamaha Student Workbook* (Alfred Publishing, 1994).

Joe Harness, *Bachelor of Music Education, University of North Texas, 1964.* Band director, Hanna HS, TX, 1965–68; Cummings MS, 1968–75; Pace HS, 1975–98, all Brownsville, TX. Band honors, performance, U.S. Capitol, Washington, DC, 1977; Musical Ambassadors European tour, Cologne and Rome, 1979, 1983; state honor band competition five times. Recipient, NBA Citation of Excellence, 2005; TBA Hall of Fame, 2006.

Anne Perry Haynie, *Bachelor of Arts/Psychology, University of Texas at Austin, 1979.* Grew up in France, Venezuela, Iran, and Norway. A non-musician, her role in the Haynie family is one of admiration and support. Since retiring as a full-time mom, she enjoys travel, golf, and volunteer work; daughter-in-law of John and Marilyn Haynie.

Jordan Haynie, *Plan II major (multidisciplinary liberal arts), University of Texas, 2003–present, studied at King's College, London.* Valedictorian, Newman Smith HS, 2003; National Merit Finalist; all-region and first division honors, flute and voice; performed leading roles in high school, college, and community theater productions; granddaughter of John and Marilyn Haynie.

Mark Haynie, *Bachelor of Arts/with High Honors, Texas Tech University, 1978; LL.D, University of Texas at Austin, 1981.* Attorney and principal in the Dallas law firm Haynie Rake & Repass, PC. He serves as General Counsel to the International Trumpet Guild. Son of John and Marilyn Haynie.

Carole Herrick, *Bachelor of Music Education, University of Texas at Austin, 1971; Master of Music/Trumpet Performance, University of Texas at Austin, 1972; Ph.D./Music Education, UNT, 1981.* Professor of trumpet, Hendrix College, Conway, AR, 1980–present; associate provost for advising and retention, 2002–present.

Larry Hodgin, *Bachelor of Arts, UNT, 1970.* United States Army Band, Washington, DC, 1970–2000. Volunteer, church and community; works in bicycle advocacy for safety, exercise, and expedition touring; police training academy; mission work for a home for orphaned girls in Honduras.

Ruth Jane Holmes, *Bachelor of Arts, UNT, 1962; Master of Music, UNT, 1964; Ph.D./Fine Arts, Texas Tech University, 1976.* Professor of music, Lubbock Christian University, 1975–present. Solo piano CDs: *Introducing Ruth Holmes; Ruth Holmes: The Christmas Album* (Holisso Records, 1996). Lubbock Christian University F. W. Mattox Excellence in Teaching Award, 1985; YWCA Women of Excellence Award for Culture and the Arts, 1997; Rotary Club of Lubbock Paul Harris Fellow for Humanitarian and Educational Programs, 1999.

Craig Hurst, *Bachelor of Music, Boise State University, 1978; Master of Music Education, UNT, 1981; Ph.D./Music Education, UNT, 1994.* Professor of music, University of Wisconsin at Waukesha, 1993–present. Two-time recipient of the Arthur M. Kaplan award in recognition of his curricular innovations and service to students. CD, *With You in My Corner.*

Gene Iles Jacob, *Bachelor of Music Education/organ and horn, UNT, 1952; Master of Sacred Music, Southern Methodist University, 1985.* Organist and music associate, First United Methodist Church, Richardson, TX, 1964–2002.

Clay Jenkins, *Bachelor of Music Theory, UNT, 1976; Master of Music/Jazz Studies, University of Southern California, 1995.* Associate professor of jazz studies & contemporary media, ECMS collegiate instructor in trumpet, Eastman School of Music, 2000–present. Solo recordings: *Rings, Give and Gather, Yellow Flowers After, Azure Eyes,* and *Matters of Time.* Performer, with Trio East, three recordings: *Range, Look at the Time,* and *Crossweave.*

Keith Johnson, *Bachelor of Arts in Music, UNT, 1963; Master of Music, University of Illinois, 1965.* Professor of trumpet, University of Northern Iowa, 1966–86; Regents Professor of Trumpet, UNT, 1986–present. Author, *The Art of Trumpet Playing* (Iowa State UP, 1981; 2nd edition Gore Publishing); *Brass Performance and Pedagogy* (Prentice-Hall, 2001).

Miles Johnson, *Bachelor of Arts/Psychology, UNT, 1980.* U.S. Air Force musician, Scott AFB, IL, 1985–96; Lackland AFB, TX, 1996–98; Allied Forces Southern Region, Naples, Italy 1998–2001; Lackland AFB, TX 2001–present.

Greg Jones, *Bachelor of Music/Trumpet Performance, Florida State University, 1982; Master of Music Education, UNT, 1986; DMA/Performance and Literature, Eastman School of Music, 1992.* CD, *Alternate Voices: Chamber Music for the Trumpet,* featuring faculty members of the Eastman School of Music and the Rochester Philharmonic Orchestra, 1998.

Pat Deemer Kimbell, *Bachelor of Music/Trumpet Performance, UNT, 1958; Master of Music/Trumpet Performance, UNT, 1959.* Music teacher, Calhoun County ISD, Dallas, TX, 1960–64; instrument methods instructor, Texas Woman's University, 1968–79; principal trumpet, Richardson Symphony Orchestra, 1962–78; active free-lance player.

Leroy Kirsch, *Bachelor of Science/Music Education, University of Illinois, 1949; Master of Music Education, University of Illinois, 1950.* U.S. Army 8th Infantry "Golden Arrow" Band, 1952–54; Band Director, Belleville (IL) Township HS, 1958–85. Active free-lance player.

Cathy Myer Kliebenstein, *Bachelor of Science/Music, University of Wisconsin at LaCrosse, 1981; Master of Music Education, UNT, 1983; Bachelor of Business Administration, East Texas State University at Commerce, 1988.* Music editor, Hal Leonard Corporation, 1998–present. Corporate accounting analyst, Kohler Company, Kohler, WI, 1988–94; private piano teacher, 1988–present.

Craig Konicek, *Bachelor of Music, Bachelor of Applied Arts, University of Minnesota-Duluth, 1976; Master of Music Education, UNT, 1980;* Free-lance trumpeter 1980–82, Minneapolis, MN; lead trumpet, Walt Disney World, 1982–87; associate director of bands, trumpet instructor, Southeastern Louisiana University, 1987–95; Minister of music, 1995 to present; First Baptist Church, Ocala Florida, 2005; publisher, *SimplyBrass* magazine; performing artist/clinician with the Edwards/Getzen Company, 1992–present; CD (with soprano/wife Jaclyn), *I'll Still Be Praising You*, 1995.

Doug Laramore, *Bachelor of Music Education, West Texas State University, 1974; Master of Music, West Texas State University, 1975; DMA, University of Oklahoma, 1990.* Professor of trumpet, *Emeritus*, East Central University, Ada, OK, 1977–2005; Who's Who Among American Teachers, 2000.

Karl Lassey, *Bachelor of Music, UNT, 1956.* U.S. Navy pilot, 1956–67; Western Airlines, 1968–87; Delta Airlines, 1987–94.

James Linahon, *Bachelor of Music, University of Northern Iowa 1973; Master of Music Education, UNT, 1975.* adjunct professor of jazz studies, Chaffey College, Ontario, CA, 1975–80; director of jazz studies 1981–92; professor of music, Fullerton College, CA, 1981–present; music producer *CBS, RCA, Warner Bros, MCA, PBS,* 17 Grammy nominations,1982–present; member, advisory board, University of Northern Iowa School of Music, 1999–present.

Joy Maynard, *Bachelor of Music Education, Evangel University, 1970; Master of Science/Education, Southwest Missouri State University, 1978: Master of Arts/Education, Oral Roberts University, 1985.* Band director, 1985–present, 18 years at Will Rogers Junior High, Claremore, OK; Site Teacher of the Year 1993, 2003, 2006.

Paul Mazzio, *Bachelor of Music, UNT, 1985; Master of Music, University of Southern California, 1989;* ITG jazz competition winner, 1982. International touring and recording artist, Woody Herman Orchestra, 1983, 1986. Active free-lance player, Portland, OR.

Scott McAdow, *Bachelor of Music Education, UNT, 1977; Master of Music/Conducting, University of Houston, 1988.* Band director, 1977–present; Langham Creek HS, Cypress–Fairbanks ISD, Houston, TX, 1991–present. Hildebrandt MS, State Honor Band, 1989; Langham Creek HS, Class V-A Honor Band, 2003, and Midwest Band Clinic performances, 2000, 2005.

Bucky Milam, *Bachelor of Arts, UNT, 1960; Master of Fine Arts, Chicago Art Institute, 1962*. Trumpet player, artist. Art displayed in Dallas, London, Tokyo Museums of Fine Art, MoMA, Chicago Art Institute; performed with Buddy Rich, Glenn Miller, Urbie Green, Henry Mancini; free-lance performer.

Charles Millender, *Bachelor of Music, UNT, 1957; Master of Music Education, Southwestern Oklahoma State University, 1975*. Played trumpet in various U.S. Air Force Bands, 1951–55; band director, 1957–85; Lawton MacArthur HS, 1971–83; Member, Oklahoma Bandmasters Hall of Fame, 1988; owner, Millender Band Supply, 1985–2005.

David Miller, *Bachelor of Arts/Music Education, Southeastern Oklahoma State University, 1987*. Free-lance musician; musical instrument repair technician, Caddo Public Schools, Shreveport, LA, 1989–present; member, Longview, TX, Symphony Orchestra, 1995–present; designer and maker of custom trumpets and accessories, 1999–present.

Ron Modell, *Bachelor of Music Education, University of Tulsa, 1957; Master of Music, University of Tulsa, 1960*. Principal trumpet, Tulsa Philharmonic, 1953–60; principal trumpet, Dallas Symphony Orchestra, 1960–69; professor of trumpet, director of jazz ensembles, Northern Illinois University, 1969–1997.

Al Moore, *Bachelor of Music Education, Texas Tech University, 1966; Master of Science/Music Education, University of Illinois, 1968; DMA/Trumpet Performance, UNT, 1981*. Professor of trumpet and horn, St. Cloud State University, St. Cloud, MN, 1971–present.

Bob Morgan, *Bachelor of Music Education, UNT, 1963; Master of Music/Composition, UNT, 1965; DMA/Composition, University of Illinois, 1974. Honorary Ph.D., Berklee College of Music, 1999*. Professor of music, Sam Houston State University, Huntsville, TX, 1965–76; director of jazz studies, Houston HS for Performing and Visual Arts, 1976–99; member, International Association for Jazz Education Hall of Fame, 2005.

Max Morley, *Bachelor of Music, 1965; Master of Music, 1967; DMA/Trumpet Performance, UNT, 1979*. Professor of trumpet, Stephen F. Austin State University, Nacogdoches, TX, 1971–91, and programming/development officer, College of Fine Arts, 1991–present; author, *Trumpet Quest*.

Remus Morosan, *Graduate, Interlochen Arts Academy, 2000. Currently enrolled at UNT, Trumpet Performance, in concurrent Bachelor of Music and Master of Music degrees program.* Winner, Romanian National Competition, 1997, 1998; winner, Timis Music Competition, 1997; music director, Maranatha Romanian Pentecostal Church, Dallas, 2003–present; recipient, John and Marilyn Haynie scholarship, 2003, 2004, 2005, and the Maxine and Johnnie Johnson scholarship, 2003; winner, UNT Concerto Competition, 2003–2004.

Leon "Ned" Nedbalek, *Bachelor of Music/Composition, UNT, 1957; Master of Music/Theory, UNT, 1957.* U.S. Air Force pilot, 1957–78 (retired Lt. Col.), Royal Hawaiian Air Service, 1978–86; Wonder View Press, 1985–present.

Bob Nero, *Bachelor of Science/Education, UNT, 1972; Master of Education, Texas A & M University at Commerce, 1990.* General manager and real estate agent with SpringsHome, Colorado Springs, 1996–present.

C. C. "Jitter" Nolen, President, UNT, 1971–79. Before his once-in-a-lifetime fishing outing on Lake Texoma with John Haynie in 1979, Jitter barely qualified as an amateur fisherman. After moving to Oklahoma City, Jitter became known as the Texas champion freshwater fisherman.

Bill Nugent, *Bachelor of Music/Trumpet Performance, 1956; Master of Music/Composition, Southern Methodist University, 1957; Ph.D./Musicology, UNT, 1970.* Chancellor, University of Arkansas; President, University of Illinois Foundation; VP/Provost, University of West Virginia; Dean, Arts and Sciences, Washington State University; Dean, School of Music, University of Oklahoma; chairman/president, *The News-Gazette*, Inc. and *WDWS* Radio, Inc., Champaign, IL.

Mike Olson, *Bachelor of Music Education, 1966; Master of Music/Trumpet Performance, UNT, 1968.* Band director, 1965–2004, Lake Dallas, McAllen, Lampasis, Tuloso-Midway, Corpus Christi, State Honor Band Finalist, 1983, 1991; member, Victoria Symphony, Corpus Christi Symphony, 1985–92; Corpus Christi Wind Symphony 1981–92, San Antonio Municipal Band (2000–present); president, Texas Bandmasters Association, 1997.

Don Owen, *Bachelor of Music Education, Stetson University, 1959; Master of Music, UNT, 1960.* Professor of trumpet, University of South Florida, 1964–2002; professor *emeritus* of music, 2002; principal trumpet, The Florida Orchestra, 1964–1989, 2nd trumpet, 1989–present.

John Parnell, *Bachelor of Music, 1960; Master of Music Education, UNT, 1961.* Band director, DeQueen, AR; McCullom HS, San Antonio, TX; Everman HS, Mansfield HS, Sherman, TX; Durant HS, OK. Durant band won Sweepstake awards 10 of 13 years. Inducted into the Oklahoma Band Directors Hall of Fame 2005; Southeastern Band Director of the Year, 2003.

Rex Perrin, *Bachelor of Music, UNT, 1956.* President of local AF of M 532, twenty years; forty-year career in automobile sales, Amarillo, TX.

Lowry Riggins, *Bachelor of Arts, UNT, 1956; Master of Science, University of Illinois, 1959.* Taught music 4th grade through college levels; associate professor of music, Northeast Louisiana University, 1964–85; honorary member of the International Double Reed Society.

Dave Ritter, *Bachelor of Music Education, UNT, 1961; Master of Music, UNT, 1965.* Professor of trumpet, director of jazz studies, director of brass choir, West Texas A&M University, 1965–2001; principal trumpet, Amarillo Symphony, 1965–2002.

Galindo Rodriguez, *Bachelor of Music, UNT, 1976; Master of Music Education, UNT, 1978; Performance Certificate, Northwestern University, 1987.* Member, Chicago Civic Orchestra, 1978–80; trumpet teacher, Boise State University, 1980–84; professor of trumpet, Northwestern State University, Natchitoches, LA, 1980–present.

Frank "Pancho" Romero, *Bachelor of Music Education, New Mexico State University, 1975; Master of Music Education, UNT, 1977; DMA, University of Oklahoma, 2001.* Owner/manager, Romero Family Music, Albuquerque, NM, 1978–91; professor of trumpet, Oklahoma Baptist University, 1991–2001; New Mexico State University, 2001–present.

Ray Sasaki, *Bachelor of Music/Mathematics, California State University at Fresno, 1972; Master of Music Education, UNT, 1975.* Professor of music, University of Illinois, 1975–2001; Frank C. Erwin, Jr. Centennial Professor in Fine Arts, University of Texas at Austin, 2001–present; St. Louis Brass Quintet.

Jay Saunders, *Bachelor of Music, UNT, 1968; Master of Music Education, UNT, 1974.* U.S. Army Studio Band, Washington, DC, 1968–71; Stan Kenton Orchestra, four tours, 1966–73; lecturer in jazz studies, UNT 1996–present.

Pat Bode Saunders, *Registered Nurse, Certified Nurse Operating Room, Bachelor of Science, Texas Woman's University, 1976*. Director, Surgical Services, Presbyterian Hospital of Denton.

Fred Sautter, *Bachelor of Arts, UNT, 1967; Master of Music, University of Washington, 1969*. Principal trumpet, Philharmonia Hungarica, 1964–66; Philharmonic State Orchestra of Hamburg, 1966–67; Portland Opera Orchestra, 1968–84; Oregon Symphony Orchestra, 1968–2006; author, *Sound the Trumpet, A Technical Book, In Video, On How to Play the Trumpet*.

James Schell, *Bachelor of Music, UNT, 1960; Master of Music, Yale University, 1964*. Faculty, University of British Columbia, Vancouver, Canada, 1964–99; chamber music coach, presented large choral works with the Vancouver Symphony Orchestra, taught theory, composed numerous choral works.

C. M. Shearer, *Bachelor of Music Education, UNT, 1962; Master of Music/Theory and Composition, UNT, 1966; DMA/Conducting, Choral Literature, University of Colorado, 1976*. Professor of music, Kent State University, 1986–present; Distinguished Teacher Award, Kent State University, 2003.

Douglas Smith, *Bachelor of Science/Music Education, Carson-Newman College, 1961; Master of Music Education, UNT, 1964; DMA/Trumpet Performance, University of Michigan, 1969*. Mildred and Ernest Hogan Professor of Church Music, 1975-present and associate dean of doctoral studies, Southern Baptist Theological Seminary, 2002–present; author/composer of numerous music articles and arrangements, including *61 Trumpet Hymns and Descants*, 3 vols., (Hope Publishing Co., 1977, 1980, 1995) and *Trumpet Hymns and Fanfares* (Lorenz, 1989).

Gary Sorensen. *Bachelor of Music Education, UNT, 1970*. Band director, AR, 1970–1973, TX, 1975–85. Instructor, math and electronics, Eastfield College, 1988–92; teacher of chemistry, physics, engineering, and mathematics, Caddo Mills HS, TX, 1988–present.

Marvin Stamm, *Bachelor of Music/Performance, UNT, 1961*. Jazz per-forming artist, Stan Kenton Orchestra, 1961–62; Woody Herman Orchestra, 1965–66; NYC studio recording artist, 1966–89; George Gruntz Concert Jazz Band, 1978–present; Westchester Jazz Orchestra, 2002–present. Recordings, *Machinations* (1967), *Stammpede* (1980), *Bop Boy* (1990), *Mystery Man* (1993), *By Ourselves* and *The Stamm/Soph Project* (2000), *Elegance* (2001), *The Stamm/Soph Project—Live at Birdland* (2005); Outstanding Alumnus Award, UNT, 2004.

Richard Steffen, *Bachelor of Music, UNT, 1974; Master of Music, UNT, 1976.* Professor of trumpet, Furman University, 1976–83; Austin Peay State University, Clarksville, TN, 1983–present.

Rick Stitzel, *Bachelor of Music Education, UNT, 1971; Master of Music Education/Jazz Studies, UNT, 1978.* Free-lance composer arranger, published by Hal Leonard Corporation, 1978–present; director of jazz studies, Tarrant County College, Ft. Worth, Texas, 1982–present; author, *Jazz Theory: A Survival Guide* (Rick Stitzel Music, 2002).

Matt Stock, *Bachelor of Science/Music Education, University of Arkansas, 1986; Master of Music/Musicology, UNT, 1996; Master of Library Science, UNT, 1995; DMA (in progress), University of Oklahoma.* Assistant professor of bibliography/fine and applied arts librarian, University of Oklahoma, 2004–present.

Sam Trimble, *Bachelor of Music Education, University of South Florida, 1970; Master of Music Education, UNT, 1971.* Professor of trumpet, New Mexico State University, 1971–82; University of Texas at El Paso, 1982–present; principal trumpet, El Paso Symphony Orchestra, 1972–present; principal trumpet/founder of El Paso Brass, 1972–present.

Ken Van Winkle, *Bachelor of Music, West Texas State University, 1980; Master of Music, UNT, 1982; DMA, University of Oregon, 1994.* Director of bands, New Mexico State University, 1985–present.

Richard Waddell, *Bachelor of Music/Trumpet Performance, UNT, 1975.* Founder, Boston Brass, 1985–97. Third-prize winner, with Boston Brass, International Brass Quintet Competition, Narbonne, France, 1992. CDs, *Fire in the Chamber, Young Fogeys, Stealing the Show;* classical trumpet instructor, Rivers Music School, Weston, MA, 2005–present.

Mike Walker, *Bachelor of Music, UNT, 1965; Master of Music, Kansas State University, 1966.* Band director, Texas schools, 38 years.

Patty Haynie Wendell, sister of John Haynie. Married Bill Wendell, 1957. Son Nick and wife Robin have two children, Robert and Matt. Son Karl and wife Merilee have three children, Brynn, Makelle, and Tyler.

Debra Millender Widdig, *Bachelor of Science/Elementary Education, Cameron University, 1982.* Elementary teacher, Central High Public Schools, OK, 1983–87; Allen, TX, ISD, 1993–99; 2004–present.

Doug Wiehe, *Bachelor of Music Education, UNT, 1952; Master of Arts, UNT, 1955; DME, University of Oklahoma, 1971*. Band director, 1953–66; assistant band director, assistant professor of band methods, music history, UNT, 1966–71; supervisor of fine arts, Brazosport ISD, 1974–1993.

Purris Williams, *Bachelor of Music Education, West Texas State University, 1954; Master of Music Education, UNT, 1968*. Band director, TX public schools, 1953–68; professor of music, University of Missouri, 1969–74; advertising/sales, 1978–present.

Thomas Wirtel, *Bachelor of Music, UNT, 1961; Master of Music/Composition, UNT, 1963; DMA/Composition, Indiana University, 1969*. Alumnus of the Stan Kenton Orchestra, Dallas Jazz Orchestra; head, jazz division, School of Music, University of Illinois, 1995–2002; leader, UI Jazz Band; awards, Rockefeller Foundation Composer in Residence grant, a MacDowell Colony appointment, 1966, Fromm Foundation Prize, 1967, and two National Endowment of the Arts jazz grants for faculty research in electronic music.

Tom Wright, *Bachelor of Music Education, UNT, 1958; Master of Music Education, University of Illinois, 1959*. Associate professor of low brass; chair, music department; head, student teacher supervision, conductor of musical theatre, Emporia State University, 1966–2001.

Cole Zeagler, *Texas A&M University finance major, 2003–present*. Graduate, Cypress Springs HS, *summa cum laude*, Cypress Fairbanks ISD, 2003; National Society of Collegiate Scholars; all-region band, 2002–2003; outstanding soloist, 2001; grandson of John and Marilyn Haynie.

David Zeagler, *Northeast Louisiana University, 1970–1972; UNT, 1972–1974*; Lead trumpet, One O'Clock Lab Band, 1974; Stan Kenton Orchestra, 1974; principal trumpet for Broadway shows in Houston, Texas, 1975–present; performed at Carnegie Hall with Houston Pops, 1976; performed at Inaugurations for Presidents Reagan and Bush; orchestra personnel manager, *Theater Under the Stars*, 2001–present; son-in-law of John and Marilyn Haynie.

Katie Zeagler, *University of Houston pharmacy major, 2004–present*; National Society of Collegiate Scholars, President's Volunteer Service Award; Certified Pharmacy Technician; graduate, Cypress Springs HS, *magna cum laude*, Cypress Fairbanks ISD, 2004; all-region band, 2001–2004; all-area band, 2002–2004; all-region orchestra, 2002–2004; outstanding soloist, 2002–2004; granddaughter of John and Marilyn Haynie.

Melinda Haynie Zeagler, *Bachelor of Science/Education, University of Houston, 1978*. Elementary teacher, Alief ISD, 1978–92, Houston ISD, 1992–2000; Teacher of the Year, Barbara Bush ES, 1995–96; librarian, Barbara Bush ES, 2000–present; daughter of John and Marilyn Haynie.

Rachel Zeagler, *Bachelor of Science/Education, Texas A & M University, 2003*. Math teacher at West Briar Middle School, Houston ISD, 2003–present; Rice University School Mathematics Project; graduate, Langham Creek HS, *cum laude*, Cypress Fairbanks ISD, 1999; all-American swimmer, 1997–99; granddaughter of John and Marilyn Haynie.

Index of Names

Note: The index does not include author/composer/publisher names listed in the Course of Study on pages 166–71 or names mentioned as part of a contributor's biographical sketch.

Gustat, Joseph 229

Hackney, C. R. 216
Hale, Anna Jean 190, 192
Hall, Gene 246
Handel, George Frideric 181
Hankins, Paul 260, 274
Hankins, Virginia Maddox 208, 260, 274
Harbaugh, John 58, 274
Hardin, Anne xii-xiii, 88, 173, *193*, 267, 274
Harding, A. A. 97, 195, 230, 249, 256, 257
Harness, Joe 62, 84, 104, 156, 274
Harvey, Paul 249
Haskins, Lauren 192
Hatch, Don 101
Haydn, Franz Joseph 65, 175, 176, 182, 220
Haynie, Anne Perry 134, *185*, 252, 253, 274
Haynie, Harvey *45*
Haynie, James *45*, 223, 263
Haynie [Gutierrez], Jessie *45*, 209
Haynie, Jordan 76, 88, *185*, 253, 275
Haynie, Lelia *45*, 206, 209, 222, 223
Haynie, Marilyn Hindsley 35, *79*, *91*, 176, 178, *185*, 190, 232, *237*, 242, 246, *248*, 249–53, 256, 258, 259, 266, 267
Haynie, Mark 40, 42, 129, 172, 179, *185*, *248*, 249–253, 267, 275
Heron, Bonnie 192

Herrick, Carole 152, 192, 275
Hindemith, Paul 231–32
Hindsley, Helene 250
Hindsley, Harold "Huck" 249
Hindsley, Mark H. 89, 93, 94, 97, 114, 176, 195, 213, 220, 230, 235, *237*, 240, 249, 250, *254*, 255–58, *259*, 259, 261, 262
Hockett, Nancy 192
Hodgin, Larry 54, 275
Hodgson, Walter 240–42
Holmes, Ruth Jane 50, 192, 275
Holt, John 87, 180
Hovhaness, Alan 181
Hruby, Alois 96, 105–6
Hughes, J. K. 206–7
Hunter, John *123*
Hurst, Craig 200, 275

Irons, Earl D. 27, 29, 57, 101, 104, 120, 127, 142, 181, 210, 214, 215, 216, *218*, 218, 219–21
Ives, Charles 178

Jacob, Gene Iles 76, 191, 245, 275
James, Harry 176
James, Harry Jeffrey 176
James, Mary Frances 250
Jeanjean, Paul 181
Jenkins, Clay 134, 276
Johnson, Keith xi, 55, *189*, 228, 265, 276
Johnson, Miles 82, 276
Jolivet, André 165, 177
Jones, Richard 3
Jones, Greg 42, 276
Jordan, Bob 126

Steinel, Michael 265
Stevens, Thomas 162
Stitzel, Rick 152, 282
Stock, Matt 152, 282
Stravinsky, Igor 235
Stubbs, Mary Ann 191

Tableman, Glenn 210
Tamez, Elida xiii
Taylor, Charlotte 192
Tenaglia & Krieger 181
Thorn, Jonathan xiii
Tomasi, Henri 165, 177
Trimble, Sam 128, 282
Tull, Charlotte Dorsey 180
Tull, Fisher "Mickey" 180

Van Winkle, Ken 120, 182, 282
VanderCook, H. A. 214
Voisin, Roger 176

Waddell, Richard 12, 72, 194, 282
Walker, Mike 144, 200, 282
Watson, R. B. 215, 216
Webb, Randol *99*
Wendell, Bill 204
Wendell, Patty Haynie *45*, 204,
  223, 282
Widdig, Debra Millender 124,
  172, 192, 282
Wiehe, Doug 2, 283
Wiley, Charles A. 180
Wiley, D. O. 216
Williams, Ernest 174, 181, 231
Williams, Purris 164, 283
Winslow, Robert 257, 261, 262
Wirtel, Thomas 92, 283

Wobisch, Helmut 176
Wright, Tom 244, 245, 283

Yount, Barton K. 259

Zeagler, Cole 80, *185*, 253, 283
Zeagler, David 21–22, 40, 164,
  185, 252, 253, 283
Zeagler, Katie 38, *185*, 253, 283
Zeagler, Melinda Haynie 40, *185*,
  248, 249–53, 284
Zeagler, Rachel 152, *185*, 253,
  258, 284